CHA

Certified Horsemanship Association

HORSEMANSHIP MANUAL

COMPOSITE

LEVEL 1 • LEVEL 2 • LEVEL 3 • LEVEL 4

Certified Horsemanship Association

CHA LEVEL 1
HORSEMANSHIP
MANUAL

Certified Horsemanship Association

HORSEMANSHIP MANUAL

LEVEL 1

TABLE OF CONTENTS

INTRODUCTION

The Level 1 CHA Manual is the beginning of your association with horses. The goals you will work towards in Level 1 include how to safely tie, groom, saddle and bridle, mount and ride a horse. You will also be able to identify various parts of your horse and riding equipment. You will develop the ability to control a horse up through a trot.

**Before you know it, you will be enjoying a
safe and enjoyable relationship with horses.**

GENERAL HORSE INFORMATION

Horse sense is the basis of horsemanship. This is the ability of a person to understand horses and even to think like a horse. **The better you understand horses, the more you will enjoy them and the better rider you will be.**

Horses are **large** and **powerful** animals, but they are also **timid** and **easily frightened**. Most horses are **gentle and obedient** if they are handled properly. If you hurt or frighten a horse you can get hurt. The first choice of a frightened horse is to run away. If he can't run away, he might kick or bite in self defense. It's a good idea to ask permission from your instructor or the horse's owner before going near a strange horse.

The following rules will help you learn how to act safely around horses. They are based on a knowledge of how horses think and often react.

HORSE SENSE • RULES AND REASONS

Rule 1. Praise often, punish seldom.
Reason Firm, gentle treatment will gain your horse's respect.
Harsh or cruel treatment will make your horse fear you.

Rule 2. Stop, look and **listen. Use caution when working around horses.**
Reason Horses are frightened by loud noises and sudden movements.
They may react in an unexpected way.

DON'T RUN OR YELL
YOU MIGHT STARTLE A HORSE

Rule 3. **Never stand directly behind or in front of a horse.**
Reason A frightened horse may kick or run over you.

Rule 4. **Horses should never be hand fed.**
Reason Fingers may be mistaken for treats and be bitten.

DON'T FEED HORSES BY HAND

FINGERS FEEL LIKE CARROTS

Rule 5. **Keep at least one horse length**
between your horse and **the horse in front of you.**
Reason Crowding a horse may cause him to kick or bite.

DON'T TAILGATE

KEEP ALERT • MAINTAIN A SAFE DISTANCE BETWEEN HORSES

Rule 6. **Check equipment for proper fit** and **have your instructor check it before you mount.**

   Reason Improperly fitted equipment may cause an accident or injury to horse and rider.

*CHECK YOUR TACK
BEFORE YOU MOUNT UP*

Rule 7. **Always use a halter** and **lead rope to tie your horse** and **never tie with the reins.**

   Reason Reins may be broken or the horse's mouth injured if tied by the bridle.

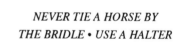

*NEVER TIE A HORSE BY
THE BRIDLE • USE A HALTER*

Rule 8. **Treat equipment with care** and **always put it away properly.**

   Reason Properly cared for equipment is easier to use and lasts longer.

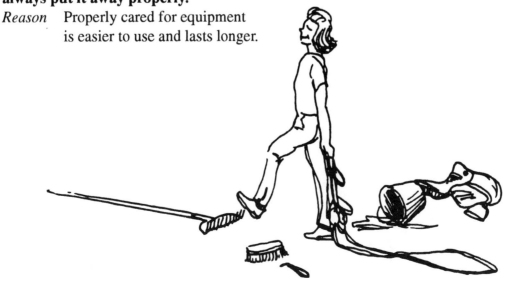

PUT EQUIPMENT AWAY PROPERLY WHEN YOU ARE THROUGH WITH IT

Rule   9. **Never wrap or tie anything attached to your horse around your body in any way.**
Reason   Being tied may result in your being dragged by your horse.

NEVER WRAP OR TIE A LEAD ROPE OR REIN AROUND YOURSELF

Rule 10. **Listen** and **learn.**
Always listen for commands from your instructor and act promptly.
Keep alert at all times when around horses.
Reason   Your instructor will help to protect you from danger and
insure that you enjoy your time with your horse.

Rule 11. Dismount to adjust clothing or equipment.

Reason Your horse may spook from unusual movement on his back.

DANGER • SNEAKERS CAN ALLOW YOUR FOOT TO GET CAUGHT IN THE STIRRUP

BE SMART DRESS THE PART

Rule 12. Dress appropriately. When riding, you should:
wear long pants
shoes with a heel or boots
proper head gear

Reason Long pants will prevent sores on your legs.
Hard shoes will protect your feet.
The heels will prevent your feet from slipping through the stirrups.
Helmets protect from most head injuries.

HORSE CARE AND HANDLING

APPROACH YOUR HORSE

When approaching a horse always consider the horse's limited field of vision.

A horse **cannot see directly behind** or **in front** without moving his head.

- Approach your horse at the shoulder or as near the neck as possible so that he can see you.
- Speak softly and call the horse's name as you approach because your horse may be asleep.
- Extend your hand and pat him on the neck or shoulder.

TIE STALL

If your horse is in a tie stall you will have to approach the horse from the rear.

- Speak to him as you enter the stall.
- Place your hand on his hip.
- Be sure to make the horse move over to give you some room.
- Walk to the horse's head and pat him on the neck.

APPROACHING A HORSE

TIED IN A STALL
APPROACH A HORSE FROM THE REAR

*PLACING A HALTER
ON YOUR HORSE'S HEAD*

HALTER YOUR HORSE

The halter and lead rope **help** you to **lead and tie your horse**. Lead ropes are attached with a clip or snap to a ring on the halter. The halter is designed to fit comfortably on the horse's head so that you can control your horse as you lead or tie him.

It is a good idea to **have the halter and lead rope ready to use when you go to catch a horse**.

Many people like to have the lead rope already attached to the halter, carrying them together as they approach the horse.

To place the halter on your horse you will need to **stand at the left side of the horse**. Most halters fasten on the left side.

• **Stand between the horse's shoulder and head.**
• Talk to your horse while stroking or patting him to let him know you are a friend.
• Slide the halter up over his muzzle on to the horse's head. The long strap (*crown piece*) should come across the horse's head right behind the ears, toward you. It should now be easy to fasten.

Some people like to wrap the lead rope around the horse's neck before putting the halter on. This gets it out of the way, and lets the horse know it is caught.

TIED TO A FENCE POST

TIE YOUR HORSE

When it is time to groom or saddle your horse you will need a way to keep the horse standing still while you work. There are several ways to do this:

Tie the lead rope to a solid object that can not be moved such as:
  • a wall with a ring in it
  • a strong fence post
  • a hitching rail or something similar
• Whenever you tie your horse, you will need to **use a quick release knot** (*see Level 2*). Always **tie at a height level with the horse's back or higher**.
• It is important not to tie the lead rope too long. If the horse decides to put his head down, he could step over the rope!

Cross ties are another common way to secure a horse. Cross ties are **usually two ropes tied high up on each side of the walkway in the stable**.
• Each rope will usually have a snap or clip to attach it to the halter.
• They attach to the side rings on the part of the halter that goes around the horse's muzzle.

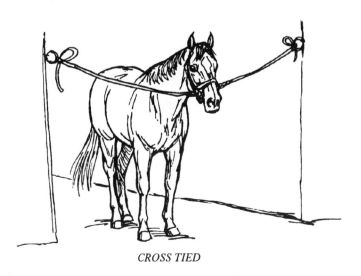

CROSS TIED

9

LEADING SAFELY

LEAD YOUR HORSE

When leading a horse with a halter and lead rope or a bridle, the procedure is the same.

You should **be on your horse's left**, leading between his head and shoulders.

- **If single reins are used and not tied together**, be sure to remove both reins from the horse's neck.
- **If the reins are tied or buckled**, bring them gently over the horse's head.

Place your **right hand about six inches from the halter or bit**, holding the lead rope or reins together.
- **Never hold on to the halter or any part of the bridle other than the reins.** The halter and bridle do not give you control of your horse if he pulls away.

Hold the excess reins or rope with the left hand. If the reins are very long, double the excess back and forth until they are short enough to hold.

Looping the excess reins or rope around your hand could be very dangerous if the horse, for any reason, decides to jump away from you.

TURN YOUR HORSE

When turning the horse;

You should **turn his head away from you** by moving your hand under his chin to the right. Continue moving around your horse as he turns to prevents the horse from stepping on your feet.

If you must turn the horse toward you;

Place your hand on his neck as you turn him to keep him an arm's length away from you.

RIGHT
PUSH HIM AWAY FROM YOU TO TURN

WRONG
DON'T PULL THE HORSE TOWARD YOUR FEET

GROOMING

Grooming is a very important part of your horse's health.

A good work over with a curry comb and brush will remove unsightly dandruff and dirt which causes saddle sores. Grooming also gives your horse's **coat a shine**, and makes your horse **feel good**.

Curry Comb:
Used on horse's body in a **circular motion** to bring the dirt to the surface. Curry comb should not be used on the face, legs, or any bony area on the horse.

Hard Brush or Dandy Brush:
Used in the **direction of hair growth** to remove the dirt. Brush in firm strokes to remove deep down dirt. Be careful on the face with this brush.

Soft Brush:
Used on the face and body to remove surface dirt and put a shine on the horse's coat.

Mane and Tail Comb:
Used on the mane and tail to remove tangles. **Start at the bottom and work towards the top**, removing tangles as you go.

Hoofpick:
Used to remove dirt, rocks and manure from the horse's hooves. The hoofpick is **held in the palm of the hand with the point away from your body**. Always clean the hoof working away from yourself.

GROOMING TOOLS

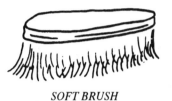

CURRY COMB

HARD OR DANDY BRUSH

SOFT BRUSH

MANE AND TAIL COMB

HOOFPICK

GROOMING • KEEP ONE HAND ON THE HORSE WHILE YOU WORK

11

When saddling a horse with a WESTERN SADDLE:

Place the **pad or blanket high on the withers**, then **slide** it backward onto the withers and back. If a blanket is used, always place the **folded edge toward the horse's withers**.

Pick up the saddle and **bring the right stirrup and cinch over the seat**.
• Holding the gullet in your left hand and the cantle in your right hand, **gently place** the saddle on the horse's back.

The **front edge** of the **pad** should be **in line with** the **center of the shoulder**. The saddle should be **centered** and placed **about three inches behind** the **front edge of the pad**.
• Place your hand under the blanket, pulling the blanket into the gullet of the saddle so it does not wear on the withers and back.

Go to the **right** (*off side*) of the horse and gently lift the stirrup and cinch down. Check the saddle and pad to be sure the pad is smooth and the cinch is not twisted.

Then from the **left** (*near side*), hook the stirrup over the horn and pull the cinch under the horse. The cinch is tied with a special knot (latigo knot).

FOLD THE STIRRUP UP OVER THE SEAT

THE BLANKET COMES TO THE CENTER OF THE SHOULDER

SET THE SADDLE GENTLY IN PLACE

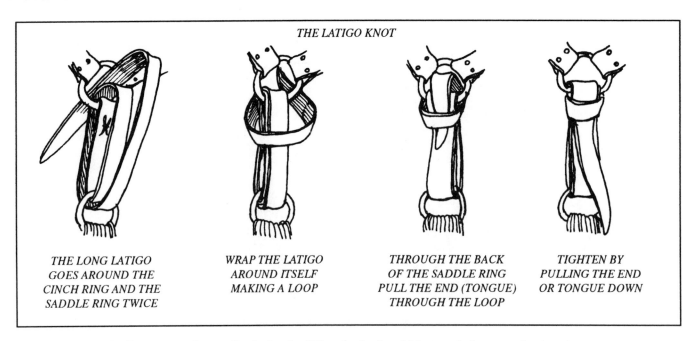

THE LATIGO KNOT

| *THE LONG LATIGO GOES AROUND THE CINCH RING AND THE SADDLE RING TWICE* | *WRAP THE LATIGO AROUND ITSELF MAKING A LOOP* | *THROUGH THE BACK OF THE SADDLE RING PULL THE END (TONGUE) THROUGH THE LOOP* | *TIGHTEN BY PULLING THE END OR TONGUE DOWN* |

Before mounting, a final check of the cinch should be made by your instructor.

**When saddling a horse with an
ENGLISH SADDLE:**

Place the **saddle pad high on the withers**, then **slide** it backward onto the back to smooth the horse's hair.

Pick up the saddle, making sure the **stirrups are run up** or the stirrups have been laid across the seat.
- Lay the **girth across the saddle.**
- Holding the pommel with the left hand and the cantle with the right, **gently place the saddle on the middle of the pad.**
- **Pull** the **pad up into the gullet** to allow the air to circulate between the horse's back and the pad.

As a general guideline, the front edge of the saddle will often just touch an imaginary line down the center of the shoulder. *(This will depend on the type of saddle and the shape of the individual horse.)*

From the **right** (*off side*), take the girth off the saddle and check to be sure the pad is smooth.
- **Attach the girth** to the **right side** of the saddle.
(The folded edge of a leather girth should be to the front.)

From the **left** (*near side*), **pull the girth under** the horse and **buckle the girth.**

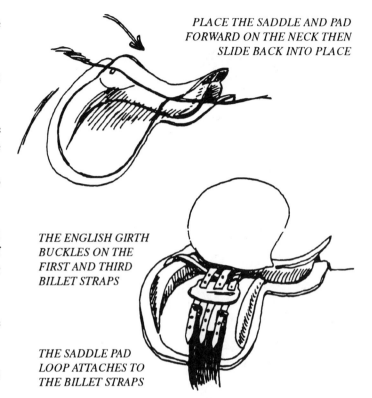

PLACE THE SADDLE AND PAD FORWARD ON THE NECK THEN SLIDE BACK INTO PLACE

THE ENGLISH GIRTH BUCKLES ON THE FIRST AND THIRD BILLET STRAPS

THE SADDLE PAD LOOP ATTACHES TO THE BILLET STRAPS

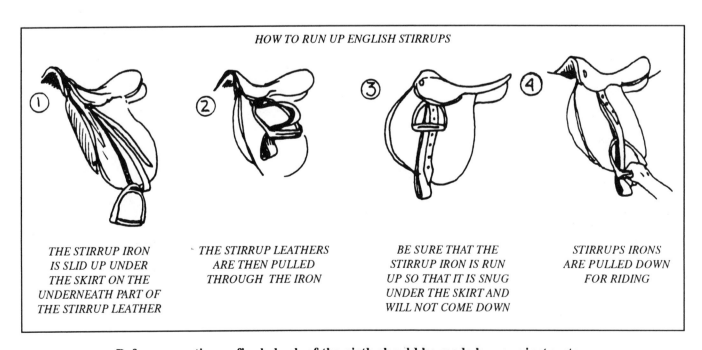

HOW TO RUN UP ENGLISH STIRRUPS

① *THE STIRRUP IRON IS SLID UP UNDER THE SKIRT ON THE UNDERNEATH PART OF THE STIRRUP LEATHER*

② *THE STIRRUP LEATHERS ARE THEN PULLED THROUGH THE IRON*

③ *BE SURE THAT THE STIRRUP IRON IS RUN UP SO THAT IT IS SNUG UNDER THE SKIRT AND WILL NOT COME DOWN*

④ *STIRRUPS IRONS ARE PULLED DOWN FOR RIDING*

Before mounting, a final check of the girth should be made by your instructor.

13

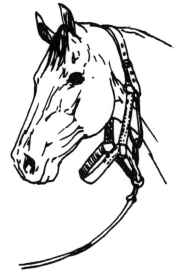

*BEFORE BRIDLING
YOU MIGHT PUT
HALTER AROUND
NECK SO HORSE IS
UNDER CONTROL*

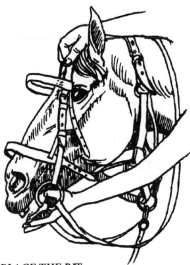

*METHOD 1
HOLD THE CROWN
PIECE IN THE RIGHT
HAND AND THE BIT
IN THE LEFT*

*PLACE THE BIT
BETWEEN THE HORSE'S LIPS
NO FINGERS IN FRONT OF TEETH*

BRIDLING

Stand on the horse's **left side** and place the **reins over the head** around his neck in order to keep the reins from falling to the ground.

Hold the crown piece in the right hand and the **bit in the left**. (*Method 1*)
• Bring the crown piece to the horse's ears.
• **Place the bit between the horse's lips**. If the horse fails to open his mouth, put your thumb in the side of his mouth and press down on the horse's bars (the area where the bit lies where there are no teeth).

Raise the crown piece and **insert the bit**.
• Slip the crown piece gently over one ear and then the other, pushing ears flat first.
• Straighten the browband and the forelock. Your instructor may suggest an alternate method.
• When using **one-eared bridles**, place the one ear in the earpiece and slide the rest of the crown piece over the other ear.

    Buckle the throatlatch loosely enough so that your **hand can be inserted breadth wise** between the throatlatch and the throat of the horse.
    Fasten the **cavesson or noseband** on an English bridle so that **one finger can be inserted** between the cavesson and the horse.
    Adjust the **curb chain or strap** so that it is **not twisted** and so that **two fingers can be inserted** between the strap and the horse's jaw.

*METHOD 2
HOLD BRIDLE
BELOW BROWBAND*

*PRESS THUMB INTO LIPS
TO MAKE HIM OPEN HIS MOUTH*

FINGERS GUIDE CURB STRAP

*WRONG WAY TO PUT
THE BIT IN HIS MOUTH*

*BUCKLE THROATLATCH
(NOT TOO TIGHT)
ENGLISH CAVESSON BUCKLES
INSIDE BRIDLE CHEEK PIECES*

PARTS OF THE HORSE AND TACK

PARTS OF THE HORSE

When working around horses there are some special words and terms that you will need to know.
Some parts of the horse are shown below.

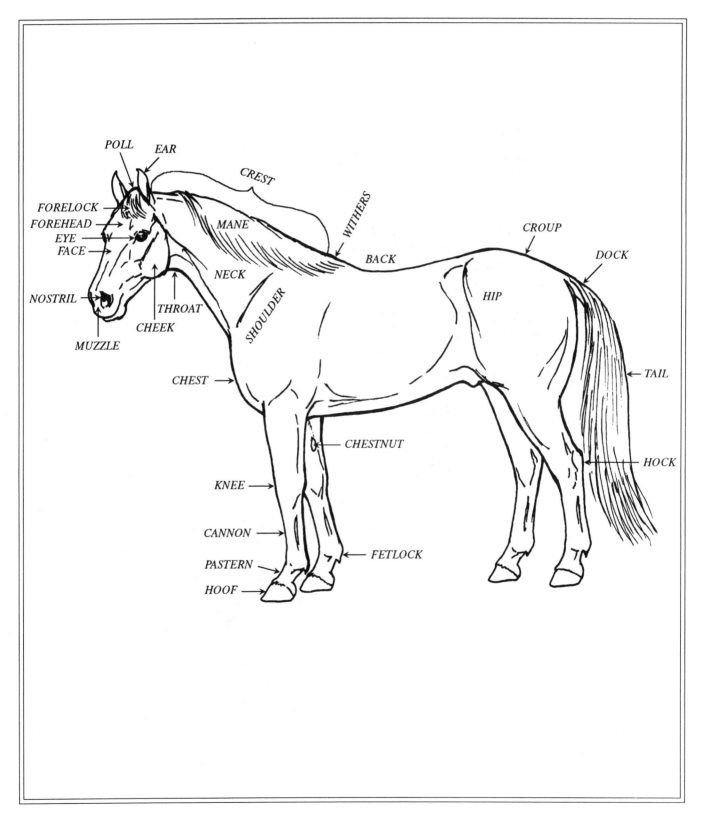

Your **tack** *(the equipment you use for riding)* should be fitted to you and to your horse. It need not be fancy or expensive but **should be safe and well cared for**. The way you take care of your equipment, your ability to talk about it and use it properly, will show if you are a horseman or not. Tack comes in a variety of forms. Be familiar with the names and use of the kind you have.

WESTERN TACK

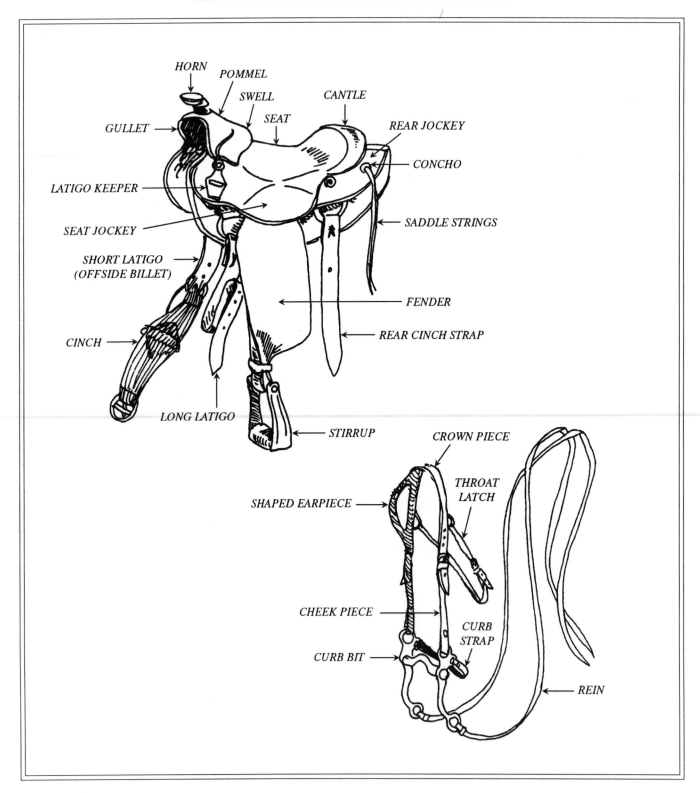

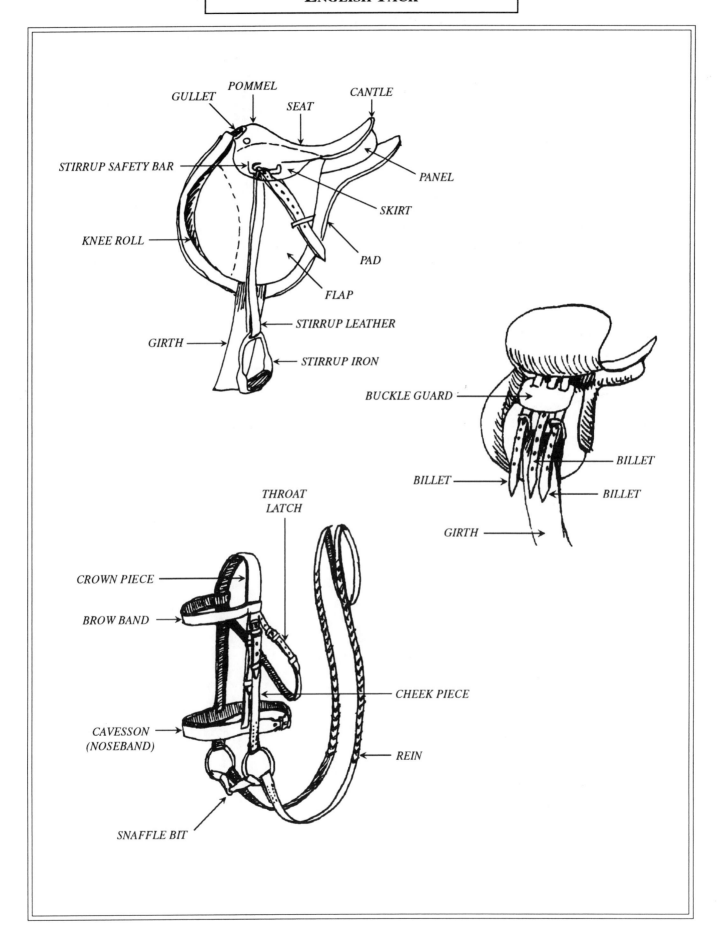

HORSEMANSHIP

Always have your instructor check the horse's equipment before mounting.

• Put the **reins over** the horse's **head**, one on each side of the neck. Stand on the horse's **left side, facing the rear of the horse**. Holding the reins in your left hand, place your left hand on the horse's neck in front of the withers with the ends of the reins on the left side.

• Take the left stirrup with your right hand and place your **left foot in the stirrup**. Grasp the pommel on the right side with your right hand. **Bounce and swing lightly into the saddle.** Mount quickly, being careful not to drag your right leg over the horse or kick your left toe into his side.

• Place your **right foot in the stirrup**. Hold the reins in your left hand and stand with weight in the right stirrup to straighten the saddle.

MOUNTING WRONG

PULLING ON BOTH ENDS OF THE SADDLE CAN MAKE IT SLIP

THIS CAN ALSO HAPPEN IF YOU FORGET TO CHECK YOUR GIRTH

DON'T POKE THE HORSE WITH YOUR TOE

DISMOUNTING

Dismounting is the reverse of mounting.

• You can **slide down** or (step down) and should **land near the horse's shoulder facing the front**.

• When sliding down, be sure to **kick your left foot out of the stirrup** and **slide down on your right hip**.

Proper dismounting procedure for both english and western riders varies little, with the exception that an english rider may place his right hand on the seat just behind the flap. Always run your english stirrups up after you dismount.

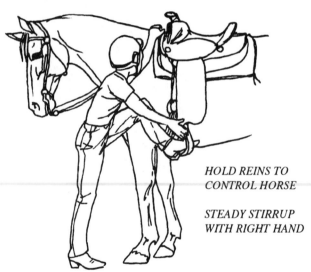

HOLD REINS TO CONTROL HORSE

STEADY STIRRUP WITH RIGHT HAND

MOUNTING

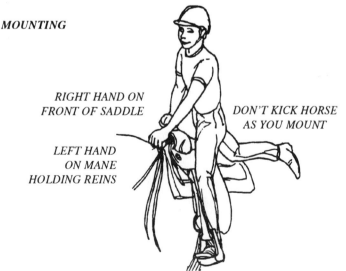

RIGHT HAND ON FRONT OF SADDLE

DON'T KICK HORSE AS YOU MOUNT

LEFT HAND ON MANE HOLDING REINS

DISMOUNTING

KICK BOTH FEET FREE FROM THE STIRRUPS

SLIDE DOWN ON RIGHT HIP FACING FRONT

BASIC SEAT AND HAND POSITION

When riding, a correct position is used to provide good control of the horse. **Good position in both english and western is basically the same.** The main difference is in the stirrup length. English stirrups are shorter than western. **A steady, secure, relaxed seat, with quiet hands is important in both.**

WESTERN POSITION

Hands & Arms: Elbows relaxed and close to sides. Reining hand held as close to pommel as possible. Right hand held loosely on the right thigh or near belt buckle.

Head: Head is held up, eyes looking ahead of the horse.

Shoulders: Both shoulders are square and even. Be careful that the left shoulder doesn't move higher than the right or twist forward as a result of holding the reins in the left hand.

Back: Upper back should be erect, sit *tall* in the saddle. Lower back should relaxed and flexing with the horse's movements.

Lower Body: Sit deep in the seat of the saddle, not back on the cantle. Keep your hip in line with your shoulder and the back of your heel.

Legs and Feet: Stirrup length is important. When standing up in stirrups with your heels lower than your toes and your knees slightly bent, there should be a space about 2 1/2" to 3" (a hand's width) between the buttocks and the saddle. Knees and thighs rolled in so that the flat part of the knee is held against the saddle. There is light contact with the horse on the inside of the calves of the legs. Ankles are flexed so that the heels are lower than the toes. Only balls of the feet are in the stirrups.

ENGLISH POSITION

Hands & Arms: Elbows relaxed and close to sides. Hands held above the horse's withers about six inches apart and held at the same angle as the horse's shoulders as seen from on top.

Head: Head is held up, eyes looking ahead of the horse.

Shoulders: Both shoulders are square and even.

Back: Upper back should be erect. Sit *tall* in the saddle. Lower back should relaxed and flexing with the horse's movements.

Lower Body: Sit well forward in the saddle. There should be a space equal to the width of a hand between your seat and the back edge of the saddle. Hip should be in line with shoulder and back of heel.

Legs and Feet: Stirrup length is important. When sitting in the saddle with feet out of the stirrups the bottom of the stirrup should just hit the ankle bone. When your feet are returned to the stirrups the knees will be bent. The knees and thighs are rolled in so that the flat part of the knee is held against the saddle. There is light contact with the horse on the inside of the calves of the legs. The ankles are flexed so that the heels are lower than the toes. Only balls of the feet are in the stirrups.

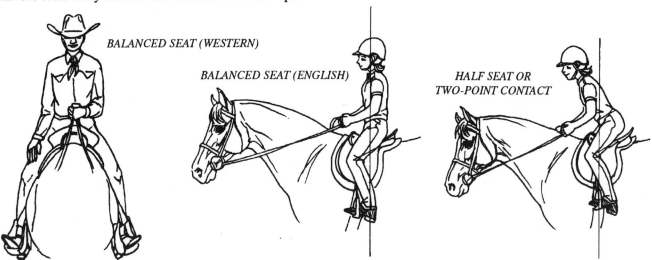

BALANCED SEAT (WESTERN)

BALANCED SEAT (ENGLISH)

HALF SEAT OR TWO-POINT CONTACT

Remember to be relaxed in your position so that you will
be able to give with the movement of your horse and ride in balanced rhythm with him.

CALIFORNIA STYLE (CLOSED REINS)

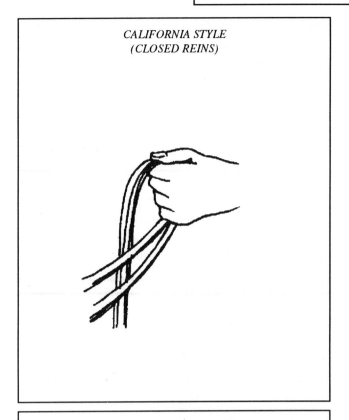

CALIFORNIA REIN HOLD

SPLIT REINS

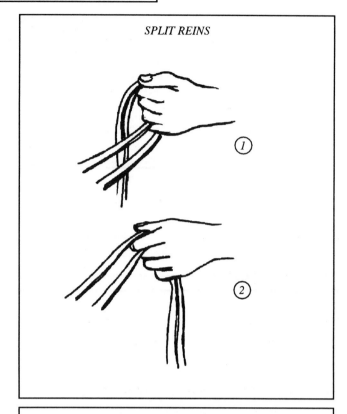

①

②

SPLIT REIN HOLDS

The reins are held in the left hand, with the end (bight) of the reins coming **out of the top of the fist**.

The end of the reins or romal is held by the right hand about **18 inches away** from the left hand.

No fingers are placed between the reins.

• 1) Hold both reins in one hand (usually the left) with the thumb up. The reins come into the hand **under the little finger, up through the hand** and **out between the thumb and index finger**. The excess rein should fall on the same side as the hand holding the reins. (The little finger may be inserted between the reins.)

• 2) Hold both reins in one hand (left) with the thumb up. The reins come into the hand **from the top** (index finger may be placed between them). They **pass through the bottom of the hand** with the excess rein falling on the same side as the hand holding the reins.

CALIFORNIA STYLE (CLOSED REINS)

SPLIT REINS

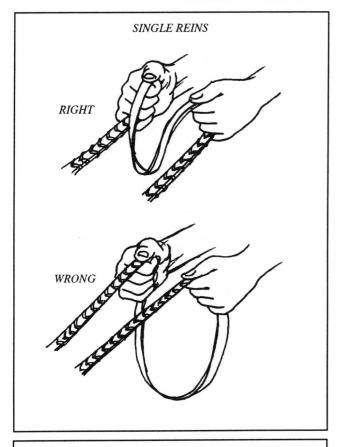

SINGLE REINS

RIGHT

WRONG

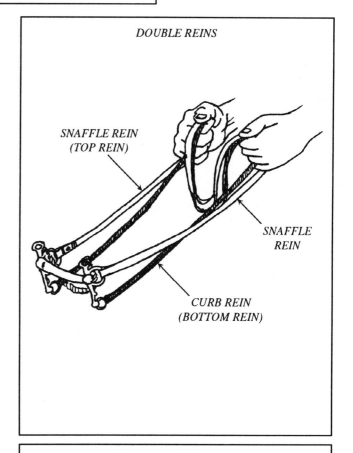

DOUBLE REINS

SNAFFLE REIN
(TOP REIN)

SNAFFLE
REIN

CURB REIN
(BOTTOM REIN)

SINGLE REINS

The reins come into each hand **between the third and little fingers, go up through the hand** and **come out between the thumb and index finger**.

Hands are held about **six inches apart** with the thumbs up and the excess rein (*bight*) falling to the right side of the horse's neck.

DOUBLE REINS

The reins are held in the same manner as single reins.

The reins come into each hand **between the third and little fingers, go up through the hand** and **come out between the thumb and index finger**.

Separate the curb and snaffle rein with the little finger:
• **curb rein on the inside**
• **snaffle on the outside**

SINGLE REINS

DOUBLE REINS

21

BASIC AIDS

As a rider, you need to have some way of telling the horse what to do.

Aids are the **means to signal the horse**. To give aid means to help. The aids help the horse **know what is wanted by the rider.**

There are **two kinds** of aids: **Natural** and **artificial aids**. A **natural aid is part of your body.**

Each natural aid has a certain way of signaling the horse. There are **four natural aids:**
1) Hands
2) Voice
3) Legs
4) Weight

An artificial aid reinforces the natural aids. They include:
- Crops
- Bats
- Spurs
- Whips

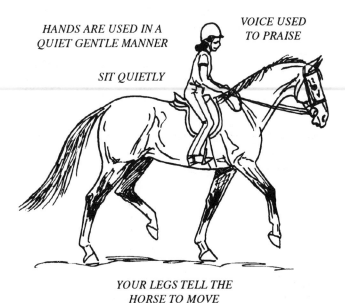

HANDS ARE USED IN A QUIET GENTLE MANNER

VOICE USED TO PRAISE

SIT QUIETLY

YOUR LEGS TELL THE HORSE TO MOVE

SHIFTING YOUR WEIGHT TELLS THE HORSE THAT HE IS TO STOP, GO OR TURN

HANDS

The hands are best when **used in a quiet gentle manner**.

- Remember the reins are attached to a piece of metal in the horse's mouth or a piece of leather around his nose. The nose and mouth are sensitive areas and can be easily injured.
- Use your hands **actively to stop** and **turn** the horse. The rest of the time, keep them in a steady position above the horse's withers.

VOICE

The voice can be **used to praise or soothe** the horse.

- By clucking or making a kissing sound, you can **tell the horse to go faster**.

Some horses are trained to understand certain voice commands. It is not necessary to yell at the horse because he has very sensitive hearing.

LEGS

The legs **tell the horse to move.**

- Squeezing with both legs will signal your horse to go forward. **Squeeze** with the **lower part** of your leg.
- Each horse is different; some will need a light squeeze while others need a stronger one.

When you are not squeezing, keep your legs **quietly by the horse's sides**. This means you can feel his sides with your lower legs without pushing against him.
- **Avoid kicking** the horse with **your heels or constantly squeezing** him. This can make the horse dull on his sides so that harder and harder kicks are needed to make him understand your signals.

WEIGHT

Weight is a very important aid.

- By **shifting your weight,** the horse **will know** that he **is to stop, go, or turn**.
- For now it is best to remember to sit quietly and move with the horse.
- Your weight is necessary to keep you and the horse in balance.

START

To walk, all four natural aids need to work. They each have a job to do.

• First, keep your **weight steady and balanced**.
• Then, **squeeze with the lower legs**.
• While at the same time you may **use your voice**. Tell the horse to walk or cluck to him.

If the horse does not move, then squeeze a little more the second time.

The **hands must be quiet** and **move with the horse's head**. Make sure you do not pull back while asking the horse to go forward.

TO WALK YOU NEED TO USE ALL FOUR NATURAL AIDS

STOP

Once you have learned to ask the horse to go forward, you will need to know how to ask him to stop. Again, all four natural aids are necessary.

• Keep your **weight balanced** and your **seat deep in the saddle**.

• With your **voice,** tell the horse to stop.
• A common word is *whoa*. Some horses are taught other sounds.

As you use your voice, shorten your reins and gently **check back with your hands, then release**.

If the horse does not stop, do it again. Continue checking gently and releasing until he stops.

Your **legs** should be **quiet and not disturbing** the horse. After the horse comes to a complete stop, reward him with a pat on the neck.

CHECK AND RELEASE

This is a method of using the reins to steady the horse.

The check and release is done by:

• A **mild pulling of the reins,** as if squeezing a sponge.
• Followed by **a release of pressure**.

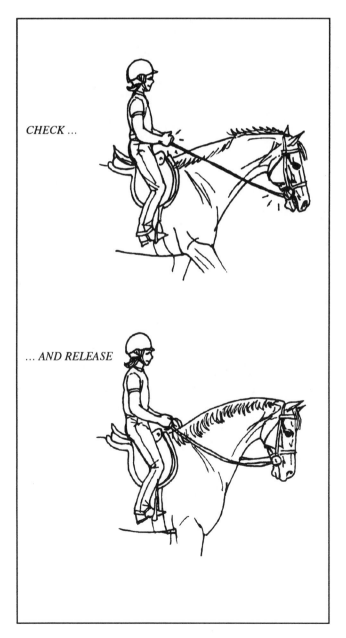

CHECK ...

... AND RELEASE

After you have mastered moving forward and stopping, you are ready to learn how to turn. Again, all the aids are necessary.

• A **turn** has **two sides, an inside and an outside.** The inside is in the direction you are turning.

• Keep your **legs quietly on the horse's sides**. If he slows down through the turn, give him a **squeeze with your lower leg**.

• You can also use your voice to encourage him to keep going.

To understand how the hands work, it is best to study English and Western separately.

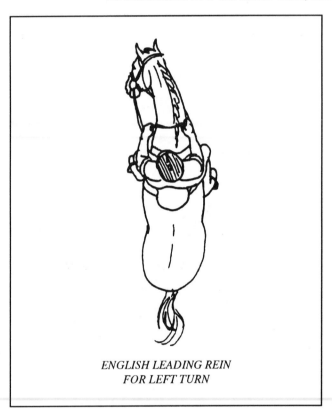

*ENGLISH LEADING REIN
FOR LEFT TURN*

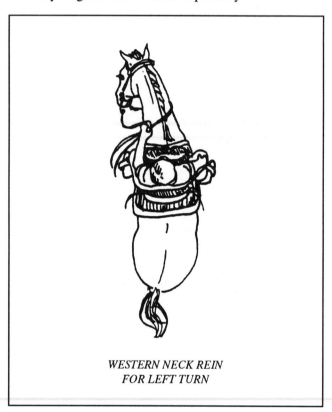

*WESTERN NECK REIN
FOR LEFT TURN*

ENGLISH

To begin a turn, you **use a leading rein**.

This means that your hand is going to lead with the rein out to the side in which you want to turn. This will pull or put pressure on the horse's mouth, on the side in which you are turning.

To turn:

Use your **inside hand** to pull the rein out away from the horse. The horse's nose will turn to the inside.

• Your **outside hand** should **gently follow** the movement of the horse's head and **not pull back**.

WESTERN

Since both reins are in the left hand, **only the left hand will move.**

• First, take your **hand** and **move it slightly** up the horse's neck.
• Then **pull across his neck in the direction you want to go** (*not back towards you*).

The rein pulling across his neck will signal him which direction to turn.
• Some horses are very sensitive and will turn if the rein is just laid on their neck. Other horses need a stronger signal.

Your instructor may prefer that you use a two handed position with a leading rein.

BASIC FIGURES

CIRCLE

A circle is **made by coming off the rail towards the center of the ring** and **going back to the rail still riding in the same direction**.

- It is especially important to sit up straight.
- To keep the horse moving by gently squeezing with your legs.
- Use only light pressure with the reins to steer.

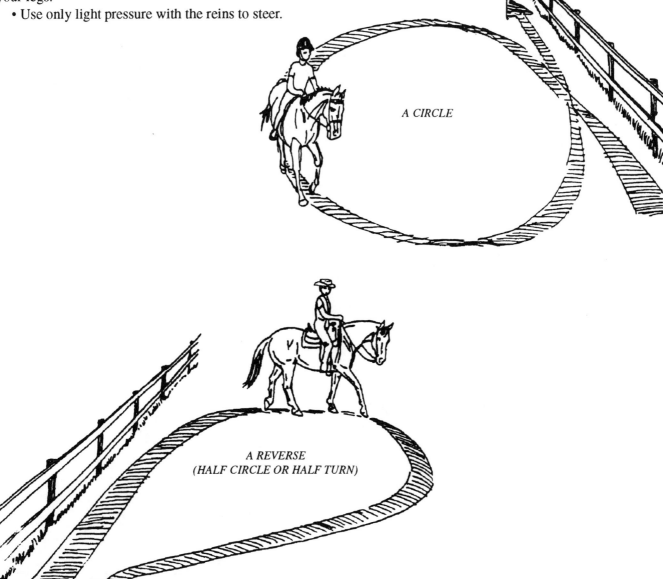

A CIRCLE

*A REVERSE
(HALF CIRCLE OR HALF TURN)*

REVERSE

To reverse, the horse is **turned off the rail toward the center of the ring and brought back to the rail going the other direction**.

This is known as a **half circle reverse** or a **half turn**.

THE TROT

Now that you can make your horse walk, turn and stop, you can begin to trot. The trot is a **two beat gait, faster than a walk.** It takes more effort to control and more practice to ride comfortably. Controlling the horse at a trot is a review of your basic aids at a walk.

Three ways of riding the trot are used to improve your balance, rhythm, and comfort. These are **sitting the trot**, a **half seat** or **two point**, and **posting**.

CONTROL AT THE TROT

The **verbal** command **trot** may be used. A *kiss* or *cluck sound* is also effective with some horses. If the horse is inclined to be lazy, be more forceful. Always **ask** the horse **gently first**. If you get no response, then tell him with a sharp squeeze and release, or a firm tap with the legs and encouragement with the voice.

• Encouragement with voice and legs may be needed to keep your horse at a steady trot. If your horse is trotting too fast, use a check and release to slow the horse down.

The **same aids** are used **to circle and turn at a trot** as when walking. Circles and turns when trotting should be **larger than at a walk** or your horse may lose his balance. Constant encouragement may be needed when circling and turning at a trot because the horse tends to slow down at this time.

To **slow** your horse **from a trot to a walk**, prepare him with a **verbal command.** Maintain your proper seat position in the saddle and **pull back firmly, but gently, on the reins**. Be sure to give **release** as your horse responds. Repeat until the horse comes to a walk. Praise your horse.

THE TROT CAN BE RATHER BUMPY UNTIL YOU KNOW HOW TO RIDE IT . . .

SITTING THE TROT

The western jog and english sitting trot are ridden in the same manner. This trot is used to develop a feel for the horse's movement and a secure seat.

In order to **sit** the trot, it is important to both **relax and sit deeply in the saddle**, rotating the hips forward so as to sit on the inside of the thighs. The shoulders should remain over the hips and not lean forward. It is very important to **keep the back relaxed so the body can follow the horse's movement**.

• Care must be taken that your **hands remain quiet**, not pulling on the horse's mouth. Keeping the back and shoulders relaxed will help you to have quiet hands.

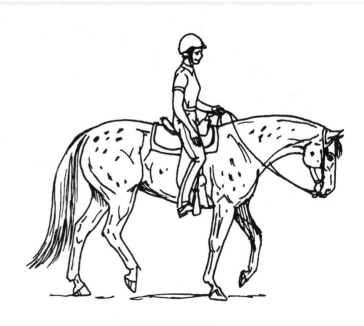

SITTING TROT OR JOG

HALF SEAT

The half seat, which is also called jumping position or two point contact, is used to help develop balance and control with your legs.

HALF SEAT OR JUMPING POSITION TWO POINT CONTACT

- The half seat position is achieved by **bending forward at the hips,** taking most of the weight in the ankles and heels. The back is straight with the seat just off the saddle. (*see also illustration on page 19*)
- Be sure while in a half seat to keep the shoulders and back relaxed. In the beginning, you may place a hand on your horse's neck or grasp a handful of mane to help you maintain your position.
- The use of the half seat position will help your balance and will strengthen your legs. It will help prepare you for posting and eventually jumping. Practice this at a halt and walk first.

POSTING

Posting is the motion of rising to the trot. It is **a forward and back motion** in which the **rider's hips move forward** (*weight out of the saddle*) **and back** (*weight in the saddle*) **on alternate beats** at the trot.

POSTING THE TROT UP AND FORWARD

Why should you learn how to post?

As you have probably learned, the trot can be a tiring and uncomfortable gait if the horse is rough or when the horse is being worked at a fast trot. If properly done, **posting makes riding the trot easier and more comfortable for the rider and the horse.**

How do you learn to post?

When a horse trots, his legs move in diagonal pairs. The left foreleg and the right hind leg move forward at the same time, and the right foreleg and the left hind leg move together. This makes the trot a two beat gait.

DOWN AND BACK

- Allow the **horse to push you forward** (*your seat will be a few inches out of the saddle*) **on one beat,** and you will **sit down in the saddle on the next beat.**
- In posting the trot, **go no higher than is necessary to get your weight out of the saddle.** The forward motion of the post comes from the hips. Your knee, lower leg and foot should be still, with your heel down.
- Be very careful not to use the reins to pull yourself up out of the saddle. This is very hard on the horse's mouth and may make him unwilling to go forward.

Posting is easy to do once you learn how. With a little patience and some practice, you will be able to add this to your list of riding skills.

EXERCISES ON HORSEBACK

Exercises will help you to develop control and coordination. They will also help you to feel relaxed on the horse. Have someone hold your horse if you are not holding the reins. Tie the reins together.

SIDE SWINGS

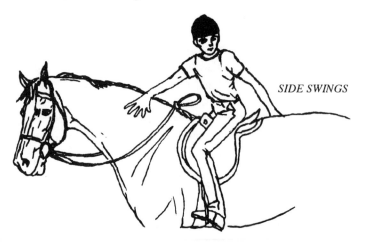

SIDE SWINGS

• With arms extended to the sides, swing the body from the waist up to the right.
• Touch the right side of the horse's neck with the left hand and the rump of the horse with the right hand.
• Swing to the left, touching the left side of the horse's neck with the right hand and the rump of the horse with the left hand.
• Rotate only the upper body, keeping hips and legs stationary and in position.

This exercise limbers the waistline and helps the rider learn to stay in balance while using the upper part of the body.

ARM SCISSORS

ARM CIRCLES

ARM SCISSORS

• Sitting straight in the saddle, drop arms to the sides. Keeping arms straight, lift them out to the side and over the head, touching the hands together.
• Then, lower them to the sides again.

This exercise is very good for limbering up the arms and shoulders.

ARM CIRCLES

• Extend the arms straight out, even with the shoulders.
• Rotate the arms toward the rear, making small circles at first and gradually making them larger.
• When arms have been rotated in the largest circles possible, reverse the direction, gradually making the circles small again.

This exercise limbers the shoulder muscles. Be sure to keep the heels down and the legs in position.

SHOULDER CIRCLES

- Sit straight in the saddle with your arms relaxed at your sides.
- First move both shoulders forward as if to touch them in front of you, then move them upwards from your sides as if to cover your ears.
- Finally, move them as far back as possible, then drop your shoulders down resulting in a rotating motion. Try to keep your arms close to your sides. After repeating this several times, return to normal position.

This exercise relaxes the tension in the neck and the shoulders.

SHOULDER CIRCLES

VAULT OFF OR EMERGENCY DISMOUNT

- On command, drop stirrups (*take feet out*), put reins in the left hand on the mane.
- Place the right hand on the pommel of the saddle and swing off.
- Land evenly on both feet. Land even with or slightly in front of the horse's shoulder, facing the front.

With practice, this can be done at all gaits. Reverse hands to dismount on the right side of the horse.

LEG SWINGS

LEG SWINGS

- Holding the reins in the proper position and keeping the upper body erect, relax the lower leg. Press in with the knees, which act as pivots for this exercise.
- Remove the feet from the stirrups.
- Swing the legs to the rear into a position parallel with the horse's back.
- Then swing legs as far forward as possible.
- After repeating this exercise a few times, return the legs to their normal position, with feet in the stirrups.

This exercise limbers the lower leg and is very good for balance.

VAULT OFF OR
EMERGENCY DISMOUNT

KICK BOTH FEET FREE
FROM STIRRUPS

SLIDE DOWN
ON RIGHT HIP
FACING FRONT

OTHER EXERCISES may also be developed and practiced with safety in mind. As you develop confidence and control, your instructor may find you can practice at a walk and trot.

Your goal as a Level 1 trail rider should be to learn how to ride safely with a group on the outdoor trails. It is recommended that all **group riding be done at a walk and in a single file manner**. The following courtesy tips will be helpful for you to know.

○ **Be attentive** to your leaders, alert to signals and to unexpected dangers.

○ **Don't tailgate!** To avoid being kicked, keep one horse length between you and the horse in front of you.

○ **Do not let your horse eat along the trail.** Teach him that while you are riding, it is not the time to eat.

○ **Always walk your horse on paved surfaces.** Trotting or turning quickly on paved surfaces can cause him to slip and fall.

○ **Always walk your horse when approaching and leaving a group of riders**, so as not to startle them.

○ When **riding uphill, use standing position.** When **riding downhill, sit in balance** with heels down. Always **walk your horse.**

RIDING DOWNHILL

SIT UP STRAIGHT AND BALANCED DOWNHILL WITH HEELS DOWN

DON'T LET YOUR HORSE EAT GRASS

BALANCE FORWARD WHEN RIDING UPHILL

If, while on the trail, **you have trouble or need to adjust your clothing or equipment**, do not do anything until **first notifying the leader**. Your leader then can stop the ride and assist you in making the necessary adjustments without endangering the others.

. . . LEANING BACK IS HARD ON YOUR HORSE

ENJOY YOUR TRAIL RIDE

LEVEL 1 REQUIREMENTS

To complete Level 1 you must be able to pass the following requirements. This can be done by performing the Level 1 Ring test, which has all the movements in it (or an alternate test made up by your instructor), or by having your CHA instructor check off each thing as you pass it. This may be done in regular riding lessons, in a group test, or an individual test.

RIDING REQUIREMENTS

_____ 1. Approach and lead a horse correctly and safely.

_____ 2. Mount with control and without disturbing the horse.
(Horse may be held by an assistant. Very small riders may mount from a safe mounting block.)

_____ 3. Dismount safely with control and prepare your horse to lead.
(Reins removed from the horse's neck and english stirrups run up)

_____ 4. Ride at a walk with good Level 1 position and control.

_____ 5. Ride at a trot around the rail with good Level 1 position and control.

_____ 6. Halt from the walk and the trot on command, with control and without hurting the horse.

_____ 7. Ride turns and reverses at the walk and trot with good Level 1 control.

GENERAL REQUIREMENTS

_____ 1. Give 5 safety rules and a reason why each is important.

_____ 2. Demonstrate 3 simple grooming steps.

_____ 3. Show how to check your equipment before riding.

_____ 4. Pass written test.

NOTES TO INSTRUCTORS ON TESTING

The goals of Level 1 are a **good foundation of safe, secure and simple basics**.

Requirements for Level 1 may be tested:
- individually
- in a group
- or by checking off as the rider passes each requirement

- Students should not be required to memorize the ring test.
- The difficulty of the horse they are riding should be taken into consideration.
- **They should be scored on their technique and safety rather than on the performance of the horse.**

The Ring Test is not a requirement in itself, but one way of testing the rider.
Alternate tests such as group tests are also acceptable.

Level 1 tests must be passed before a rider may take the Level 2 tests.

MULTIPLE CHOICE (select the best answer)

1. The first choice of a frightened horse is to:
   a) Neigh loudly
   b) Stand and paw the ground
   c) Run away

2. When approaching a horse you should approach him:
   a) At his shoulder
   b) From the front
   c) From the rear

3. A horse should be tied up with:
   a) The bridle reins
   b) A rope attached to his bit
   c) A halter and lead rope

4. When leading a horse safely, you should:
   a) Walk on his left halfway between his head and his shoulder
   b) Walk in front of him
   c) Walk on his right halfway between his head and his shoulder

5. To remove tangles from the horse's mane or tail:
   a) Start at the bottom and work up through the tangles
   b) Comb downward through the tangles
   c) Use scissors to remove bad tangles

6. When riding, your eyes should be:
   a) Looking down to be sure your horse is behaving
   b) Looking at your hands, seat and heels to be sure that they are in position
   c) Looking ahead to see where you are going

7. To stop your horse, you should:
   a) Pull on the reins very hard to make him obey you
   b) Say *Whoa* loudly several times
   c) Say *Whoa* and then check and release on the reins

8. When riding at the trot, you should keep your hands:
   a) Up in the air and out to the sides for balance
   b) Quiet, not pulling on the horse's mouth
   c) Tight on the reins for balance and to keep the horse under control

9. When approaching a horse in a tie stall:
   a) Place your hand on his rump and move him over
   b) Speak to him and get his attention
   c) Stand behind him as you enter the stall

10. When mounting, you should never:
    a) Hold on to your reins
    b) Dig your toe into the horse's ribs
    c) Ask your teacher to check your equipment

TRUE OR FALSE

__ 1. Feeding treats to horses can get your fingers nipped.

__ 2. When leading with a lead rope, you can wrap the leftover rope around your hand.

__ 3. You should speak to your horse before touching him.

__ 4. Saddling is done from the left side.

__ 5. When riding properly, your heels should be higher than your toes.

__ 6. On trail rides, you should not let your horse eat grass.

__ 7. Going uphill, lean back for better comfort and safety.

__ 8. The clothes you wear for riding don't matter except for show.

__ 9. A rubber currycomb is used to scrub in circles or against the way the hair grows.

__ 10. When you turn your horse while leading him, you should usually push him around to the right.

SHORT ANSWERS (fill in the missing word)

1. When riding Western, the reins are usually held in your _____ hand.

2. The four natural aids are:
   1. _____
   2. _____
   3. _____
   4. _____

3. Squeezing with your legs tells your horse to
   _____

4. If you make a turn which takes you off the rail, into the center of the ring, and then back to the rail going in the opposite direction, it is called a
   _____

5. When a rider rises up and down with the beats of the trot, he is _____

FILL IN THE PARTS OF THE TACK

*You may fill in **either** the parts for English or Western saddle and bridle,*
according to which seat you ride or which your instructor requires.

Western Tack

Western Bridle Parts to choose from:

Cheek piece
Crownpiece
Curb bit
Curb Strap
Reins
Shaped Ear piece
Throatlatch

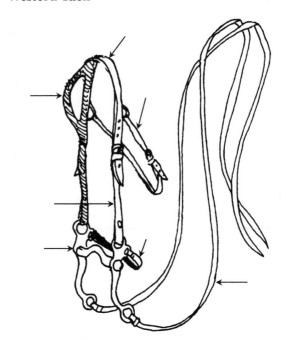

Western Saddle Parts to choose from:

Cantle
Cinch
Concho
Fender
Gullet
Horn
Latigo Keeper
Long Latigo
Pommel
Rear Cinch Strap
Rear Jockey
Saddle Strings
Seat
Seat Jockey
Short Latigo
Stirrup
Swell

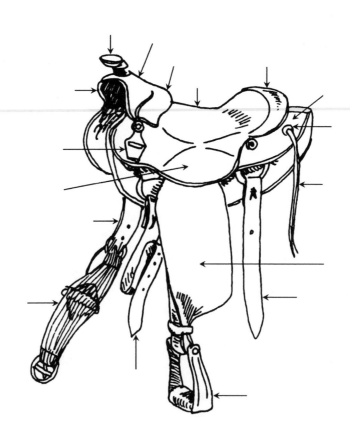

English Tack

English Bridle Parts to choose from:

Browband
Cavesson
Cheek piece
Crownpiece
Rein
Snaffle bit
Throatlatch

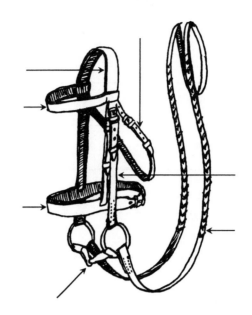

English Saddle Parts to choose from:

Billets
Buckle guard
Cantle
Flap
Girth
Gullet
Knee roll
Pad
Panels
Pommel
Safety stirrup bar
Seat
Skirt
Stirrup iron
Stirrup leather

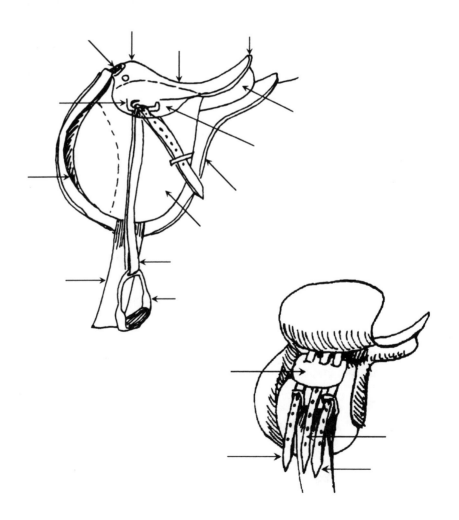

LEVEL 1 RING TEST • SCORE SHEET

Name: _____ Place _____ Date _____

		POINTS	COMMENT
1. Leading to O	(5 pts.)		
2. Safety check and mount at O	(10 pts.)		
3. Walk to C (control & equitation)	(10 pts.)		
4. Trot or jog to B (control & equitation)	(10 pts.)		
5 Stop at B thru the walk. Continue trot or jog to M	(10 pts.)		
6. Reverse at M to B	(10 pts.)		
7. Trot or jog to E (control & equitation)	(10 pts)		
8. Transition to walk at E. Turn and walk to center of arena X	(10 pts.)		
9. Stop and pause at X	(10 pts.)		
10. Dismount at X	(10 pts.)		
11. Prepare the horse to lead , at walk lead horse out of arena	(5 pts.)		

Total = 100 pts.   TOTAL
Passing score 70%.   SCORE

Scoring:

0 = Not performed	6 = Satisfactory
1 = Very bad	7 = Fairly good
2 = Unsatisfactory	8 = Good
3 = Poor	9 = Very good
4 = Insufficient, not good enough	10 = Outstanding
5 = Sufficient, fair	

Passing scores are 5 and over.
Please note that **10 means outstanding, not perfect,** (10 is a possible score, though rare).

• An alternate ridding test may be used. This is only a suggested one.
• Instructors may require posting and very small riders may have assistance in mounting.

PASSING: _____ Yes _____ No _____ Instructor's signature _____

Remember that the **goals** of Level 1 are a **good foundation of safe, secure and simple basics.**

Name: _____ Place _____ Date _____

Letter		Directions	You are scored on		Points	Comment
1. To O		Lead horse (saddled)	Leading safely and correctly	(10 pts.)		
2.	O	Check tack and mount *(Assistant will hold horse)*	Safety check and mounting properly (Control of horse, not disturbing horse while mounting)	(10 pts.)		
3.	A	Enter ring at walk Turn to right along rail Continue to C	Position, seat and control at a walk Not cutting corners	(10 pts.)		
4.	C	Jog or trot (posting optional) Continue jog or trot to B Without breaking gait	Position, seat and control at jog or trot Good corners	(10 pts.)		
5.	B	Halt through the walk	Control while stopping (10 pts.) Not hurting the horse while stopping			
6.	B	Continue trot to M	Ability to get horse to trot from B (10 pts.)			
7.	M	Reverse without breaking gait In half circle, returning to rail at B	Turning and control while reversing At the jog or trot.	(10 pts.)		
8.	B	Continue jog or trot to E Without breaking gait	Position, seat and control at jog or trot Good corners	(10 pts.)		
9.	E X	Turn and walk to center of ring (X) Stop in front of judge	Position and control While turning and stopping	(10 pts.)		
10.	X	Dismount, prepare horse to lead Leave arena Leading horse at walk	Dismounting safely In control of horse Preparing and leading horse Correctly and safely	(10 pts.)		

Total = 100 pts.
A score of 70% is considered passing.

TOTAL SCORE

Scoring:

0 = Not performed	6 = Satisfactory
1 = Very bad	7 = Fairly good
2 = Unsatisfactory	8 = Good
3 = Poor	9 = Very good
4 = Insufficient, not good enough	10 = Outstanding
5 = Sufficient, fair	

Passing scores are 5 and over.

Please note that **10 means outstanding, not perfect,** (10 is a possible score, though rare).

• An alternate ridding test may be used. This is only a suggested one.
• Instructors may require posting and very small riders may have assistance in mounting.

PASSING: _____ Yes _____ No _____ Instructor's signature _____

Remember that the **goals** of Level 1 are a **good foundation of safe, secure and simple basics.**

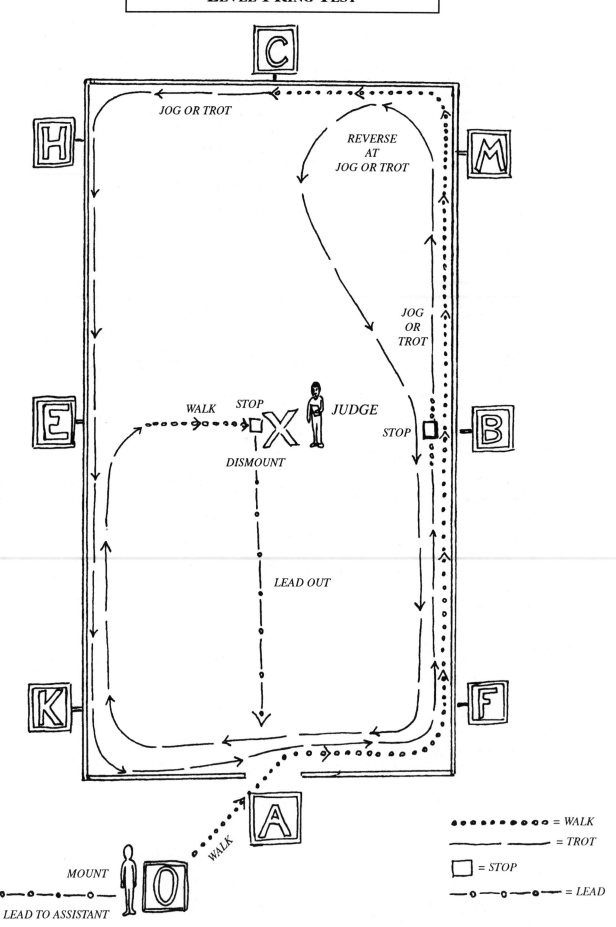

LEVEL 1 RING TEST

C

JOG OR TROT

H

REVERSE
AT
JOG OR TROT

M

JOG
OR
TROT

E

WALK   STOP   X   JUDGE

STOP

B

DISMOUNT

LEAD OUT

K

F

A

MOUNT   O   WALK

LEAD TO ASSISTANT

•••••• = WALK

——— = TROT

▭ = STOP

—o—o—o— = LEAD

CHA LEVEL 2
HORSEMANSHIP
MANUAL

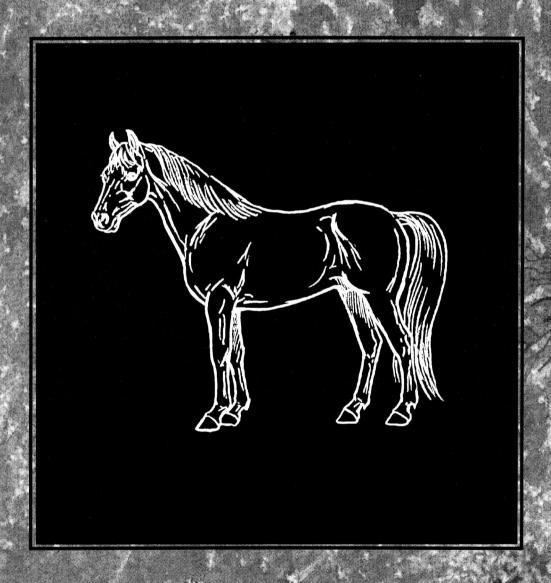

Certified Horsemanship Association

HORSEMANSHIP MANUAL

LEVEL 2

© Copyright 1983 CHA
© Copyright 1996 CHA
© Copyright 1999 CHA

TABLE OF CONTENTS

INTRODUCTION

Having passed CHA's Level 1, you have learned to safely ride your horse with some confidence. You can use the four aids to control your horse at the walk, trot, stop, circle and reverse. You have been introduced to approaching, haltering, leading, grooming and tacking up of your horse.

In this section you will learn more about how the aids work and how to put them to better use. You and your horse will develop a unique partnership as you better understand his nature and develop more balance.

GENERAL HORSE INFORMATION

Like dogs, cats or any other kinds of pets, horses can be fun, safe and enjoyable companions.

However, just as a dog must be trained and treated properly, or he will become a nuisance, **a horse must be handled correctly** if he is to be useful, safe and happy.

The key is to **understand why** horses act the way they do.

- You then need to know how to **tell** them what you **want them to do** in ways that horses can understand.
- Since horses don't understand human language, your actions teach your horse what you want and how to behave.

FEARFUL

Horses are very **big, powerful** and **fearful** creatures.

If they are frightened, they will try to run away from whatever scares them. They can be scared and startled by many things that don't bother people.

Things that may frighten a horse are:
- Loud noises
- Sudden movements
- Things that move toward them suddenly
  (*like a piece of newspaper blown by the wind*)

When a horse is nervous or frightened, he will often calm down if someone gives him confidence by keeping him under control.

Be kind but firm, soothing him with quiet words.

If you act frightened or nervous, your horse may become more frightened himself. He will feel that something must be wrong if you are frightened.

HABIT AND TRAINING

Horses **obey** humans **through habit** and **training**. They don't know that they are bigger and stronger, or they would realize that they don't need to obey us.

When you handle a horse, you are either helping his training or hurting it.

If you always handle horses properly, using the same rewards and punishments they are used to, they will keep their training and remain obedient.

Poor handling by abuse, cruelty or spoiling, untrains horses and spoils their behavior.

REWARD AND PUNISHMENT

Horses are trained by reward and punishment.

They learn how to obey commands and to do or not to do certain things, by connecting these things with **pleasant** (*reward*) or **unpleasant** (*punishment*) feelings.

A horse can only **pay attention** to a reward or punishment for about **3 seconds**.

This means that the pleasant or unpleasant feelings must come **immediately** after the horse has done something right or wrong.
- A few minutes later will be too late. He won't understand why he is being rewarded or punished.

HORSES ARE FEARFUL CREATURES

REWARDS

Rewards are not always feed, carrots or apples. They can also be:
- Kind words
- Petting
- A break from work
- Releasing the pressure of the bit or your legs is a reward when the horse obeys your signals.

PUNISHMENT

Punishment isn't always such things as being hit with a crop or jabbed with spurs.

- Punishments to a horse can also be:
  - A harsh, sharp voice
  - A stronger aid with your legs or the reins
  - Not being allowed to do what he wants to do

Rewards and punishments should **fit the situation** and must **be fair**.

If a horse doesn't understand why he is being punished, or if he is punished too hard or too long, he will look for ways to get away from a rider who hurts and frightens him.

You must also be sure that your horse isn't allowed to get a reward for something that he should not do. If he learns that jerking the reins out of your hands gains him a tasty mouthful of grass, he will do it again and again to get the reward.

Some riders may abuse their horses by **punishing** them **accidentally**.

Even if you love horses and mean to be kind, if you pull on the reins to stay in the saddle, or lean back and give your horse a backache, he will think that he is being punished.

**Good riding means not hurting or abusing
your horse even accidentally.**

*REWARD CAN BE THE RELEASE
OF THE PRESSURE OF YOUR LEGS*

PUNISHMENT CAN BE A STRONG AID

CRUELTY

Cruelty is not the same as abuse.

A rider is cruel if he **hurts his horse** or **does unsafe things** with him **on purpose**. It may be because he has lost his temper or is showing off.

*THERE IS NO EXCUSE

FOR CRUELTY

AT ANY TIME*

HORSEMAN'S TALK

If you want to talk with horse people, you should know the terms they use to describe horses and horse items.

Here are some of the most common terms:

○ **Stallion** • is a mature male horse that can be used for breeding (*Can be a father*)

○ **Mare** • is a mature female horse over 4 years old (*Can be a mother*)

○ **Foal** • is a young horse of either sex still with its mother (*A baby horse*)

○ **Filly** • is a young female horse under 4 years old (*A girl horse*)

○ **Colt** • is a young male horse under 4 years old (*A boy horse*)

○ **Weanling** • is a young horse of either sex that has just been taken away from its mother (*It is usually between 6 months and 1 year old*)

○ **Yearling** • is a horse that is officially one year old (*Some horses, regardless of their actual birth date, have an official birthday on January 1 of the next year after their birth*)

○ **Gelding** • is a male horse that has been castrated or altered (*Most male riding horses are geldings*)

○ **Pony** • is a mature horse of either sex that will never grow taller than 14.2 hands (58 inches) (*Do not confuse with a foal or baby horse that may be larger when it grows up*)

○ **Mule** • is a cross between a female horse and a male donkey

○ **Tack** • is bridles, saddles and horse equipment

○ **Green** • is an untrained or inexperienced horse

○ **Off side** • is the right side of a horse

○ **Near side** • is the left side of a horse

○ **Hand** • is the way a horse is measured, one hand equals 4 inches (*measured from the ground to the withers, the highest part of his backbone*)

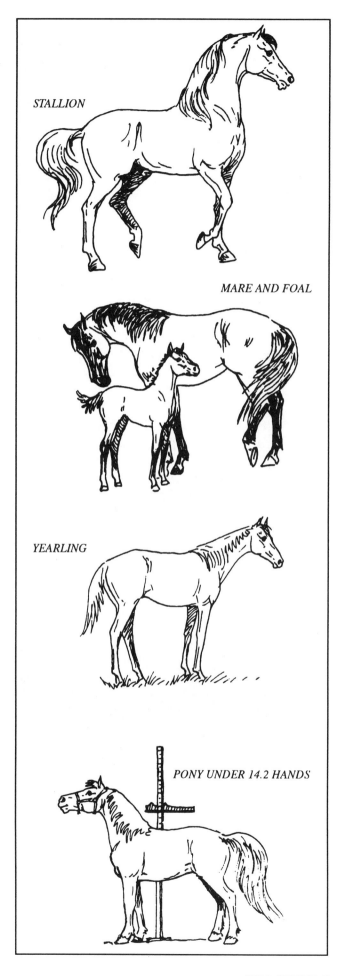

STALLION

MARE AND FOAL

YEARLING

PONY UNDER 14.2 HANDS

5

HORSE COLORS AND MARKINGS

In order to identify a horse, you should know the terms for the basic horse colors and markings.

COMMON HORSE COLORS

○ **Sorrel or Chestnut** • a reddish brown horse with reddish, brown or tan mane and tail. Legs are the same color as the body. Their legs may also have white markings. Chestnut runs from very light reddish brown to red or very dark liver color.

○ **Bay** • a brown horse with black legs, mane and tail. Body color runs from light brown, reddish brown to very dark brown, but legs, mane and tail are always black (*they may also have white markings*).

○ **Brown** • a very dark brown, almost black coat with lighter brown highlights on the muzzle, the flanks and inside the legs. Mane and tail are always black. They are hard to tell from dark bay.

○ **White** • white horses are born white. They have pink skin and usually blue or pink eyes.

○ **Pinto** • white plus large patches of black, brown, chestnut or any other color.

○ **Gray** • born dark with dark skin. Hair becomes whiter with age until pure white. A gray may range from **iron gray** (*nearly black*) to **dapple gray, white gray or flea-bitten gray** (*with tiny flecks of black or brown*).

○ **Black** • coal black without brown highlights.

○ **Dun** • sandy yellow, reddish or brown, usually with darker legs, a dark stripe down the back, and a dark mane and tail.

○ **Buckskin** • A light to dark yellow dun with black mane and tail.

○ **Palomino** • golden body color with white mane and tail. Can be a light to very dark gold color.

○ **Roan** • mixture of white hairs and one other color (*chestnut, bay or black*).
A chestnut roan is called a **strawberry roan** or **red roan**. A black roan is called a **blue roan**.

COMMON FACE MARKINGS

STAR   *STRIP*   *BLAZE*   *SNIP*   *BALD FACE*

Star • is a spot of white in the forehead

Strip • is a narrow strip of white down the face

Blaze • is a wide stripe of white down the face

Snip • is a spot of white on the muzzle

Bald face • is a white face extending across or including

at least one eye and down on sides of face

LEG MARKINGS

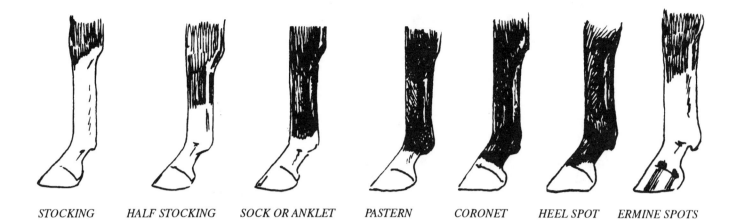

STOCKING *HALF STOCKING* *SOCK OR ANKLET* *PASTERN* *CORONET* *HEEL SPOT* *ERMINE SPOTS*

Stocking • white extending to knee or hock

Half stocking • white part way up cannon bone

Sock or anklet • white includes fetlock

Pastern • white to bottom of fetlock

Coronet • white ring around coronet of hoof

Heel spot • white spot on one heel

Ermine spots • black or colored spots in a white leg

OTHER MARKINGS

BRAND

(A MAN MADE SCAR)

FREEZE BRAND

(HAIR GROWS IN WHITE OR MAY BE HAIRLESS)

Brand • A man made scar left by a hot iron used to identify a horse with a special design. Brands are usually hairless.

Freeze brand • A brand made by a cold instrument instead of heat. It causes the hair to grow in white (or the skin may be hairless) in the shape of the brand.

Scars • left by injuries. May be hairless or hair may grow in white.

7

In Level 1 you were introduced to some of the parts of the Horse. Here are some more parts for you to be familiar with in Level 2 in order to be a better horseman and to understand about your horse.

PARTS OF THE HORSE

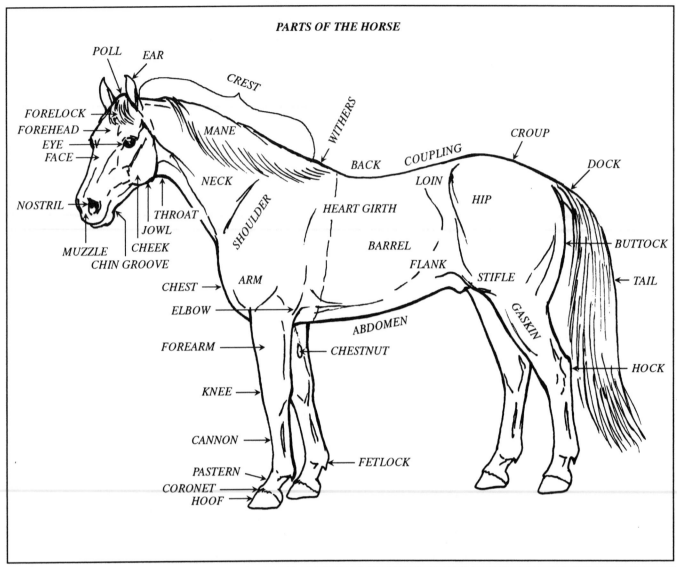

PARTS OF THE HOOF

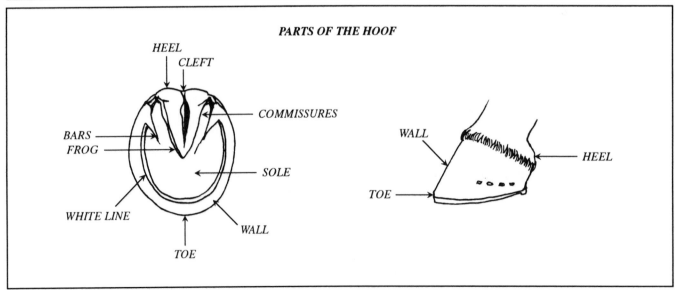

HORSE CARE AND HANDLING

In Level 1 you learned to groom and tack up a horse. Now you will learn more about horses and their needs along with the daily chores that are necessary to keep them happy and healthy. This is part of being a good horseman. It will be useful if you ever plan to have a horse of your own.

CATCHING HORSES

To catch a horse:

- You need to be quiet and confident.
- If you have a halter or lead rope, put it over your shoulder and out of sight.
- Hold your hand out as if you were offering a treat.
- Speak to the horse pleasantly.
- Walk slowly up to his left side, near the shoulder.
- If he starts to move away, stop.

When you get up to the horse's left shoulder:

- Scratch his neck gently.
- Slide your hand along his neck.
- Take his halter gently.
- If he isn't wearing a halter, **slip a lead rope around his neck** right behind his ears, to hold him while you slip his halter on.

Sometimes a horse that doesn't want to be caught will come up to you if you are quiet and patient and ignore him. Pretend that you are **interested in another horse** or **something** you have **in your hand.** Quick moves will scare him away and might make him kick or run off.

When leading a horse, even if it is for a short distance, **ALWAYS USE A LEAD ROPE.**

If anything should spook him while you are holding him with just your hand on the halter, he can get away and/or you may get hurt especially if you hold on.

TURNING OUT HORSES

Turning a horse loose:

- Lead him through the gate.
- Make him turn around and face you while you shut the gate.
- When he is standing still, remove his halter or unsnap the lead rope.

Never let him rush through the gate or pull away from you. He will become wild and hard to handle when you are letting him go.

Don't chase him or encourage him to jump away when you let him go. It can make him learn to kick.

It is **safer** for the horse if his **halter** is **removed** when he is turned loose. He can get a leg caught in the halter or the halter caught on an object and hurt himself very badly. This means, however, that he will not be as easy to catch as when the halter is left on.

IT IS SAFER FOR YOUR HORSE IF YOU REMOVE THE HALTER

ALWAYS USE A LEAD ROPE

QUICK RELEASE KNOT

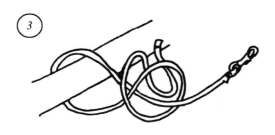

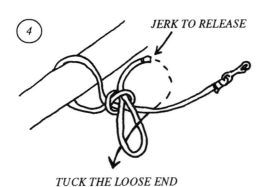

JERK TO RELEASE

*TUCK THE LOOSE END
THROUGH THE LOOP
IF YOUR HORSE PLAYS
WITH THE ROPE*

Horses should **always be tied with a halter and lead rope, NEVER a bridle and reins**. Horses may pull back and injure their mouth or break an expensive bridle if this rule is not followed.

When you tie a horse up, **always tie to something solid** that he cannot break or pull loose. If he should pull back and break off a piece of board, he might run and drag it in a panic and get badly hurt.

Tie a horse at the **level of his back or a little higher**. Tying him low may make him pull on the rope. He can get a foot over it and get hurt.

Give him only **enough rope** for **his nose to stretch to the ground**, no more or he can get hung up in the rope. A good test is to see (*if you took the halter off the horse*) if the top of the halter would just touch the ground. This is a safe length of rope for most tying.

For saddling, it is recommended to tie shorter.

QUICK RELEASE KNOT

The best knot to use is a **Quick Release Knot** (also called a *safety knot*). This is a jerk loose release knot that can be pulled loose quickly if a horse should pull back and fight the rope.

TYING TOO LONG IS DANGEROUS

COOLING OUT A HOT HORSE

When a horse is hot and sweaty, he needs to be **cooled down gradually** so that he will be comfortable and will not get chilled. Improper cooling out can make a horse very sick.

• First, you will need to **walk** a hot, sweaty horse until he is **breathing normally**.
• You should **always walk** for the **last ten minutes** of your ride. This will help you bring your horse in cool.
• If he is very hot and tired, **dismount** and **loosen** the **girth** on the saddle.
• Your horse will be happier if you take off the bridle and replace it with a halter.
• Leave the saddle **in place with the girth loose** to let the circulation return to normal slowly in the areas compressed by the saddle. After his **breathing returns to normal**, you may remove the saddle.

If the weather is hot, you may **wash** your **horse** down with **plain water** (*tepid, not hot or cold*) to remove the sweat and salt.
• Use a sweat scraper to squeeze the water out of his coat until he is almost dry.
• Then, **cover him with a cooler** (*a light cover*) if it is breezy and **walk him** around until he **feels dry and cool** when you touch him **between the front legs**.

A hot, tired and sweaty horse may be very thirsty, but he should **not be allowed to gulp large amounts of water,** especially cold water. This can make him seriously ill.

Instead, **set out a pail of slightly warm water** and **walk a large circle;** let him have **a few sips each time you pass the bucket.** By the time he is cool and dry he will probably have had all the water he wants. He can then safely be put in his stall with a bucket of water without becoming sick.

*TIE AT THE PROPER LENGTH
ONLY ENOUGH ROPE FOR HIS
NOSE TO STRETCH TO THE GROUND*

*TIE AT THE PROPER LENGTH
SHORTER FOR SADDLING*

WASH YOUR HORSE DOWN AND COVER HIM WITH A COOLER

11

STABLE CHORES

There are some chores that have to be done every day if you have horses.
These include **cleaning stalls or corrals**, **watering** and **keeping the aisles and stable area clean**.
You can help around the stable if you learn how to do these chores properly and pitch in when they need doing.

STALL CLEANING

If your horse lives in a stall, it **must be cleaned every day** or else it will become a filthy, smelly prison cell for him.

• Wet, dirty bedding can lead to thrush, a foot infection that rots the horse's feet.

• Flies also breed in manure and soiled bedding.

To clean a stall:
• Take the horse out and tie him somewhere else.
(*Unless your instructor tells you otherwise.*)
• Pick up the piles of manure and wet spots with a pitchfork and throw them into the wheelbarrow or muck basket.

Before the horse returns to his stall, the stall should be bedded down. There are different kinds of bedding you can use. The most common kinds of bedding are:
• Straw
• Shavings
• Sawdust
• Peanut hulls

You should add enough new bedding to make up for what you took out, but don't waste it.

Spread the bedding around. (*Put the old clean bedding in the spots most likely to be soiled. You may want to spread the new bedding in the cleaner areas of the stall.*)

• Regularly **check stalls for hazards** that could hurt the horse.
• Take a broom and **sweep the cobwebs** off the walls while you look the walls over for nails or splinters.
• Be sure that there are **no sharp edges** on anything metal, or **holes** in panes of glass that he could poke his nose through and get hurt.

If you see signs that horses are **chewing the wood**, ask your instructor for some wood preservative to paint over the spot.

WATERING

Horses need plenty of **clean water available at all times**, except when the horses are hot and sweaty. They may drink as much as 20 gallons on a hot day.

• The bucket or trough they drink from **must be clean** because horses hate to drink dirty, slimy water.

• Water buckets should be **emptied** and **rinsed out** and the slime scrubbed out with a brush as often as they need it, usually every day.

• When you fill water buckets, notice if the horse drinks or not. Let him have all he wants, then leave him with a full bucket.

CLEANING THE AREA

Clean, neat aisles and areas not only look better, they are safer for people and horses. You aren't as likely to trip over a rake or bump into something that shouldn't be there if you keep the area picked up and neat.

Some chores that need to be done frequently:

1. **Pick up after your horse.**

   If he drops manure, clean it up.
   Don't leave a mess for somebody else.

2. **Rake up hay and trash.**

   Makes the area neater; reduces a fire hazard.

3. **Put tack and tools back where they belong.**

   Rakes and forks can hurt you if you step on them.

   Tack lying around may get dumped in the dirt and/or be lost or broken.

4. **Pick up papers and trash.**
   Keep dangerous trash away from the stable.

   Glass bottles around a barn may lead to broken glass and cuts.

   Loose wire or baling string can trip a horse or a person.

   Nails can get stuck in the horse's feet, causing serious injuries.

HORSES AND PONIES FOUND IN AMERICA

There are many kinds of horses that have been developed to serve man in different ways.

○ **BREED** • is a horse that comes from the **same ancestors** and has been bred according to a particular standard.
○ **PUREBRED** • is a horse with **both parents of the same breed.**
   (*Not a thoroughbred which is a particular breed of horse*)
   Purebred horses may be registered with their breed club or association, which makes them more valuable.
○ **GRADE** • is a horse of **mixed breed** or those that are mostly one breed, such as a "*grade Morgan*".
○ **TYPE** • is a kind of horse that is built well or has a talent to do a particular job, regardless of breed.
   (example "*hunter type*" or "*western stock horse type*")

There are many breeds in the world. The following are some of the best known breeds in this country.

HORSE BREEDS

THE GRADE HORSE	ARABIAN

THE GRADE HORSE

Just like dogs, not all horses are blue blooded aristocrats. Like the mutt you get from the pound, the grade horse has a **mix of many different ancestors.**

They may be beautiful or something less than handsome, but they can still be as good as a fancy purebred. Don't look down on a grade horse just because he doesn't have papers or fancy breeding.

Handsome is as handsome does, especially in a camp riding horse or a family pleasure mount.

Sometimes it is fun to try to figure out what breeds make up a grade horse. They might have Arabian ears, a Quarter Horse rump or Thoroughbred speed.

The possibilities are many!

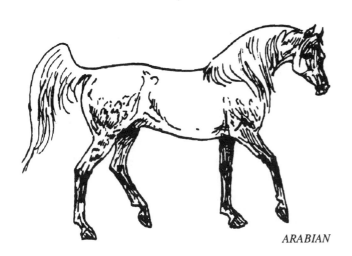

ARABIAN

ARABIAN

They are sometimes called the *"Father of Breeds"* because most riding horses trace back to the early Arabian. They originated in the Middle East and were bred by Bedouin tribes of the desert. Arabians are the **oldest pure breed** existing today. The Bedouins used Arabian horses as war horses and prized them highly, even keeping them in their tents. They were ridden by Mohammed and his warriors. Some were taken back to Europe by the returning Crusader knights. An Arabian horse was a princely gift.

Arabians are **small to medium size**, about **14 to 15.2 hands** and around **900 to 1000 pounds**. They have **dark skin** which withstands desert sun better, and are found in most **solid colors**.

The Arabian has a beautiful **wedge shaped head**, broad and deep at the forehead and **dished** in the **face**, with a delicate teacup muzzle and wide nostrils. Their eyes are large, dark and expressive. The **ears are small** and turned in at the tips. Their **necks** are gracefully **arched** and set into a sloping shoulder. They will usually have a long flowing mane. Arabians have a very short, strong back because they have **one less vertebrae** than other horses. The **croup** should be **high and level** and the **tail** is **carried** in a **high arch**. The legs are fine, hard and trim. An Arabian should move with a proud walk, a floating trot and a graceful canter.

Having been developed in the desert, Arabians have great endurance. They are **hot blooded, sensitive and intelligent, with spirit and courage**. Arabians are very versatile and do many jobs well. Pleasure riding is one of their main uses. They also excel in endurance riding, dressage, cutting and driving.

13

THOROUGHBRED

QUARTER HORSE

THOROUGHBRED

The Thoroughbred was developed in the late 1600's for racing in England. All Thoroughbreds trace back to three Oriental stallions imported into England about that time, the **Darley Arabian**, the **Byerly Turk** and the **Godolphin Barb**.

These small, light and fiery stallions gave the English racehorse the hot blood, speed, and courage of the Arabian. The great race horse families of **Eclipse**, **Herod** and **Matchem** all trace back to these three sires, and all modern Thoroughbreds go back to those early horses.

Thoroughbreds were raced in England in four mile distance races. Today they race from five furlongs to $1\frac{1}{2}$ miles on the flat. They also steeplechase or race over jumps, and are among the finest hunters and show jumpers. Many of the horses on our Olympic teams are Thoroughbreds or part Thoroughbred. They excel in polo, jumping, dressage and three day eventing. A Thoroughbred makes a fine pleasure horse in the hands of a good rider and most are built to jump well.

Thoroughbreds are registered with the Jockey Club. All Thoroughbreds are considered to have an **official birthday on January 1** of the next year after their birthday, regardless of their true birth date.

They are tall, about **15.2 to over 16.2 hands** and light, about **900 to 1000 pounds**. Like their Arabian ancestors, they have fine, thin skin and are sensitive, which along with their **hot blooded**, **competitive nature** can make them a handful for an unskilled rider. They have small refined heads, sloping shoulders, sharp withers and long, lean muscles. Their legs are thin and fine but tough.

Thoroughbreds usually move with long, low strides and are beautiful to see at the gallop.

QUARTER HORSE

The Quarter Horse is a distinctly **American breed**. He descended from **Chickasaw Indian ponies** found in the Southeast and used by the colonists for quarter mile races. Later, English Thoroughbreds like **Janus** were bred to the Quarter Horse for more speed and the characteristic muscling. Quarter Horses were taken west by explorers and settlers. They followed wagon trains, herded cattle and raced in short brush races. The best known early families were **Steeldust** and **Shiloh**. The King Ranch in Texas developed a modern type of Quarter Horse for cattle work from their stallion, **Old Sorrel**. These working cow horses were tough, hardy and had quiet dispositions. Recently they have been crossed with the Thoroughbred for racing.

Quarter Horses are sturdy, compact and built like a good athlete. They stand **14.2 hands and taller**, and weigh between **1000 and 1250 pounds**. They have tremendous muscle development, which gives the breed its explosive speed and turning ability. Quarter Horses should have **well developed hindquarter and forearm muscles** and a powerful, compact body carried over clean, well proportioned legs. The head has a deep, muscled jaw, straight face and **small fox ears**. They come in **all solid colors** (*bay, brown, chestnut, black, grey, dun, roan and palomino*). Spots or paint markings are not allowed.

The Quarter Horse is a versatile, athletic animal with a **quiet disposition**. They are used extensively for ranch work, cattle work, rodeo events, cutting, western pleasure and speed competitions. They also make a fine trail horse, english pleasure horse, hunter and jumper. Quarter Horses have made the Olympic jumping team. They are the fastest horse in the world for short sprints, topping the Thoroughbred at distances under a half mile. Quarter Horses are raised and ridden all over the country for pleasure, work, show, racing or just fun.

MORGAN

AMERICAN SADDLEBRED

MORGAN

The Morgan is another truly **American breed**. All Morgans trace back to a single sire, a small bay stallion named **Figure**. He was foaled in New England just after the Revolutionary War. His sire may have been an English Thoroughbred called True Briton, captured from a Tory. He is said to have also carried Arabian blood. When Figure became famous as a sire, his owner, Justin Morgan, gave the little stallion the name **Justin Morgan**.

A tough, compact but beautiful horse, he had to earn his keep by plowing, winning trotting and running races, and even winning bets on how much weight he could pull after a hard day's work. His colts turned out to be superior horses, compact, powerful and speedy, with their sire's beauty and willingness. His most famous sons were **Sherman**, **Woodbury** and **Bulrush**. In the 19th century, Morgans were versatile utility horses, fancy carriage horses, farm horses and cavalry mounts. **Winchester**, a Morgan ridden by General Sheridan, became a hero of the Civil War. The Morgan gave speed and trotting ability to the Standardbred harness racer.

Morgans today are still **compact** and **powerful,** but they show more refinement and not many pull plows any more. They range in height from **14.2 to 15.2 hands**. They have fine, intelligent heads with large eyes and **small ears**, a **well arched neck**, **short back**, **flat croup** and fine, hard, strong feet and legs. They come in **solid colors** such as bay, chestnut, brown and black.

They move with **high, stylish action** and usually have a **spirited but cooperative disposition**. One word that describes the Morgan is versatile. He is used for all kinds of pleasure riding, driving, trail riding, dressage, parades and jumping. He is a great family pleasure horse.

AMERICAN SADDLEBRED

The American Saddlebred is the **peacock** of the show ring, delighting the crowd as he shows off his high action and **show biz personality**. He is also a pleasure mount with easy gaits and an intelligent, trainable nature. The Saddlebred was developed by planters in the South who needed an easy gaited horse to carry them through the fields all day and that would look fancy for Sunday visiting. They bred the Saddlebred from **Arabian, Thoroughbred and Morgan stock,** crossed with **easy gaited pleasure horses**.

Saddle horses performed the **walk, trot, canter and singlefoot** (*a smooth fast gait that is easy on the rider*). Later on, the people with fine saddle horses began to exhibit them in horse shows where their gaits, manners and beauty were judged. Saddlebred horses became popular as fine harness horses and stylish park mounts in the cities during the late 1800's. Today, the American Saddlebred is primarily an english pleasure and show horse. Show horses are shown as **three gaited** (*walk, trot and canter*), or **five gaited** (*walk, trot, canter plus the slow gait and the thrilling rack, developed from the singlefoot*). They also compete as fine harness horses in formal driving classes.

Show saddle horses have their feet grown long for high action and their tails set in a brace for show appearance, but pleasure Saddlebreds are ridden with normal feet and tails, both english and western. American Saddlebreds are **tall (15.2 to 16 hands), proud and elegant** looking, with a **long arched neck**, small refined head, **flat back and croup** and a **high tail carriage** and **solid colors**. They naturally have a somewhat **high action** and smooth, collected gaits. The Saddlebred is **showy** but **calm and intelligent**, so he is a favorite of trick, circus and movie horse trainers.

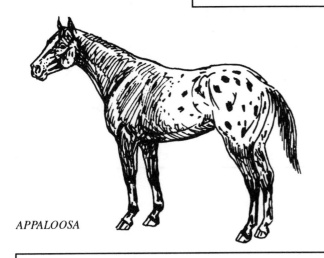

APPALOOSA

PINTO AND PAINT

APPALOOSA

The Appaloosa is a **color breed**, meaning that these horses have **special color patterns** as well as other breed characteristics.

Horses with Appaloosa spots were known for centuries in Asia, the Middle East and Europe. They probably reached this country along with the Spanish explorers. Some of the horses escaped and ran wild and later were caught and used by the Indians. When Lewis and Clark made their expedition they found that the Nez Perce Indians along the Palouse River raised horses with distinctive spots. These horses got the name Appaloosa from the Palouse country. The Nez Perce used them as buffalo hunting horses and as war horses, fighting a long campaign against the U.S. Cavalry. When the Indians surrendered, the Appaloosa breed nearly died out, but a few survived as tough western cow ponies.

Modern Appaloosas are larger and more refined than their Indian pony ancestors, having typical stock horse type conformation. They range from **14.1 to 16 hands** and weigh between **900 and 1100 pounds**. Appaloosas are used for ranch and cattle work, pleasure riding both english and western, trail riding, rodeo events, and hunting and jumping. They are tough and hardy with plenty of stamina. Distinctive Appaloosa characteristics include a **white sclera** or **ring around the eye** which resembles a human eye, **mottled skin** on the face, muzzle and under the tail, and **striped hooves**. Appaloosas come in **five different color patterns**. They include the **blanket** (*white over the hips, sometimes with small spots*), **leopard** (*white horse with small dark spots all over*), **snowflake** (*dark body with small white spots all over*), **marble** (*mottled colour*) and **frost** (*dark body with white spots or frosting*).

PINTO

The Pinto is another **color breed**, going back to the Indian ponies and before them, to horses brought over by Spanish explorers. The name Pinto is a Spanish word meaning "*painted*".

They may be a **piebald** (*black and white*) or a **skewbald** (*any other color and white*) and come in **two color patterns**.
• **Tobiano** pattern, the white seems to work down from the back and the edges of the spots are smooth and clear.
• **Overo** pattern, the white seems to work upward from under the belly and the edges of the spots are jagged and lacy.

A Pinto **can be a horse or a pony** and may be of **any other breed or combination of breeds** besides having the Pinto color.

PAINT

The Paint is a fairly **new breed** of Pinto colored horses with stock horse conformation. To be considered a Paint the horse **must have Pinto color** and also have **Quarter Horse or Thoroughbred breeding** and a typical **stock horse build**. All Paints are Pintos, but not all Pintos can be registered as Paints.

Paints are used for typical western activities like ranch work, rodeo events and cutting. They are also used for english and western pleasure riding, showing and trail, and are raced over short distances. Pintos are used according to their type, western or english. Their flashy color makes them favorites for parades, rodeos and cowboy movies.

PONY BREEDS

Ponies are not young horses but are **naturally small animals that will never grow larger than 14.2 hands**. There are numerous pony breeds, but many ponies are part horse. They are considered ponies because of their size, not their breeding. True ponies are tough and hardy. They often were small because they had to survive under adverse conditions with little feed.

SHETLAND PONY

WELSH PONY

SHETLAND PONY

The Shetland Pony is the **smallest** of the pony breeds, **11.2 hands or smaller**. They developed hundreds of years ago on the cold, rocky islands north of Scotland. Shetland ponies had to be tough and hardy to survive the fierce cold and scarce feed. Because they were small but strong, they were used to carry peat for fuel and to work underground in the coal mines.

In America, the Shetland breed was refined and developed into a miniature show pony with a thinner neck, smaller head, finer legs and higher, fancier action than the original Island type. These ponies are usually shown in harness as fine harness ponies, as roadsters, which are miniature trotting speed ponies or in children riding classes.

Shetland ponies come in **solid colors** and with **pinto markings**. They are **strong**, and can be kept on little feed and in small quarters. Shetlands are small enough for little children to handle them easily. They are **very intelligent** and **sometimes stubborn**, so they must be well trained, especially if they are to be used by very small children. Shetland ponies have always been popular for children because of their small size and great intelligence. They are a favorite of circus trick trainers because of their beauty, small size and quickness to learn.

PONY OF THE AMERICAS

Pony of the Americas or POA is a **new breed** which combines the size of the Welsh with the conformation of the Quarter Horse and the coloring of the Appaloosa. They are **11.2 to 13 hands** and are usually ridden and shown western. They make a fine intermediate pony for a child too big for a small pony and too small for a horse.

WELSH PONY

The Welsh Pony was a refugee from persecution hundreds of years ago in the mountains of Wales. King Henry VII, wishing to encourage the breeding of larger horses, decreed that *"all nags of small stature shall be put to death."* The wild Welsh ponies survived, living on sparse feed, high up in the Welsh mountains. Later, they were crossed with Arabian blood which produced a small, hardy and unusually beautiful pony.

Most are somewhat larger than the Shetland Ponies. Some are **as large as 14.2 hands** and are used for adult riders as well as children. The Welsh pony's Arabian blood gives them a small, refined head with large eyes and **often** an **Arabian dished face**. They show the Arabian influence in the trot, which appears to float over the ground. Welsh ponies are natural jumpers and are often used as hunter ponies. They also drive well and are fine children's riding ponies. Welsh ponies come in **all colors except pinto**. They should be **refined** and **compact**, with smooth muscling, clean legs and heads and well arched necks. Like the Shetland, they are extremely **intelligent** and **often very spirited**.

*POA OR
PONY OF THE AMERICAS*

HORSEMANSHIP

ADJUSTING YOUR STIRRUPS

Now that you are past the beginning stage, you should be able to adjust your own stirrups to the right length for the kind of riding you are doing. It is important to get your **stirrups even**, or you may ride crooked in the saddle and off balance. **Too long** a stirrup will make you point your toes down and dangle your legs. If your stirrups are **too short** they will push you too far back in the saddle and can make it hard to sit smoothly. You may have to shorten or lengthen your stirrups for certain activities like jumping or working on the sitting trot.

ENGLISH STIRRUPS

You can **check** the approximate length of the **stirrup** leathers **before you mount**.

- Pull the stirrup iron all the way down to the end of the leather loop.
- Place your fingertips on the stirrup bar.
- The stirrup iron should reach to your **armpit**. This will give you approximately the right length of your stirrups when you mount.

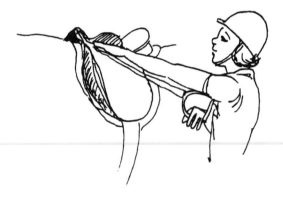

*CHECKING
ENGLISH STIRRUP LENGTH
BEFORE MOUNTING*

To check the stirrups when you are mounted:
- Sit in the middle of the saddle with your feet hanging straight down.
- The bottom of the irons should tap your feet at just about the ankle bone.

For riding the **sitting trot and canter**, the stirrups should be just below the ankle bone. For **jumping or a more forward seat**, the stirrups should be just above the ankle.

Right at the ankle bone is a good all around length.

When you are on your horse adjusting your stirrups, **keep your feet in the irons** and **hold your reins**.

To **adjust your stirrups** to the proper length, pull on the end of the stirrup leather until the buckle slides out where you can reach it. Hold the outside of the buckle and pull up on the strap.

- To **shorten** the leathers, pull the buckle higher on the leather, closer to the saddle.

- To make them **longer**, slide the buckle down farther from the saddle.

- When you have adjusted the stirrups, check the length again and be sure that they are even.

- Pull the buckle back up under the skirt so that it will not rub your leg and cause discomfort.
- The spare end of the stirrup leather can be tucked back under your leg and held by the tab or keeper on the saddle.

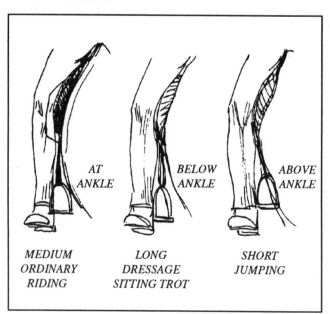

AT ANKLE	BELOW ANKLE	ABOVE ANKLE
MEDIUM ORDINARY RIDING	LONG DRESSAGE SITTING TROT	SHORT JUMPING

WESTERN STIRRUPS

Western stirrups cannot be checked from the ground. You will have to **mount to check the length.**

• Stand straight up with both feet in the stirrups. Keep your heels lower than your toes and your knees bent.
• When standing up, there should be **a space about 2 1/2" to 3" (a hand's width) between your seat and the seat of the saddle.**

• If you can't fit any fingers between you and the saddle, or if you can't stand up with your heels down, your stirrups are **too long.**
• If you can fit a whole fist between your seat and the saddle, your stirrups are **too short.**

Western stirrups are easier to **adjust from the ground.** You may have to dismount to fix the stirrup length if it is too long or short. The stirrup leathers may have buckles or a slide fastener.

• To **shorten** the stirrups, slide the fastener or buckle up closer to the saddle.
• To make them **longer,** slide it down.
• Be sure to get both stirrups even.

Never slip your feet into the stirrup straps instead of the stirrups if the stirrups won't go short enough for your legs. You could get a foot caught in the strap, which is very dangerous.

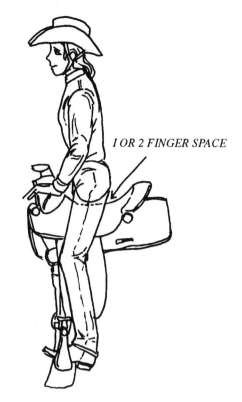

1 OR 2 FINGER SPACE

*CHECKING
WESTERN STIRRUP LENGTH
AFTER MOUNTING*

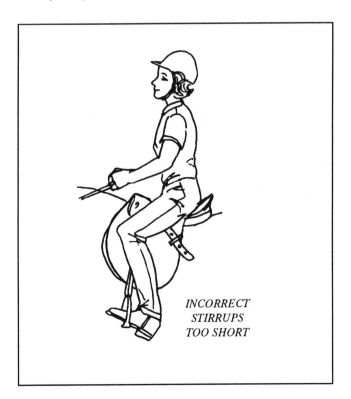

*INCORRECT
STIRRUPS
TOO SHORT*

*INCORRECT
STIRRUPS
TOO LONG*

BALANCE OF HORSE AND RIDER

The kind of riding that is most often taught today is called **Balanced Seat**.
This means that you ride by balance, not by muscle grip. Balance is more important in a rider than strength.
To be comfortable and secure on a horse, you need to be in balance with him in everything he does.

CENTER OF GRAVITY

To understand the balance of horse and rider, you need to know where your center of gravity is and where your horse's center of gravity is.

The center of gravity is **an imaginary spot** where you or the horse are **in balance**. You might think of the center of gravity as the **balance point**.

When you are sitting in a **normal riding position**, your center of gravity is just about in your **middle**, near your stomach.

The **horse's center of gravity** is near his **middle** too, just about under the saddle.

Your center of gravity is **right over his**, so you are **in balance at the halt**. You don't need to hold on in order to stay in the saddle.

**WHEN THE HORSE MOVES,
HIS CENTER OF GRAVITY MOVES TOO.**

When he steps into a walk, his center of gravity goes **forward** just a bit.

If he goes faster, it moves forward more.

• To stay in balance as he starts to move, you must **move your center of gravity forward** just enough to be **with** your horse.

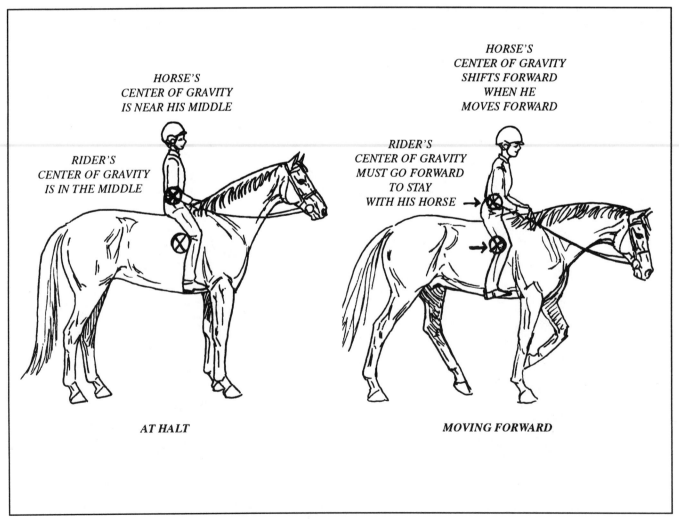

HORSE'S
CENTER OF GRAVITY
IS NEAR HIS MIDDLE

RIDER'S
CENTER OF GRAVITY
IS IN THE MIDDLE

AT HALT

HORSE'S
CENTER OF GRAVITY
SHIFTS FORWARD
WHEN HE
MOVES FORWARD

RIDER'S
CENTER OF GRAVITY
MUST GO FORWARD
TO STAY
WITH HIS HORSE

MOVING FORWARD

BEHIND THE MOTION

If he suddenly went forward fast and you didn't bend forward with him, you would be **behind the motion**, and may be left behind your horse, sitting on the ground.

*IF YOUR HORSE JUMPED FORWARD
AND YOU LEANED BACK
YOU'D BE BEHIND THE MOTION*

AHEAD OF THE MOTION

When the **horse slows down or stops, his balance comes back** and **yours must also come back**.

If you straighten up smoothly with your horse, you will feel as if you both stop together.

If your horse suddenly puts on the brakes and you keep leaning forward, you will find yourself **ahead of the motion**, and possibly biting the dust or hugging your horse around the neck.

*IF HE STOPS SUDDENLY
AND YOU KEEP LEANING FORWARD
YOU WILL BE AHEAD OF THE MOTION*

EXERCISE FOR BALANCE

Riding behind the motion or ahead of the motion is sometimes done on purpose by expert riders for special purposes. Ordinarily a rider should try to be **with the motion** and balanced with his horse at all times in any gait that his horse is in.

You can control where your balance is by keeping your **legs in the proper position** with your **heels down, leaning forward from your hips**.

To test your balance, **try to stand up without holding on to the reins, horse or saddle**.

*EXERCISE
TO CHECK YOUR BALANCE*

*STAND UP IN YOUR STIRRUPS
WITHOUT HOLDING ON
NO HANDS*

• If you are truly **in balance**, you will be able to keep your position without holding on.

• If you are **behind the motion**, you will **sit down** with your legs in front of you and not be able to stay up in the saddle.

• If you are **ahead of the motion**, you will feel as if you are going to **topple over** onto the horse's neck with your legs in back of you.

21

BALANCE IN TURNS

When you turn your horse, you should feel securely balanced with him.
Your horse may lean into a turn slightly, especially as you progress to faster gaits.

○ **Your body should stay in line with the horse's backbone**
so that you lean just as much as he does and no more.

○ **If you lean too much,**
you may feel as if you might fall over to the inside and you will put your horse off balance.

○ **If you lean to the outside of the turn,**
it will make your back crooked and you may slip sideways across the saddle.

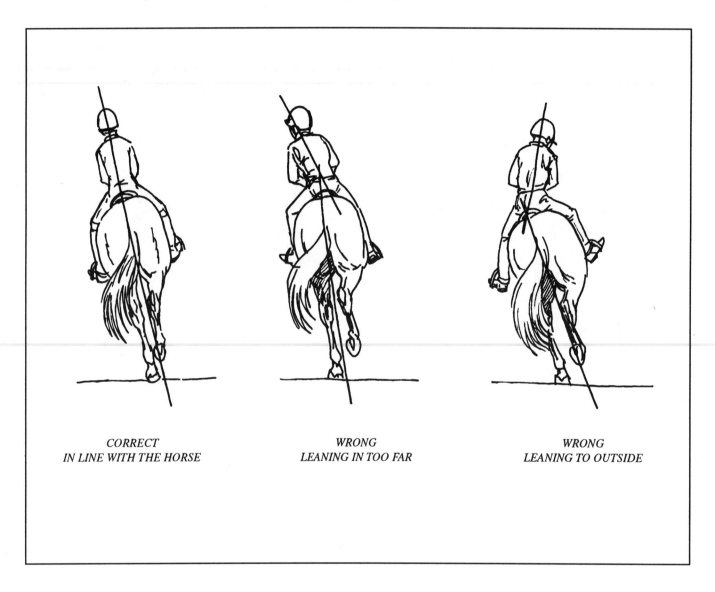

CORRECT
IN LINE WITH THE HORSE

WRONG
LEANING IN TOO FAR

WRONG
LEANING TO OUTSIDE

Your instructor can tell by watching you from behind if you are in balance on the turns.

ASK, TELL AND COMMAND

To be sure that your horse obeys you, the best method is the **three stage method**:

ASK, TELL and COMMAND.

When you want your horse to do something, you should **first ASK him**, giving him the lightest possible signal and a chance to respond willingly. (*This could be a gentle pressure on the reins, a quietly spoken voice command or a touch of your legs.*) If the horse does not mind you, he may have a good reason. Is he confused by your signal, frightened or maybe not paying attention?

If you are sure that you gave a clear signal and he is just not paying attention, or if he does not want to do what you have told him, **TELL him by giving a stronger, clearer signal**.

If he still does not obey, you will need to now **COMMAND him to respond**.
• A command might be a sharp kick or a strong, firm pressure on the reins to make him obey.
• As soon as he starts to do what he was told, it is important to **reward him by relaxing the pressure** (*stop kicking or release the pressure on the rein*) and by **giving him an approving word or a pat**.

Don't continue to punish him by hitting or acting angry **after he has started to obey you**, even if he wasn't behaving himself earlier. If you don't reward him when he starts to behave correctly, he won't understand what you want.

Don't be afraid to be firm and just as stubborn as the horse is when insisting that he do as you say. **If you use the ASK, TELL and COMMAND system, your horse has the best chance to understand and obey you and earn his reward.**

Some things that you should work on in handling and riding your horse are:

• Keep your horse's attention on you only.

• Ask your horse to respond promptly to your signals, but be reasonable.

• Never punish him when you have made the mistake and given him the wrong signal.

• Don't let your horse eat grass while you are riding or when he has a bit in his mouth.

• If your horse makes an angry gesture at another horse (like flattening his ears or threatening to bite or kick), **correct him by immediately** taking him out of reach of the other horse and by using a sharp voice command.

• Insist that your horse listen to you and obey you about staying in his gaits, starting and stopping.

If you let him start or stop when he wants, he may start disregarding your signals. If he stops or changes his gait without being told, make him go back to what he was doing until you give him the signal to change.

• Use the smallest and lightest signals that you can to get your horse's attention and to ask him to obey you.

Don't forget to reward when he does as you ask.

BASIC GAITS OF THE HORSE

WALK

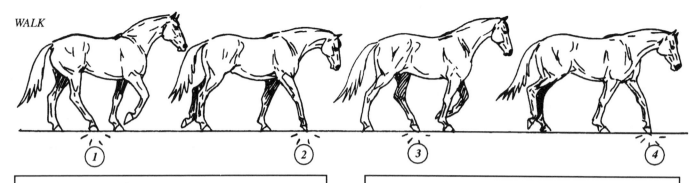

THE WALK

The walk is **a slow, flat footed gait** with **four beats**, about **3 to 4 miles per hour**.

The horse steps **first** with his **right hind foot**, then the **right front foot**, then the **left hind** and finally the **left front**. Because it is slow, steady and even, the walk is easy to ride and easy on the horse. A horse should walk calmly but with long strides, using his legs and muscles and stretching his neck for balance.

A good rider relaxes and lets his seat go with the movement of the walk and lets his arms and hands relax to permit the horse to stretch his neck.

Walking is good:
- to warm up the horse's muscles before hard work.
- to cool him out after work.
- to relax and calm him.

It helps to develop a horse's muscles when he is made to walk energetically.

THE TROT AND JOG

The trot is **a two beat gait** in which **the diagonal** (opposite corners) **front and hind legs move and hit the ground together as a pair**. It has **suspension**, which means that part of the time the horse is off the ground. This is what gives the trot its bounce.

The trot, which is about **6 miles per hour**, is faster than the walk. The trot should be even and regular with a steady **1-2, 1-2 rhythm**. At the trot the horse's head does not bob up and down as it does in the walk unless your horse is lame.

A **jog** is **a soft, slow trot without as much speed, suspension or bounce as a regular trot**. Most western horses are trained to jog as it is easier to ride in a western saddle. A jog should be even, steady and relaxed.

Jogging and trotting are **good exercise** for both horse and rider. The rider can ride posting, sitting, or balancing in two-point position. A good rider can do all three. The trot and jog are used a lot for the training of horses and many practice exercises for riders. The trot and jog also cover the most ground while being the least tiring for the horse, so they are used for long distance riding.

TROT OR JOG

CANTER OR LOPE

THE CANTER AND LOPE

The canter is **a three beat gait with suspension.**

In the **LEFT LEAD**, the **right hind leg pushes off** the ground. Then the left hind and the right front feet hit the ground at the same time. Next, the left front foot, or the leading leg, hits the ground. Finally, the period of suspension comes when all four feet are off the ground.
• In the **RIGHT LEAD**, the **left hind leg hits first.**

The canter is **a medium gait,** about **8 to 10 miles per hour**. It should always be **done on the lead which is to the inside of the turn or circle**. When cantering on the wrong lead, a horse could slip or stumble.

The **lope is a slow, relaxed canter** which is done on a loose rein when riding western.

The **rider** usually **sits up tall** in the saddle when cantering and should keep his **seat deep and relaxed** to follow the rolling movements of the horse's back.

THE GALLOP

The gallop is a horse's **natural speed gait**. It is very much like a canter speeded up.

The gallop **has four beats** instead of three and the **suspension is longer**. The horse pushes off harder, reaches farther with his legs and stays up in the air longer between strides than he does in the canter.

A riding horse should always be ridden in a **hand gallop, which is a gallop that is under control**.

Running a horse all out is dangerous and poor horsemanship and should not be done except on a racetrack. Galloping is exciting to horses and should be practiced only by good riders.

Too much galloping can make a horse wild and hard to control.

GALLOP

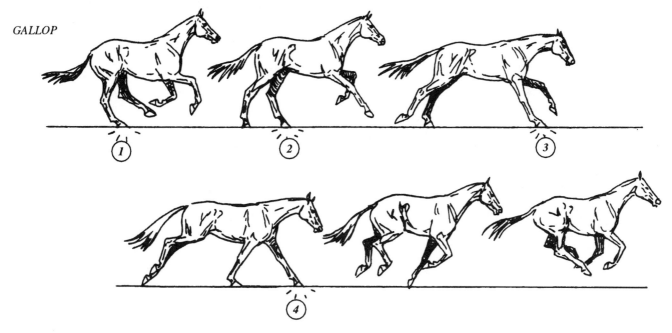

1) WAKE UP WITH LEG AID

2) KEEP HORSE IN CHECK

3) SIGNAL YOUR HORSE

4) SIT UP AND RELAX YOUR LEGS, BACK AND ARMS

LEARNING TO CANTER OR LOPE

When you have a good seat and control at the trot, the next step is learning to canter or lope.

• The canter or lope is slightly faster than the trot or jog, but it should be a smooth, delightful, rolling motion, something like a merry-go-round.

To canter or lope, you need to learn:

• How to get ready for the lope or canter.

• How to signal the horse to do it.

• How to ride the lope or canter.

• How to slow down or stop afterwards.

PREPARE FOR THE LOPE OR CANTER

○ **WAKE UP:**
• You must first wake up your horse.
• Squeeze with your legs or use a little kick if your horse needs it.
• You can also use a voice command if your horse is trained to one.

○ **KEEP your HORSE IN CHECK:**
• Even though you wake up your horse, you must keep him slowed down or he may just trot fast instead of cantering.
• If he goes faster, **check and release** on the reins until he slows down again.

○ **CHECK your SEAT and POSITION** and be sure:
• Your heels are down.
• You are sitting tall.
• Your reins are the right length so that you will be ready to sit correctly when he canters on.

○ **SIGNAL your HORSE:**
• Give the **command for the lope or canter** that your horse has been trained for.
• Your instructor will tell you exactly how to give the proper leg and rein aid so that he knows he is to lope or canter, not just trot on.
• You may also need to use a voice command.

○ **When you are ready to STOP cantering:**
• **Sit up tall** and **check and release** on the reins until your horse slows down into a trot.
• Use a **voice command** to slow down.
• If the trot is quite fast, it may be easier on you to post, and then to slow down to a sitting trot, and then to a walk.

26

AIDS FOR THE CANTER OR LOPE

LATERAL AIDS

Lateral means to be **on the same side**.

- With a lateral aid, you will use your outside leg and outside rein together or your inside leg and inside rein together.
- Sit up straight in your saddle, keeping your heels down and body relaxed.
- Move your outside leg behind the girth while your inside leg remains at the girth.
- Do not let your arms flap around but keep them quiet at your sides.

For English:
- Use a **direct rein with your outside hand**.
- As you squeeze with your outside leg, turn the horse's nose slightly to the outside.

For Western:
- **Neck rein** to turn the horse's head.

DIAGONAL AID

Diagonal means to be on **opposite corners**.

- For this you will need to use your outside leg and inside rein.
- Sit up straight in your saddle, keeping your heels down and body relaxed.
- Move your outside leg behind the girth while your inside leg remains at the girth.
- Do not let your arms flap around but keep them quiet at your sides.

For English:
- Use a **direct rein with your inside hand**.
- As you squeeze with your outside leg, turn the horse's nose slightly to the inside.

For Western:
- **Neck rein** to turn the horse's head.

You can **begin** a canter **from a walk, trot or jog**.

If you begin from a trot, give a very clear signal with the outside leg. Otherwise, the horse may just trot faster. If he trots faster and faster before cantering, you will be bounced out of balance.

- Check your horse back gently with the reins and signal again, rewarding him with a pat on the neck if he does it well.

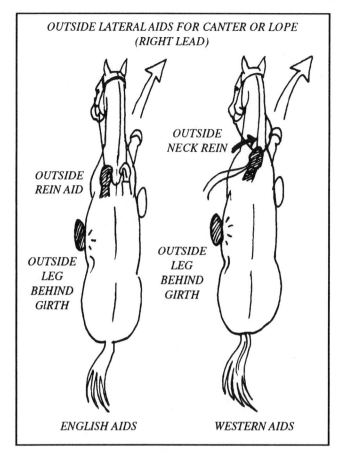

OUTSIDE LATERAL AIDS FOR CANTER OR LOPE (RIGHT LEAD)

OUTSIDE NECK REIN

OUTSIDE REIN AID

OUTSIDE LEG BEHIND GIRTH

OUTSIDE LEG BEHIND GIRTH

ENGLISH AIDS   WESTERN AIDS

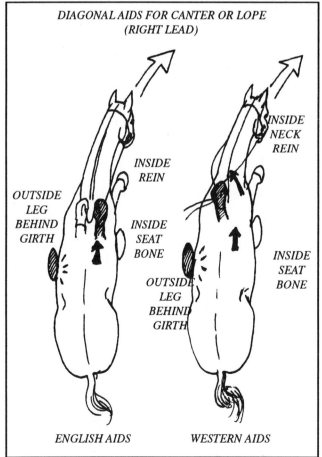

DIAGONAL AIDS FOR CANTER OR LOPE (RIGHT LEAD)

INSIDE NECK REIN

INSIDE REIN

OUTSIDE LEG BEHIND GIRTH

INSIDE SEAT BONE

OUTSIDE LEG BEHIND GIRTH

INSIDE SEAT BONE

ENGLISH AIDS   WESTERN AIDS

Your instructor will tell you whether your horse is trained for a lateral or diagonal signal.

27

RIDING THE CANTER AND LOPE

The canter or lope can be the most enjoyable gait of all if you ride it well, but it can be fast and bouncy if your seat isn't good.

• You should try to **sit to the canter or lope**, not post, bounce, or stand up.
• Sitting tall and balanced with good posture will help, as will relaxing your legs and back.
• Your hands may bounce around at first, so your instructor may want you to keep them steady by holding the mane or a neckstrap or by resting your hands on the horse's neck.
• Bouncy hands will jerk on the horse's mouth and make him stop loping or cantering when he shouldn't. The mistake is not the horse's fault.

When you canter **around a turn**, the horse's lean is more noticeable because he moves faster. It is especially important to lean with the horse, not to over lean or to lean the wrong way (*see balance in turns page 22*).

Imagine what would happen if you leaned too far when riding a bicycle around a fast turn, or if you leaned the wrong way!

BREAKING THE CANTER STRIDE

You may have trouble **keeping** your horse **in a lope or canter**. Some lazy horses are even hard to keep in a trot. Slowing down to a trot or a slower gait without being asked to is called **breaking** and it is an annoying habit that some horses have.

• First, be sure that **you are not making the horse break** by pulling on the reins by accident.
• Then, as you canter, try to tell when the horse feels like he is about to break. He will usually tip you off **by slowing down** or perhaps **putting his head down**.

• If you think that your horse is thinking of breaking, catch him with a sudden leg squeeze or kick **before he has a chance to break**. You can also give your horse a cluck or voice command.

• When he responds and stays in the canter or lope, give him a pat and a word of praise.
• If he breaks, get him right back to work as soon as you can. Some very lazy horses may need a tap of a crop to keep their minds on their work. If this is needed, your instructor will show you how to use the crop.

CANTER LEADS

When loping or cantering, your horse **should be in the proper lead** for any turns he makes. However, at this stage of your riding, you will be more concerned with learning to ride and control the new gait than about leads. Giving your horse the proper aids or signals for the canter or lope tells him to take the proper lead.

• At this stage you should not be trying to make sharp turns or circles at the canter, so a wrong lead will not be too serious a problem. In the next level you will learn to recognize the proper lead and correct mistakes.

SPEED CONTROL

Speed control is **important for safety** in the canter or lope. You must let your horse go fast enough to keep cantering or loping without breaking down but he should not get out of control or feel like he is picking up speed.

If he seems to be **going too fast**, sit up straight and use a repeated check and release on the reins in rhythm with his canter or lope until he slows down.

Some things to remember about the canter or lope are:

1. Prepare your horse. Don't surprise him with an unexpected signal to canter.

2. Horses like to go faster towards other horses and the barn. They may be stubborn and reluctant to go away from the other horses, the barn, or the ring gate.

3. All beginning loping and cantering should be done in an enclosed ring. Trying this out on the trail could cause you to get out of control.

4. Sit tall in the saddle and relax. Try to let your seat go with the roll of your horse's back. Stiffening up will make you bounce and gripping with your heels may tell your horse to go faster than you want.

5. Don't make sharp turns or let your horse cut the corners while loping or cantering.

6. Cantering and loping takes energy. Don't overwork your horse.

POSTING ON THE CORRECT DIAGONAL

In your Level 1 classes, you learned that when a horse trots, his legs move in diagonal pairs. The left foreleg and right hindleg are one pair or diagonal, and the right foreleg and left hindleg are the other pair or diagonal. You learned that the motion of your body in posting is related to these diagonals. Now it is important to learn to post on the correct diagonal.

First, you need to remember what the terms inside and outside refer to.

• The **outside** refers to the side of the horse that is closest to the rail.

• The **inside** refers to the side of the horse that is furthest away from the rail.

• The diagonals are termed inside or outside, or left or right, according to the **foreleg** that is **extended**.

When **posting**, your **body should**:

• **Rise when the** *outside* **shoulder moves forward.**

• **Sit when the** *outside* **shoulder moves back.**

For example, if your horse is circling to the **left**, you will **post** or rise **on the right diagonal**, when the **right foreleg and left hindleg are extended**, and you will **sit** when these two legs are on the ground and the **left foreleg and right hindleg are extended**.

By posting to the outside diagonal to **reduce strain**, the **inside hindleg takes the weight when the rider sits**. As this leg has less distance to travel when on the circle, circling is much easier for the horse.

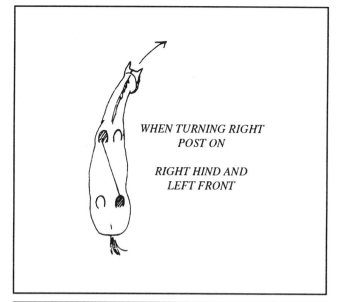

WHEN TURNING RIGHT
POST ON

RIGHT HIND AND
LEFT FRONT

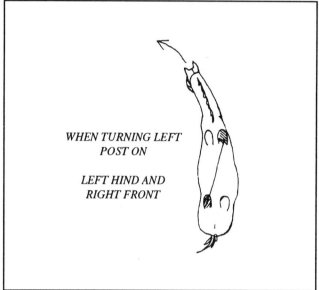

WHEN TURNING LEFT
POST ON

LEFT HIND AND
RIGHT FRONT

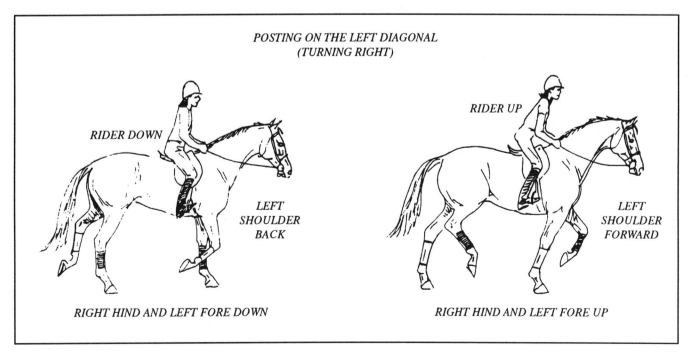

POSTING ON THE LEFT DIAGONAL
(TURNING RIGHT)

RIDER DOWN

LEFT
SHOULDER
BACK

RIGHT HIND AND LEFT FORE DOWN

RIDER UP

LEFT
SHOULDER
FORWARD

RIGHT HIND AND LEFT FORE UP

29

PREPARATION FOR JUMPING

When you have a secure seat and good basic control, you can begin preparing for jumping. Learning to jump is no different than learning to walk, trot and canter. However, you must master each step before going on to the next one or trying to jump even a little higher.

When you plan to jump, you must use the proper equipment for your own safety and the horse's comfort.
• **Always wear a helmet** for jumping exercises.
• You also should **learn to jump in an english saddle**. The western saddle makes it hard to learn a good jumping position and most curb bits are too severe for jumping. Western riders will sometimes hop over a fallen log. You can do the pre-jumping exercises riding western, but don't ask your horse to go over jumps higher than his knees.

Don't use a **bareback pad** with stirrups as a substitute for an english saddle. This kind of pad can slip around underneath the horse if you should lose your balance.

THE JUMPING POSITION

The jumping position is the best position to put you in balance with your horse over a jump. It is the same position you learned in Level 1 when you practiced a Half Seat or Two Point Position at the walk and trot.

For jumping exercises you should **shorten your stirrups** a **hole or two** so that they reach to **just above your ankle**.

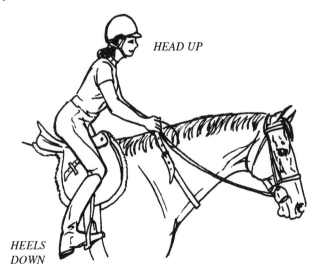

HEAD UP

HEELS DOWN

JUMPING POSITION (HALF SEAT)

JUMPING POSITION CHECKLIST

○ **Heels** down.

○ **Feet** placed in the stirrups with the stirrup under the ball of the foot. (not toeing excessively in or out)

○ **Lower legs** stretched and gently but firmly hugging the horse's side.

○ **Knees** relaxed, springy and resting on the saddle, not pinching in.

○ **Thighs** rolled inward.

○ **Seatbones** out of saddle.

○ **Upper body** inclined (closed) forward from the hip joint, in balance with the horse.

○ **Shoulders** back and square.

○ **Head** up.

○ **Eyes** looking up and straight ahead at *target*.

○ **Arms** relaxed and close to sides (elbows not out).

○ **Hands** on or near horse's neck with the reins the right length for good control.

When releasing the horse's head over the jump, hold the mane or neckstrap firmly about one foot ahead of the saddle.

○ **Stirrups** adjusted so that they touch just above the ankle bone when legs hang straight down.

PRE-JUMPING EXERCISES

FINDING YOUR SPRINGS

• In Jumping position bounce gently without hitting the saddle with your seat.
• Feel your knees and ankles spring. These will take up the shock when your horse trots or lands over a jump.

Next, trot in jumping position, feeling the horse **bounce** your heels down.

JUMPING POSITION

• **Bend forward at the hips** and **close your body angle** until you are balanced at the halt.

• Put **both reins in one hand** and reach up with the **other** to **hold a piece of the mane** about one foot ahead of the saddle.

(*Your instructor may prefer to have you hold onto a neckstrap placed in this spot.*)

The mane hold is to keep you from accidentally hurting your horse's mouth while you practice your jumping position.

• Now move into a walk, staying up in jumping position. Don't let your seat hit the saddle!

This will **strengthen your legs** until you can stay up in jumping position for several times around the ring at a walk or a slow trot.

EYE CONTROL

Your **eyes direct your horse** straight over poles or a jump. He can feel where you are looking because you **shift your head and weight** when you look down, left or right. If you look down, the horse will know that he can stop or go around the jump. You must use your eyes to **aim** your horse straight over a jump. When you turn your eyes it tells your horse to turn.

• Start with a pair of jump standards set up on the rail without a rail between them (*an invisible jump*). Pick out a **distant target** in the middle of the **jump** at eye level like a branch or leaf in the distance.

• Ride toward the target, staring at it as you pass between the standards. If your horse drifts to one side, make him move back over but don't take your eyes off the target.

• At the end of the line, halt your horse and check to be sure that he is perfectly lined up with your target.

• If he's a little crooked, move him over before you give him a pat and go on.

• Just before you get to the corner, look around for the next target.

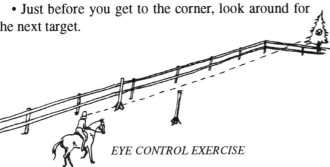

EYE CONTROL EXERCISE

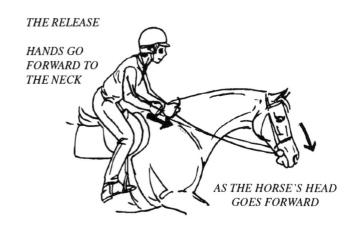

THE RELEASE

HANDS GO FORWARD TO THE NECK

AS THE HORSE'S HEAD GOES FORWARD

THE RELEASE

Every time you jump, you owe your horse a release so that he can stretch his neck and jump without being hurt by the bit. If you don't release him properly, he will find that jumping hurts him and he will stop wanting to jump for you.

The first release is the **mane release**. There are other releases you may learn later.

• In the mane release, you **hold the mane** or **hook your fingers in a neckstrap** to anchor your hands on the top of the horse's neck about **one foot ahead of the saddle**. This keeps you from hurting his mouth when he stretches his neck. Your arms will learn to stretch out with his movement.

• Always release with both hands together.

• Keep the reins held normally in both hands as you grab the mane or neckstrap.

When you begin jumping, you should **release several strides** before the jump or practice pole (*30 feet or more away*). This gives your horse time to get ready to jump on his own.

• It may be necessary to use a chute or wings on the jump when you are releasing early.

• Expert riders wait until the horse jumps to release. However, you should not release your horse just before the jump. This will surprise him and is called **dropping the horse**.

Once you have released, hold the mane or neckstrap **until your horse is over the jump and has taken a stride or two**. Then, pick your hands up gently.

31

CAVALETTI AND PRACTICE POLE

RIDING OVER CAVALETTI IN JUMPING POSITION

CAVALETTI OR TROTTING POLES

Cavaletti or trotting poles are a series of poles laid one after the other, about 4 to 4 ½ feet apart.

• They make the horse trot steady, pick up his feet and stretch his neck down to watch where he is putting his feet.
• They give the rider a little extra bounce which prepares you for real jumping and helps you get your heels down.
• You should ride over cavaletti in jumping position, releasing at the first pole with your hands on the mane or neckstrap.

With practice, you may be able to ride over trotting poles in a chute with your reins tied and *no hands*, just like the balancing exercise in Level 1.

PRACTICE POLE

A practice pole is a make-believe jump with a pair of standards and a pole resting on the ground.

• It gives you practice in all the basics of jumping, but the horse probably won't lift himself off the ground enough to be noticed.

• Use practice poles to check yourself before actually jumping.

TROTTING POLES IN A CHUTE
REINS TIED AND NO HANDS

32

FIRST JUMP

The first actual jump should be a **crossrail**, which looks like a flattened X with the center **no more than six inches high**.

If you have practiced your basics well, you will find that as your horse trots over the small jump it is easy to:

- Balance in jumping position
- Aim straight for your **target**
- Sink your heels down
- Release and hold the mane

In the beginning, all your jumping should be done at the trot.

The canter might get your horse going too fast and jumping too big for a beginning jumper.

Don't be in a hurry to raise the fences. You must practice over practice poles and low fences until your basics are really good.
- If you rush into higher fences before you are ready, you may make mistakes that can hurt you or your horse.

Your instructor will tell you when you are ready to jump higher safely.

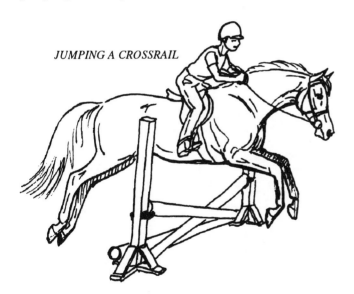

JUMPING A CROSSRAIL

BASIC JUMPING PROBLEMS

GETTING LEFT BEHIND

Getting **left behind** happens to most riders sooner or later. You fall behind your horse's balance and sit down hard on the saddle, thumping his back and your seat, often grabbing the reins to stay on.

This is **unfair to your horse** because he gets **punished** in the back and the mouth for jumping.

To avoid getting left behind:
- Get in jumping position
    about 30 feet before the fence
- Keep your heels down
- Release and hold the mane properly
- Stay up in jumping position
    for 30 feet or so after the jump

GETTING AHEAD

Don't fall into the opposite problem, **getting ahead**. This happens when a rider tries to make a leap into jumping position **just as the horse jumps**, or worse, **just before he jumps**.

It **upsets the horse's balance** and can throw the rider right off, or he may wind up ungracefully hugging his horse's neck.

To avoid getting ahead:
- Get up into jumping position early
- Wait for the horse and let him do the jumping
- Keep your eyes up and on your target
- Keep contact with your lower leg
- Keep your heels down

Remember that **jumping is hard work for any horse.**

He should not be asked to jump **too many fences in one session**, or be pounded by being jumped hard and high every day.

This may make him hate jumping and can even make him lame.

WESTERN PATTERNS

Now that you have achieved good balance and better control, you can learn to ride your horse through patterns for practice, fun, and later for competition. These patterns **test your memory and your ability to ride and maneuver your horse**. They should be ridden perfectly at slow speeds (walk and jog) before you try to ride them faster.

CLOVERLEAF BARREL PATTERN

For the cloverleaf barrel pattern three barrels are set up in a triangular pattern with a start and finish line marked out by cones. Although a right hand pattern is drawn, it is possible to run a left hand pattern.

To do it as fast as possible, you have to work on riding your horse **straight from barrel to barrel** (*swinging wide wastes time*).

• You must **go around the barrel** as close as you can **without hitting it**.
• You also need to go wide enough to keep the horse going forward.
If you turn too tight, he'll hit the barrel (*a penalty*).

Ride the pattern looking ahead to where you want your horse to go. Be sure and pay attention to your turns and straight lines to the barrels.

The better you stay in balance with your horse, the better he can turn and keep going.

You may want to have your instructor time you as you practice the barrel pattern at a jog and trot, but don't get too fast and rough in the competition.

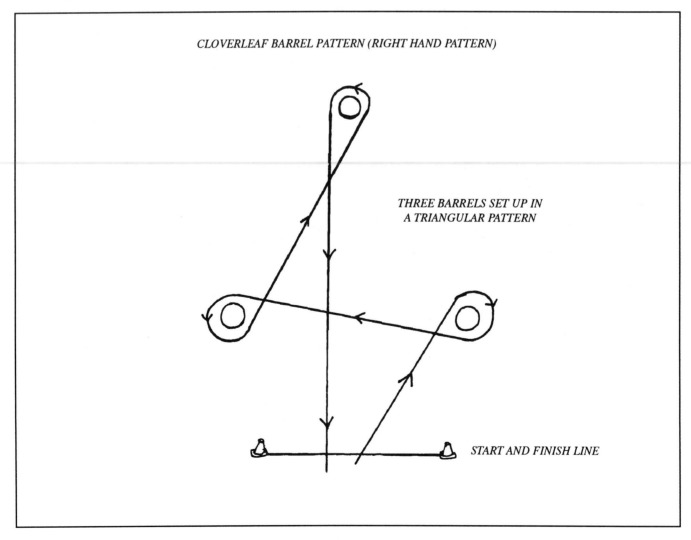

CLOVERLEAF BARREL PATTERN (RIGHT HAND PATTERN)

THREE BARRELS SET UP IN
A TRIANGULAR PATTERN

START AND FINISH LINE

POLE BENDING PATTERN

This pattern tests the horse's ability to make repeated turns to the right and left as he weaves in and out of poles (*you can also use cones or barrels set in a line*).

To ride the pattern:

- You ride **straight** to the far end of the poles.
- Then you **weave in and out** around the poles back to the near end.
- **Turn around** the end pole and begin to **weave back** to the far end.
- Now **turn** the last pole and ride **straight** back across the finish.

Like the cloverleaf pattern, this is a timed event in horse shows. It can be run starting to the right or the left.

This pattern should be practiced at the walk and jog at first, as it requires very good balance and skill at changing leads when done in a lope or gallop.

- When you ride the pattern at the jog, practice shifting your weight slightly for each turn around a pole.
- Rein your horse with a little gentle touch of the rein on his neck.
- Make the end turns round so that your horse won't hit the pole (*a penalty*), but not so wide that he loses time.
- Ride straight on your way down to the end and back to the finish.

As you practice trotting the pattern, you should find that your horse and you become more skilled at turning and maneuvering.

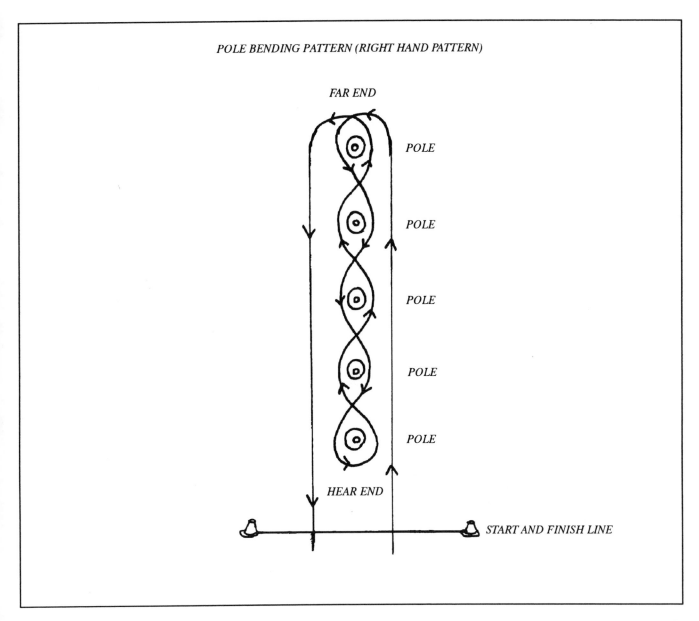

POLE BENDING PATTERN (RIGHT HAND PATTERN)

FAR END

POLE

POLE

POLE

POLE

POLE

HEAR END

START AND FINISH LINE

SOME TYPES OF TRAIL OBSTACLES

MAILBOX

BRIDGE

STREAM

LOGS

TRAIL OBSTACLES

The long awaited time has now come for you to perform greater events with your horse. Encountering various kinds of obstacles such as water, logs, jumps, etc., can be both fun and challenging depending on how well prepared you are.

The key to getting your horse through or over such obstacles is your ability to communicate with your horse effectively. **Good communication is accomplished through the use of the four natural aids**. At this level, it will be important to use them together.

For example, should you and your horse approach a stream on the trail, the horse may either resist or plunge through it. Your goal is to not allow him to resist and balk, or to run on after crossing it.

• To do this, you will need to **urge him forward into the stream**, giving him time to look about.
• At the same time use your hands to keep him from shying to the right or left.
• As he enters the stream, let him have more freedom with his head, yet still continue to move him through the obstacle.
• Once you have arrived at the other side, check your horse if he is impatient.
• You should sit upright and move with the horse to use your weight to your advantage.
• Occasional verbal commands may be helpful.

Performing such feats as walking or trotting smoothly over logs, quietly crossing streams, or taking a jump in stride will reveal your ability to use your aids well.

When you continue to have great difficulty with an obstacle, it is a **sign** that either **you are misusing the aids** or that you have encountered **an obstacle beyond the training of the horse**.

For example, if your horse continues to knock over a barrel you are trying to go around, it may indicate that you are using your hands too abruptly or perhaps throwing your horse off balance by leaning.

This will be an important time to pay attention to your instructor who will provide you with obstacles either in an arena or on the trail for you to practice your skills on.

TRAIL RIDING

In Level 1 you had your first trail riding experience at the walk. Now that you have a better seat and control at the trot, you can add trotting on trails. You should not canter or lope on trails until your instructor feels that you have made good progress cantering in the ring and will be able to handle your horse safely enough to canter on trails. At this point, you can work on perfecting your trail riding skills and control.

STARTING OUT AND STOPS

Always **wait until everyone is mounted and ready** before moving off.

• If the group starts to leave while someone is getting on or fixing his equipment, their horse will also want to leave and may get out of control.

• If anyone has to stop to fix something or put on or take off a jacket, **everyone should stop and wait** while it is taken care of.

• It isn't safe to put on or take off a jacket while mounted. Your arms are stuck behind your back for a moment, and a jacket may look strange to your horse and frighten him. **Dismount to fix your clothes.**

HAZARD WARNINGS

If you should see a hole in the trail or a hazard like a coil of wire:
• Point to the hazard as you pass it
• Tell the rider behind you

English riders use the term **ware**, which is short for **beware**. You can say, *"ware hole"* or *"ware wire"*.

Each rider should **pass the warning back** to the rider behind him until it reaches the end of the line, where the last rider says *"okay"*.

It is also courteous and safer to pass back a warning like *"prepare to trot"* before you move into a faster gait.
• **Horses will copy each other**. A rider can be taken by surprise if you take off at a faster gait without warning.

RATING YOUR HORSE

As you ride farther and at faster gaits, you will have to exercise control and good judgment. You must *rate* your horse, which **means controlling his speed** to keep him in the proper place in line.

Long distance riders seldom gallop or go fast as this tires a horse quickly.
• Instead they **rate their horses** to a **ground covering gait** that is easy on horse and rider and can be performed for a long time without tiring.
• This is usually a **long striding walk or a trot**.

When riding with others, you should stay in **single file**. Your horse should be about **one horse length** behind the next horse.
• If he is closer, he may annoy the horse ahead and get himself kicked.
• If he lags farther back he may dawdle and stop to graze, or catch up quickly when you aren't ready.

Use your **leg aids** to make him move out if he's **slow**. Squeeze and relax your leg. Use a kick, if he is really lazy and refusing to move.

If he **crowds the horse ahead**, use a **check and release** on the reins as often as necessary to make him stay in his proper place in line.

RATE YOUR HORSE TO A GROUND COVERING GAIT

A LONG STRIDING WALK OR A TROT

RIDING UPHILL

Whenever you ride uphill, **stand up and balance forward** so that it is easier for your horse to climb.

• Put your hands forward to let him stretch his neck. When riding up a steep hill, you may need to rest your hands on the neck or hold the mane.

• Use a check and release if necessary to keep him from rushing or lunging up a steep hill.

• Keep moving when you reach the top. If you stop, others on the hill behind you will have to stop, too.

RIDING DOWNHILL

When riding down a hill or a steep place, **sit straight and tall with your weight balanced over your legs.**

• Before you start down, check and release to slow your horse down and signal him to be careful.

• Keep his **front legs straight in front of his hind legs.** If he should get sideways, he is more likely to slip.
• Let him **have his head** enough **to see where he is going,** but don't let him go fast down a hill, especially a steep place.

• At the bottom, keep moving slowly under control. If you speed up, other horses on the slope behind you may hurry to catch up.

• **Walk down hills** and do not go faster.

*PUT YOUR HANDS FORWARD
WHEN RIDING UP A STEEP HILL*

STREAMS AND MUDDY PLACES

If you cross a stream or a muddy place slow down to a walk. A horse can sprain an ankle or lose a shoe if he goes fast through deep mud.

Give your horse an **extra leg squeeze** and **keep** him **walking straight through.** If you let him stop, he might paw and play in the water, or even lie down and roll.

• If you feel him lower his head and sag his knees, use your legs hard, give a **stern voice command** and even hit him if you have to, to keep him moving forward.

Some horses are reluctant to cross water. They will usually **follow** another horse across.

• Keep your heels down and hold on to the mane or saddle, as your horse might try to leap across the water.

Use the same technique as in training over trail obstacles. Keep the horse f**acing straight** over the stream and **urge him steadily with legs and voice.**

WALK DOWN HILLS

RIDING ALONG ROADS

If your trail ride follows a road or highway, all the riders should ride in **single file as far off the pavement as possible**.

• Pavement is bad to ride on because it is hard on your horse's feet and legs. Also, horseshoes are very slippery on pavement.

If you absolutely must ride on a paved surface, keep to a walk.

When you ride on the shoulder of a road, keep a sharp eye out for broken glass or other trash that could injure your horse.

Horses and auto traffic are a dangerous combination, so it is good to avoid highways whenever possible.

• If you must ride along a highway, you should obey your state's traffic laws regarding which side to ride on.

• If it is possible, **ride on the left side**, facing the traffic, so that your horse will not be surprised by cars coming up from behind.

• **All riders** should stay on the **same side** of the road and should be alert and on watch for traffic.

• When you notice a car coming, pass the warning back or ahead to all riders.

When you must cross a road or highway, all riders must line up and cross together.

If some horses are left behind on the opposite side of the road, they might try to cross the road and join the other horses, even if traffic is coming.

• The trail guide and the rear guard rider will:
   • Stop the group
   • Check for traffic
   • Then call for a flank turn

• All riders are to turn at once and cross side by side.
• As you reach the other side, turn back into line.

Sometimes it is easier and safer for all to dismount and lead horses across, then remount on the other side.

• This is up to the instructor or trail guide.

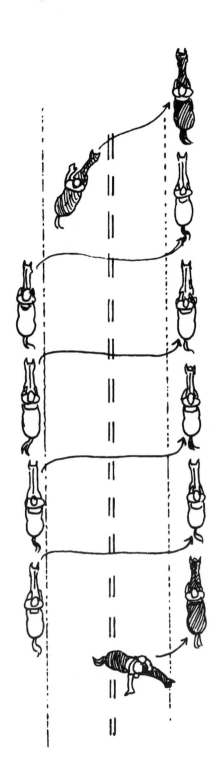

*CROSSING A ROAD
WITH A FLANK TURN*

39

LEVEL 2 REQUIREMENTS

To complete Level 2 you must be able to pass each of the following requirements. This can be done by performing the Level 2 Ring Test, which has all the movements in it (or an alternate test made up by your instructor), or by having your CHA instructor check off each thing as you pass it. This can be done in regular riding lessons, as a group test, or an individual test.

RIDING REQUIREMENTS

_____ 1. Mount and adjust your stirrups to the proper length.
   (*Western riders need not adjust stirrups from the saddle, but should check stirrups for proper length.*)

_____ 2. Dismount and prepare the horse to lead.(*Reins over horse's head, english stirrups run up correctly.*)

_____ 3. Do a tack check (*saddle and bridle*) on both sides and tighten girth if needed.

_____ 4. Ride with good position and balance for Level 2 at **walk and trot or jog**:
   __ a. Walk   __ b. Sitting trot   ___c. Jumping position   __ d. Posting (*optional for western riders*)

_____ 5. Demonstrate good Level 2 control by:
   __ a. Riding at least twice around the ring at a jog or trot without breaking the gait.
   __ b. Halting on command without unnecessary roughness to horse.
   __ c. Keeping the proper distance when riding in a group or on the trail.
   __ d. Riding at a jog or trot without breaking gait:
      __ 1. Simple reverses
      __ 2. Circles
      __ 3. Western pattern (*optional for english riders*)

_____ 6. Put the horse into a lope or canter and ride at least once around the ring with good Level 2 seat and control.
   (*Correct leads desirable, but not required.*)

_____ 7. Post on the correct diagonal both directions of the ring. (*optional for western riders*).

GENERAL REQUIREMENTS

_____ 1. Show how to cool out a hot horse properly.

_____ 2. Demonstrate how to tie a proper quick release knot for tying a horse.

_____ 3. Understand how to clean a stall, clean the stable area and stable chores.

_____ 4. Pass written test.

TRAIL REQUIREMENTS

_____ 1. Give 5 rules for safety when trail riding.

_____ 2. Demonstrate the following:
   __ a. What to do if you see a hazard like a hole or wire.
   __ b. Keeping a safe distance from other horses and staying in your place in line.
   __ c. How to ride over or through a simple trail obstacle (like a creek, stepping poles or a muddy spot).
   __ d. How to ride uphill and downhill.

JUMPING REQUIREMENTS

(Optional • Jumping is NOT required to pass any CHA level.)
However, it is recommended that riders pass the Level 2 Jumping Test before beginning Level 3 jumping.)

_____ 1. Demonstrate jumping position at a walk and trot in good balance.

_____ 2. Ride over practice poles and cavaletti in jumping position at trot.

_____ 3. Jump a low crossrail (*under 1 foot high*) at a trot showing:
   __ a. Good jumping position ___ b. Balance ___ c. Correct release ____d. Good control

The goals of Level 2 are to be improve the **use of the aids** and to **develop more balance**.
Level 1 and 2 tests must be passed before a rider may take the Level 3 tests.

Requirements for Level 2 may be tested:
- individually
- in a group
- or by checking off as the rider passes each requirement

- Students should not be required to memorize the ring test.
- The difficulty of the horse they are riding should be taken into consideration.

The Ring Test is not a requirement in itself, but one way of testing the rider.
Alternate tests such as group tests are also acceptable.

LEVEL 2 • WRITTEN TEST

MULTIPLE CHOICE (select the best answer)

1. Horses learn to obey because of:
   a) Sugar, carrots and petting
   b) Cruelty
   c) Reward and punishment
   d) Natural instincts

2. A horse can pay attention to reward or punishment for about:
   a) An hour
   b) Three seconds
   c) Three minutes
   d) As long as you want to ride him

3. A baby horse of either sex is a:
   a) Foal
   b) Colt
   c) Pony
   d) Filly

4. A horse that will never be taller than 14'2 hands high:
   a) Miniature horse
   b) Foal
   c) Pony
   d) Stunted in growth

5. When cooling out a hot horse, you should:
   a) Walk him until he is breathing normally
   b) Give him plenty of cold water immediately
   c) Put him in his stall to stand and dry off

6. A walk is a:
   a) Two beat gait
   b) Three beat gait
   c) Four beat gait
   d) Fast gait with suspension

7. When a rider is in balance with his horse, his center of gravity is:
   a) Ahead of the motion
   b) Behind the motion
   c) Up in the air
   d) Right over the horse's center of gravity

8. When tying a horse, you should:
   a) Tie him at the level of the withers
   b) Use a quick release knot
   c) Give him only enough slack for his nose to touch the ground
   d) All of the above

9. When riding the canter or lope you should:
   a) Post as in the trot
   b) Sit down
   c) Stand up
   d) Lean back

10. When riding on trails in a group you should:
    a) Stay right up against the horse ahead
    b) Stay at least one horse length back
    c) Stay 30 feet or more behind the next horse
    d) Ride side by side with your friends

test continued on next page

MATCHING

Colors:

____ Bay

____ Chestnut or Sorrel

____ Palomino

____ Appaloosa

____ Pinto

____ Brown

____ Grey

____ Roan

A. Gold body color, white mane and tail

B. Small spots all over body or over hips

C. Brown body with black legs, tail and mane

D. Reddish brown with red, brown or light mane and tail

E. Mixture of white hairs makes lighter color like strawberry

F. Almost black with brown highlights in muzzle, flanks and legs

G. Born dark, gets light with age until white

H. Large spots of white and other color

Horseman's Terms:

____ Mare

____ Colt

____ Foal

____ Filly

____ Stallion

____ Gelding

____ Green

I. Father horse

J. Untrained or inexperienced horse

K. Mature female horse, mother horse

L. Altered male horse

M. Young female horse under four years

N. Young male horse under four years

O. Young horse of either sex, still with its mother

Breeds:

____ The Shetland Pony Club sets a height limit of

____ The Father of breeds is the

____ The Welsh ponies are any color except

____ The Appaloosa got it's name from the

____ The Pinto was brought to America by the

P. 14.2 hands

Q. Brown

R. Palouse River

S. Arabian

T. 11.2 hands

U. Spanish explorers

V. Thoroughbred

W. Spotted

WRITE IN
The correct name of each face marking shown:

A. _____

B. _____

C. _____

D. _____

A   *B*   *C*   *D*

The correct name of each leg marking shown:

E. _____

F. _____

G. _____

E   *F*   *G*

FILL IN THE PARTS OF HORSE (place the correct number in front of the correct part of the horse)

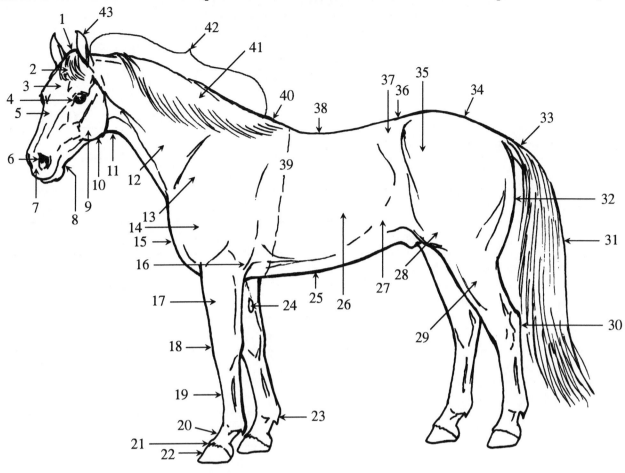

_____ Abdomen
_____ Arm
_____ Back
_____ Barrel
_____ Buttock
_____ Cannon
_____ Cheek
_____ Chest
_____ Chestnut
_____ Chin Groove
_____ Coronet

_____ Coupling
_____ Crest
_____ Croup
_____ Dock
_____ Ear
_____ Elbow
_____ Eye
_____ Face
_____ Fetlock lock
_____ Flank
_____ Forearm

_____ Forelock
_____ Forehead
_____ Gaskin
_____ Heart girth
_____ Hip
_____ Hock
_____ Hoof
_____ Jowl
_____ Knee
_____ Loin
_____ Mane

_____ Muzzle
_____ Neck
_____ Nostril
_____ Pastern
_____ Poll
_____ Shoulder
_____ Stifle
_____ Tail
_____ Throat
_____ Withers

FILL IN THE PARTS OF THE HOOF

(Hoof parts to choose from)
Bars
Cleft
Commissures
Frog
Heel
Sole
Toe
Wall
White line

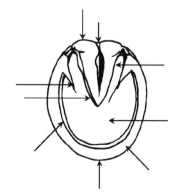

(Based on 5 points each, a total of 100 points)

Name: _____ **Place** _____ **Date** _____

		POINTS	COMMENT
1. Safety check, stirrups adjusted, mount at O	(5 pts.)		
2. Walk to B	(5 pts.)		
3. B to E Jog or trot	(5 pts.)		
4. E to A Posting trot (Western may continue at jog)	(5 pts.)		
5. A Circle, (posting trot)	(5 pts.)		
6. A to B Trot or jog, (half seat)	(5 pts.)		
7. B to M Transition to walk	(5 pts.)		
8. M to M Canter or lope	(5 pts.)		
9. M to H Transition through trot and walk to halt at H	(5 pts.)		
10. H to H Trot or jog	(5 pts.)		
11. At K Reverse	(5 pts.)		
12. E to C Posting trot	(5 pts.)		
13. At C Circle, (posting trot)	(5 pts.)		
14. C to B Trot or jog (half seat)	(5 pts.)		
15. B to F Walk	(5 pts.)		
16. F to F Canter or lope	(5 pts.)		
17. A to K Transition through trot and walk to halt at K	(5 pts.)		
18. K to A Walk and reverse	(5 pts.)		
19. Overall control	(5 pts.)		
20. Overall equitation	(5 pts.)		
Possible 100 points Passing score 70%	TOTAL SCORE		

Scoring: 1 = Not performed   2 = Unsatisfactory   3 = Sufficient, fair   4 = Good   5 = Outstanding

PASSING: _____ Yes _____ No _____ Instructor's signature _____

(Based on 10 points each, a total of 120 points)

Name: _____ **Place** _____ **Date** _____

	Letter	Directions	You are scored on		Points	Comment
1.	O	Check tack and mount	Mounting correctly			
		Tighten girth if needed	Safety check of tack			
		Adfust stirrups or check length	Not disturbing horse			
			Correct stirrup length	(10 pts.)		
2.	A	Enter ring at walk	Seat, position and control			
		Turn to the right along rail to B	At walk and sitting trot			
	B	Trot or jog,, sitting	Staying on rail			
		Continue to E at jog or trot	Not breaking or cutting	(10 pts.)		
3.	E	(Posting trot on correct diagonal)	Posting well			
		(Western may continue at jog)	Correct diagonal			
	A	Circle left, width of ring	Control during circle			
		(Posting trot, on correct diagonal)	Not breaking gait	(10 pts.)		
4.	A	Jog or trot, (in Half Seat)	Balance, position and control			
		Continue along rail to B	Half Seat	(10 pts.)		
5.	B	Sit down and walk	Aids, seat and cantrol			
	M	Prepare to canter or lope	During canter or lope			
		(may jog if necessary)	Not breaking gait			
	M - M	Lope or canter	Correct lead desirable but not required			
		Continue once around ring back to M		(10 pts.)		
6.	M	Jog or trot	Control stopping from lope or canter			
	C	Walk (prepare for the halt)	No unnecessary roughness			
	H	Halt, pause 5 seconds				
		Continue at jog or trot		(10 pts.)		
7.	K	Sitting trot or jog	Control			
		Reverse at sitting trot or jog	Not breaking during reverse	(10 pts.)		
8.	E	(Posting trot on correct diagonal)	Posting, correct diagonal			
	C	Circle right width of ring	Circle	(10 pts.)		
9.	C	Jog or trot, (balancing in Half Seat)	Balance, position and control			
		Continue to B		(10 pts.)		
10.	B	Sit down and walk	Aids, seat, control			
	F	Prepare to canter or lope	Not breaking			
		(may jog if necessary)	Correct lead desirable but not required			
	F - F	Lope or canter				
		Contine once around ring, back to F		(10 pts.)		
11.	F	Trot or jog	Control without unnecessary roughness			
	A	Walk (prepare for the halt)				
	K	Halt, pause 5 seconds, Walk on		(10 pts.)		
12.	H	Reverse at walk	Aids, smoothness			
	A	Exit ring at walk	Control during reverse	(10 pts.)		

Total = 120 pts

A score of 70% is considered passing

TOTAL SCORE [ ]

Scoring:
0 = Not performed	3 = Poor	6 = Satisfactory	9 = Very good
1 = Very bad	4 = Insufficient, not good enough	7 = Fairly good	10 = Outstanding
2 = Unsatisfactory	5 = Sufficient, fair	8 = Good	

Passing scores are 5 and over. Note: **10 means outstanding, not perfect** (10 is a possible score, though rare).

PASSING: _____ Yes _____ No _____ Instructor's signature _____

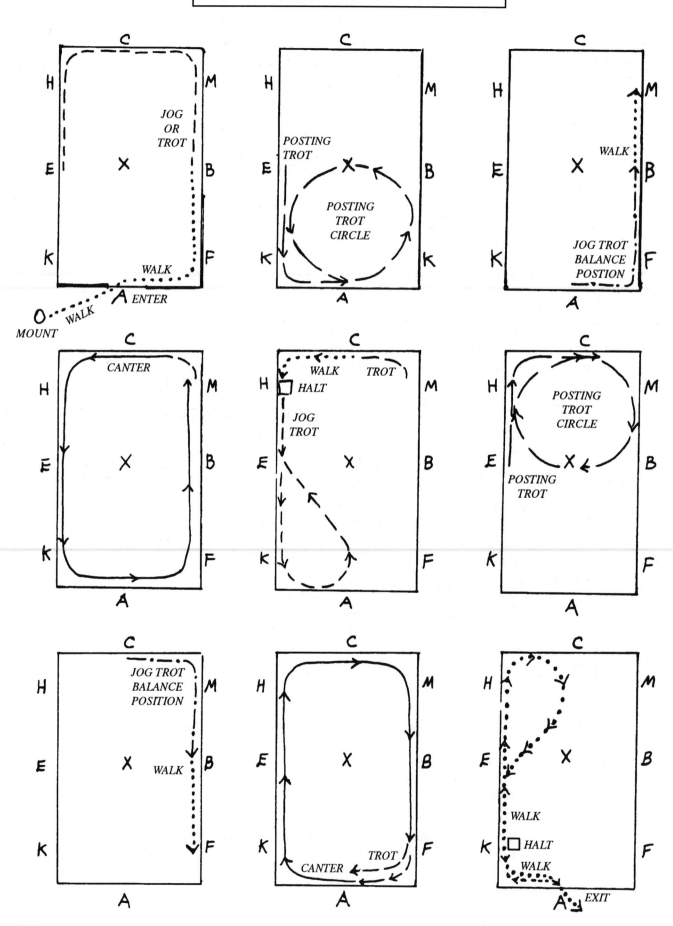

Certified Horsemanship Association

CHA LEVEL 3
HORSEMANSHIP
MANUAL

Certified Horsemanship Association

HORSEMANSHIP MANUAL

LEVEL 3

TABLE OF CONTENTS

INTRODUCTION

Knowledge alone will never make you a good horseman, yet knowledge with a lot of horse experience will put you on the road to becoming a Level 3 rider. In this level, you can look forward to learning many things that will equip you to be a horse owner, including what kind of riding equipment you'll need. Your riding ability should enable you to obtain diagonals and correct leads, to jump higher and smoother, and to pass through or around obstacles with ease and increased speed. You will find this level a great challenge and a lot of fun.

GENERAL HORSE INFORMATION

HORSE BEHAVIOR

Horse behavior will teach you the characteristics of the horse and give you an understanding of the horse's reasons for certain actions or habits. When you know why a horse does something, you will be better prepared to respond to him properly. It is important that you know the horse's traits and instinctive responses. They vary to different degrees in every horse, but they are common to all.

TRAINING HORSES

You will be more successful in riding and training horses to obey you if you use what you know about horse psychology.

Horses are **easy to handle** if they are **trained fairly and consistently** and if you try to **understand why they behave as they do**.
• However, if your instructions are confusing or inconsistent, your horse will never know what you want and he may become stubborn, nervous or just hateful.

Horses that are hard to handle are often that way because they were handled or ridden badly in the past.

HERD INSTINCT

All horses possess a **strong group or herd instinct**. In their wild state there was safety in numbers.

For this reason, an untrained horse will not leave the group unless he is forced to, and even then, he may attempt to remain with other horses.

Another way the horse shows his group instinct is in his desire to **mimic other horses**.

• If one horse shies they will all shy.
• When one bucks they all want to act up.
• If one horse runs they will all run.

The horse never loses his herd instinct, but it **can be controlled with training**.

This instinct is used to an advantage in training a young horse. If a young untrained horse is ridden along with a steady, well trained horse the young horse will mimic the older horse.

PECKING ORDER

All horse groups have a **system of rank** or *pecking order* with a boss horse at the top.

The boss horse acts as herd leader and gets to eat and drink first. He can pick on any horse below him. At the bottom of the pecking order is the weakest horse who must give in to all the others.
Horses **determine their place** in the herd by **bluffing, making threats of biting and kicking** and sometimes by **actual fighting**.
• Once all know their place there is little fighting.
• A new horse has to test all the others to find out where he stands.
• Often the herd boss is an old mare, rather than a stallion or gelding.

When horses are **being ridden** and **handled**, they should **respect humans** as if they are **the boss horse**.
• **Never let a horse** get away with **threatening you** or he may decide that you are lower on the pecking order. He may feel free to push you around or even bite or kick at you.
• You should not be mean and harsh, but he must accept you as his leader.

Sometimes horses try to **boss other horses while** they are **being ridden or handled**.
• This should **not be allowed**. The rider should put the bossy horse firmly under control and keep him away from the horse he is picking on.

3

MEMORY

A horse's **memory is excellent**. He remembers when he got a reward and what for, and things that were unpleasant, hurtful or frightening.

Some horses have an **exaggerated fear of certain objects or situations** because they connect them with painful or frightening memories.

Memory works for you as it helps a horse to remember his training and keep the good habits he has been taught.

HOMING INSTINCT

Horses always **go more willingly toward the stables than away from them**. This is because they have a strong homing instinct. They have a good sense of where home is and a strong desire to be there.

Because of the strong homing instinct, your horse can be trusted to find the way home.

It is also important to **make your horse walk when returning to the stable**. A horse that is allowed to run home can be very difficult or dangerous to handle.
• If someone left the barn door open and the ceiling is low, you may find yourself lying on the ground with a sore head and body.

DEFENSES

Nature has given horses **speed** and an **instinct to run from danger**.
• They also have **defenses** such as **kicking, biting** and **striking with their front legs** which they may use if they are cornered and danger threatens.

A horse's **first means of protecting himself is to run**. You need to remember this when riding or handling a horse around anything that might frighten him.

Horses **can be trained to obey their riders** even **when their instinct tells them to flee**. For instance war horses learned to obey their riders even in battle.

To overcome a horse's instinct, it takes good riding and training. The horse must have confidence in his rider.

A horse is most frightened of losing his ability to run away. He may become panicky if he is trapped, entangled or made helpless when he is frightened.

HABIT

One of the **strongest traits** of horses is their **sense of habit**. Horses get nervous when faced with new situations. They like to do things the same way over and over again. It gives them a sense of security.

If your horse does something two or three times, he is on the way to forming a habit, good or bad.

It is important to see that the habits he forms are those you want, and to change his routine quickly if he begins to form an undesirable habit.

If your horse learns that you always stop and dismount by the ring gate, he may form the habit of stopping and refusing to move, hoping that you will get off. You can break the habit by dismounting at different places and insisting that he go past his favorite stopping place.

POSSESSIVENESS

Horses can be **possessive about** their **food**, their **stall**, or their **friends**.

For this reason it's a good idea not to bother a horse while he is eating his grain. He may think that you are teasing him or trying to take it away from him and may get angry.

A mare may be very protective of her foal.

COURAGE AND LAZINESS

Most horses are a **little lazy** about working for people.

Horses like to do things the easy way and they don't make any more work for themselves than they have to. This leads them to find ways to **cheat** when the **work gets hard or boring**, just like kids look out the window in school.
• Some horses are very lazy, especially if their work is unpleasant or if they have to put up with poor riders.

Horses are surprisingly **generous**.

They will often continue to **obey their riders even after they are tired or hurting**. This is a special kind of **courage** that horsemen call *heart*.

A good horseman values his horse's heart or courage and does not abuse it.

The horse's ears and actions are the key to his emotions. He can tell you what he is paying attention to and how he feels by the way he uses his ears and the way he acts. Following are some tips to his emotions.

Ears forward but relaxed
interested in what's
in front of him.

Ears turned back but relaxed
listening to his rider
or what's behind him.

Ears pointed stiffly forward
alarmed or nervous about what's
ahead. Looking for danger.

Ears pointed left and right
relaxed, paying attention
to the scenery on both sides.

Ears stiffly back
annoyed or worried about what's
behind him; might kick if annoyed.

Droopy ears
calm and resting,
horse may be dozing.

Ears flattened against neck
violently angry, in a fighting mood.
May fight, bite or kick.

OTHER SIGNS YOU SHOULD NOTICE ARE:

• **Tucking the tail down tightly.**
  Danger to the rear.
  Horse may bolt, buck or kick.
  Watch out if ears are flattened, too!

• **Switching the tail.**
  Annoyance and irritation:
    at biting flies, stinging insects or
    tickling bothersome actions of a rider or another horse.

• **Droopy ears and resting one hind leg on toe.**
  Calm and resting, horse may be dozing.
  Don't wake him up by startling him!

• **Wrinkling up the face and swinging the head.**
  Threatening gesture of an angry or bossy horse.
  Watch out for biting or kicking.

HORSES' SENSES

Horses have **highly developed senses** that enable them to **detect changes** in their surroundings. They affect how the horse will think and act. Horse trainers and riders need to be aware of horses' senses and how horses feel and respond. Many riders do not realize how finely developed a horse's senses are and how sensitive he can be.

TOUCH

Horses use touch to **examine strange objects**.

They will **look, sniff and then feel** the object with their muzzle and lips. The horse's **sense of touch is very sensitive**. He can feel a fly land on his skin and is able to detect a very light touch or pressure.

We depend on his sense of touch in most riding and training. Horses are trained by applying and removing pressure, sometimes gentle pressure and sometimes painful pressure.

The tongue, lips, and bars of the mouth are especially sensitive places where we apply pressure with the bit.
• If too much pressure is used, the horse may become **dead to pressure** (this is called a hard mouth). This doesn't mean that he no longer feels it, but that he has learned to ignore all but the most severe pressure.
• A **dead sided** horse or a **hard mouthed** horse still has his sense of touch, but his reactions have been spoiled by insensitive riders.

SMELL AND TASTE

These senses are related quite closely. Horses have a **keen sense of smell** and can detect odors that humans cannot. Horses may **recognize** familiar horses or people **by their familiar scent**. Horses can **detect** substances with a **slightly different taste**.

Some horses are very clever about sniffing out and refusing to eat medicine in their feed.
• Horses may refuse to drink water that tastes or smells different from that which they are used to.
• Some of the horse's homing instinct may be his ability to smell the familiar scent of home, even at a great distance.

HEARING

A horse's **hearing** is **very acute**.

His **ears can swivel** like radar screens to seek out sounds in any direction.

He can **hear very soft sounds**, like a rustle in the bushes which might conceal a predator.

Since their hearing is very acute, it is not necessary to shout voice commands at horses to make them hear. They can hear you just as well if you talk quietly to them. Horses understand the tone of your voice. They know if you are angry or pleased with them.

*THEY HAVE A
KEEN SENSE OF SMELL*

*HEARING IS VERY ACUTE
HE CAN HEAR VERY SOFT SOUNDS*

*EARS CAN SWIVEL
TO SEEK OUT SOUNDS*

Horses' eyesight is **geared to finding danger**.

They **don't** have very **accurate vision close up**, but they can **detect** even a **tiny movement** at a **distance**.
• It might be a predator sneaking up on them.

Horses' eyes are unique in a way which affects the way they behave.

○ A horse's eyes are **set** on the **sides** of his **face**.

○ He can see a **different picture** out of **each eye** and can see **back** almost to his **tail**.

○ He **cannot see directly behind** him or **right under his nose**.

Horses also become alarmed if something suddenly appears above or behind their heads where they cannot see it. They instinctively fear anything attacking them from above, because they are helpless when attacked from above.

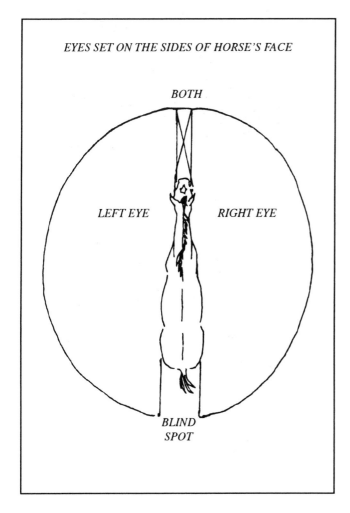

EYES SET ON THE SIDES OF HORSE'S FACE

BOTH

LEFT EYE   *RIGHT EYE*

BLIND SPOT

The **lens** of the **horse's eye doesn't change shape** as ours does.

Instead, the horse **changes** his **head position to change his focus** from close to far away.

Holding his **head high** lets him **focus on distant objects** and **lowering** his **head** lets him examine something **close**.

HORSES CHANGE THEIR HEAD POSITION

*RAISING THE HEAD HIGH
LETS HIM FOCUS ON DISTANT OBJECTS*

*LOWERING THE HEAD
LETS HIM EXAMINE SOMETHING CLOSE*

HORSE CARE AND HANDLING

HORSE FEEDS AND FEEDING

Horses were intended by nature to be **grazing animals**. Good **pasture** is the most **natural diet for horses**.

When we ask horses to work for us, they have less time to eat and greater needs for nutrients, so quite often we have to feed them differently.

• Horses need water, salt, roughages (bulk feed like hay or grass) and sometimes concentrates (grain and supplements).

GRASS AND SALT LICK

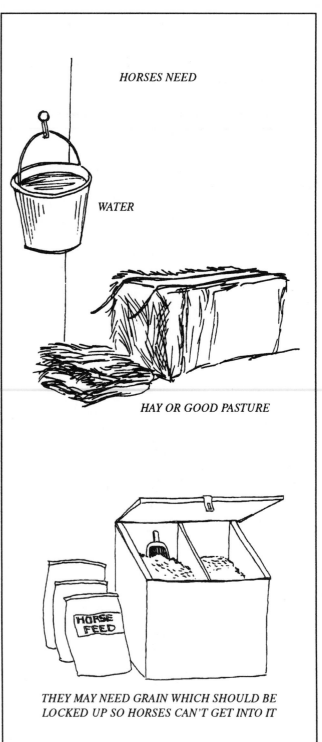

HORSES NEED

WATER

HAY OR GOOD PASTURE

THEY MAY NEED GRAIN WHICH SHOULD BE LOCKED UP SO HORSES CAN'T GET INTO IT

WATER

Horses need **clean water** available **at all times**, **except** when they are **overheated**.

• They drink an average of **12 gallons a day** but may need more in hot weather or when being worked hard.

SALT

Horses **lose salt as they sweat**.
• This vital mineral must be replaced or the horse may not be able to function during hot weather.

• Salt can be given in salt licks, or loose salt can be added to the feed.
• Some salt licks contain trace minerals to supplement the horse's diet.

ROUGHAGE

Roughage consists of grass, hay and certain other forms such as **pellets or cubes.**

Pasture should not be considered part of the horse's feed unless it is a good pasture with nutritious plants. Weedy or over grazed pastures will not support a horse.

HAY

Hay may be:

- O **Grass** hay
  (timothy, bermuda grass or orchard grass)
- O **Legume** hay
  (clover, alfalfa)
- O **Mixed** hay
  (example: timothy and alfalfa)
- O **Oat** hay

• Legumes hays are more nutritious than grass hays.

• **All hay should be:**
  • green
  • leafy
  • sweet smelling

• **Dusty or moldy hay** makes horses cough and can cause permanent lung damage.

• **Brown, tough and stalky** hay has little nutritional value to a horse.

Hay is usually **measured by the section or flake**. A horse usually **receives around 20 pounds**, or about **five sections a day**, but this varies widely.

HAY SUBSTITUTE

O **Pellets or cubes** contain hay that is **ground and pressed into shapes** are another form of roughage. This is often used where hay is expensive and hard to obtain.

O **Sugar beet pulp** is sometimes used as a hay substitute for horses that are allergic to hay dust.

CONCENTRATES

Concentrates are primarily **grains**, although **vitamin** and **protein supplements** are also concentrates.

• **Concentrates contain more nutrients per pound than roughage does.**

Horses can become **very sick from overeating concentrates**, because their digestion is not able to handle the overload.
  • Roughages do not cause the same problem.

Here are some common horse feed grains.

- O **Oats** may be fed whole, crimped or rolled.

- O **Barley** is similar to oats and is often steamed and rolled.

- O **Corn** has more calories per pound than other feeds. It is usually fed in winter.

- O **Bran** is ground from the husk of the wheat plant. It is a slightly laxative feed.

- O **Soybean meal** and other **legume meals** are used to increase the protein in a feed.

- O **Sweet feed** is mixed grain containing molasses. Horses like the sweet taste.

- O **Complete feed** is a type of pellet feed containing grain and roughage. It takes the place of hay and grain.

Grain is usually **fed in two or three small feedings per day**. Any **changes in feed**, especially in grain, must be **made over a week or two** to prevent upsetting the horse's digestion.

Some horse owners feed a vitamin and mineral supplement as well as grain.

This may be necessary if the feed is not of good quality, but usually is not required if the diet is well balanced otherwise.

SOME RULES AND FEEDING PRACTICES

1) **Horses should be fed according to their individual needs.**
   Different horses need different amounts of feed to stay in good shape.
   The right amount is that which keeps
   - that animal healthy,
   - at the right weight and looking good
   - with enough energy to do his work.

2) **Feeding should be done on a regular schedule** as horses become upset if feeding times are irregular.

3) **All feed must be clean, good quality** and not spoiled or moldy.
   Moldy or bad feed can make a horse sick or even kill him.

4) **Never feed horses grain right after hard work** when they are hot or **just before they work.**
   This may cause colic or stomach ache.

5) **Feed should be kept off the ground** and fed in a way as to keep it from being contaminated by manure.
   Horses take in parasite eggs along with dirty feed and suffer damage internally from worms.

6) **Horses are very eager to get their feed** and often fight with each other about it.
   They should be tied or separated for feeding or the weak and timid horses may get none.
   An experienced horse person should be in charge of feeding.
   They should be sure that horses are under control and that helpers are safe during feeding.

7) **Changes in a horse's appetite may indicate sickness.**
   Notice each horse's eating habits and any changes.

8) **Do not bother a horse while he is eating his grain.**
   He may think you are teasing him and bite or kick.

9) **Grain and concentrates must be locked up** so that a horse cannot get into them.
   Horses can literally eat themselves to death on such feeds and will if they have a chance.

INSECT AND FLY PROTECTION

Horses suffer a great deal from stinging and biting insects along with flies in hot weather. Face flies, which do not sting, gather on horses' faces and drink from their eyes and lips, spreading germs and irritating their faces.

• Horses should be protected against flies by fly spray, a wipe-on fly repellent or anti-fly stick which is applied to their faces.

• Some horses need special net bonnets to protect their eyes and ears or a plastic browband with strips which brush flies away.

Watch out for horses' feet and tails when flies are bad. Horses kick and stamp, not knowing that they may step on you by accident, and the tail can hurt if it hits your face or eyes.

EQUIPMENT

BITS AND BITTING

There are many **different kinds of bits**, but **all** are **meant to communicate with and control** the horse **by pressure**, not to hurt him. Different bits work in different ways and some are better for different horses or different kinds of riding. It's important to know how the bit you use works, so that you can use it to control your horse but not hurt him.

PRESSURE POINTS

All bits **work on one or more pressure points** on the horse's head.
The horse learns that pressure in a certain place means to slow down, stop, turn or change his head position.

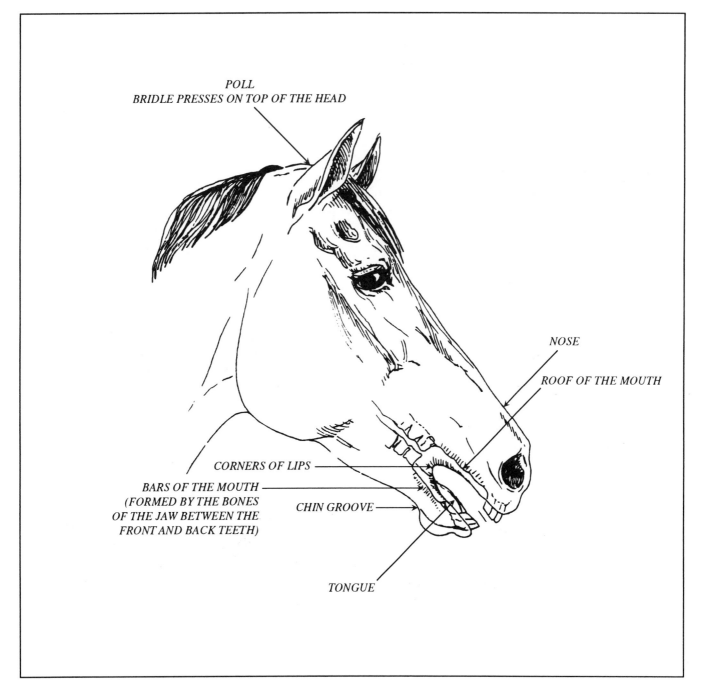

POLL
BRIDLE PRESSES ON TOP OF THE HEAD

NOSE

ROOF OF THE MOUTH

CORNERS OF LIPS

BARS OF THE MOUTH
(FORMED BY THE BONES
OF THE JAW BETWEEN THE
FRONT AND BACK TEETH)

CHIN GROOVE

TONGUE

11

DIRECT PRESSURE BIT

*THE SNAFFLE
A DIRECT PRESSURE BIT*

Direct Pressure bits are the **simplest**. They **pull directly backwards** or **sideways on the mouth or nose**.

• If you use two ounces of pressure on the reins, the horse feels two ounces of pressure on his mouth or nose from the bit.

SNAFFLE BITS

The **snaffle bit** is the **most common direct pressure bit**. It consists of **two rings joined by a mouthpiece** which may be **straight or jointed**.

• The mouthpiece can be made with various kinds of surfaces (*examples: stainless steel, copper, rubber*).

Snaffle bit rings may be:
• **Round**
• **D shaped**
• **Eggbutt** with a special nonpinch hinge
• **Made with cheeks** which help in turning

The snaffle bit is simple to use and understand, so it is often used on green horses or by beginning riders.

• It is usually mild, but snaffle bits can be made severe.

SOME TYPES OF SNAFFLE BITS

BAR SNAFFLE

Eggbutt Rings

Bar Snaffle is often used on draft horses. Very mild, pulls straight back on tongue, lips and bars of mouth.

JOINTED SNAFFLE

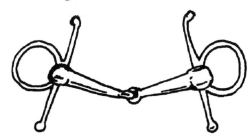

Full Cheek

A **Jointed Snaffle** is hinged in the center to give a looser action and **nutcracker effect on the bars of the mouth**. It is fairly mild and very common.

RUBBER SNAFFLE

Dee Ring

A **Rubber Snaffle** is covered with rubber for a mild effect on the horse's mouth.

TWISTED SNAFFLE

Loose Rings

A **Twisted Snaffle** is made of twisted metal. The edges create severe pressure on the mouth.

LEVERAGE BIT

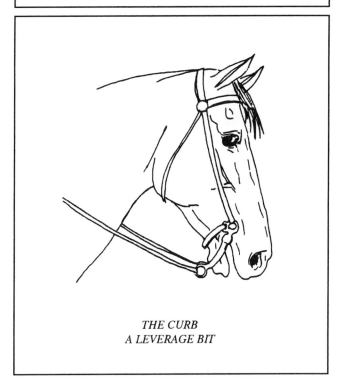

*THE CURB
A LEVERAGE BIT*

Leverage bits multiply the **pressure** the **rider uses on the reins.**

• If the rider puts two ounces of pressure on the reins, the horse might feel four or six ounces of pressure on his mouth.

Leverage bits **can be more severe**, so they should be used only on horses that have been trained to understand and obey pressure.

Leverage bits should be used **only by riders with trained, sensitive hands.**

CURB BITS

The **curb bit** is the **most common leverage bit.**

The curb bits **squeeze** the horse's **whole lower jaw,** putting **pressure** on the **bars of the mouth, the chin groove** and the **tongue.**

• They also put **some pressure downwards on the horse's poll.**
• The **longer the shank** and the **tighter the curb strap,** the **more severe** the curb bit.
• Some curb **mouthpieces** are more severe than others.

Curb bits are best used with **a gentle check and release method with a light or loose rein.**

• If you pull steadily on a curb, it makes the horse's mouth first hurt and later go numb.
• He is apt to toss his head and fret.

Curbs are usually used in western riding, where most riding is done on a loose rein.

They can be used for english but are usually combined with a snaffle bit as they are too severe for jumping.

PARTS OF THE CURB BIT

The curb bit has several basic parts:

○ **Mouthpiece** • which often has a port
○ **Port** • an arch which gives room for the tongue, concentrates the pressure on the bars of the mouth
○ **Bridle rings** • at upper end of bit
○ **Shank** • long side pieces which give the bit its leverage
○ **Rein rings** • rings at lower end of shank
○ **Curb strap or curb chain** • which is necessary for the bit to work with leverage

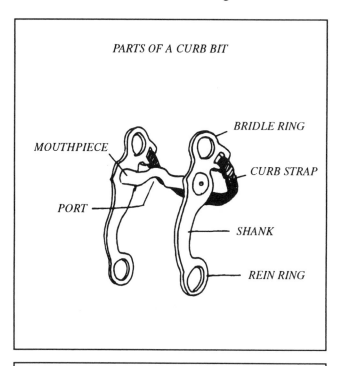

PARTS OF A CURB BIT

MOUTHPIECE

PORT

BRIDLE RING

CURB STRAP

SHANK

REIN RING

SNAFFLE AND CURB BITS

The snaffle and curb bit should be **adjusted** to rest firmly in the **corner of the horse's mouth,** forming **a slight wrinkle in the lip.**

13

SOME TYPES OF CURB BITS

LOW PORT CURB

A **Low Port Curb** gives the horse a **little tongue room**. It is usually easy on the horse.

HIGH PORT CURB

A **High Port Curb** removes the pressure from the tongue and **puts** more **pressure on the bars**.

ENGLISH CURB

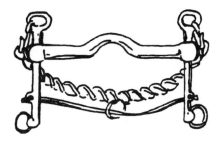

A **English Curb Bit** is used combined with a snaffle bit. It is often used in dressage.

JOINTED CURB OR TOM THUMB

A **Jointed Curb** or **Tom Thumb** is a **short shank** curb often mistaken for a snaffle because of its jointed mouthpiece. It has a **strong nutcracker effect on the bars** of the mouth.

GRAZING BIT

A **Grazing Bit** is a curb with **swept back shanks** so that they can drag along the ground when the horse eats grass. It is a traditional western bit.

HALF BREED CURB

A **Half-Breed Curb** is a **medium or high port** curb with a **cricket** or **roller**. The roller gives the horse something to play with and roll with his tongue. It pacifies some nervous horses.

SPADE BIT

A **Spade Bit** is a special curb with a **very high, molded port that resembles a spoon**. The **spade touches the roof** of the horse's mouth and **can be very severe**. It is **only for experts**.

An old saying is "*that to handle a spade, you should be able to ride with reins made of thread.*"

TYPE OF PELHAM BIT

RUBBER PELHAM

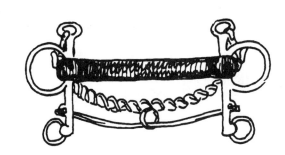

The **rubber pelham** has a hard rubber mouthpiece.

PELHAM BITS

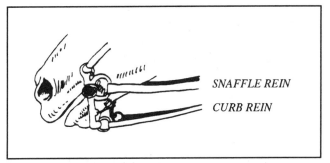

SNAFFLE REIN
CURB REIN

A **Pelham Bit** is a compromise between **a curb and a snaffle**.

• It is a **double action bit** that can work like either one, **depending** on which **pair of reins** you use.

• It looks like a curb bit, but has an **extra set of rings attached to the mouthpiece** for snaffle reins as well as curb reins at the bottom of the shank.

The rider must handle **double reins**, using the **wider snaffle reins** (*top reins*) when he wants a mild snaffle action and the **narrow curb reins** (*bottom reins*) when he wants curb action.

Pulling back on **all four reins at once** causes a general pull back on the horse's mouth which isn't precisely curb or snaffle.

Pelham bits work well for turning, so they are used in polo and are good for english horses that need a little more control than a snaffle.

KIMBERWICKE BIT

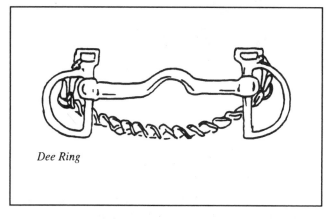

Dee Ring

The **Kimberwicke Bit** is a variation of the pelham bit. It looks like a curb, having a **curb chain, a port mouthpiece** and **upper rings**.

• Instead of shanks it has a **dee-shaped ring**.
• The reins can slide around this ring for a partly curb, partly snaffle effect.

This bit has **only one set of reins**, so it is preferred for beginners or for riders jumping who don't want to handle double reins.

It is **fairly mild but stronger than a snaffle**.

OTHER EQUIPMENT

BOSAL

A bosal is a **braided rawhide or rope loop around the horse's nose**, right at the **end of the nasal bone**.

It works by **direct pressure** and is handled with **two hands on the reins**.

It is a training device that takes skill to handle properly for control.

BOSAL

DROPPED NOSEBAND

A dropped noseband is used to **prevent a horse from evading the bit** by gaping his mouth wide open.

• It rests **lower on the nose** than the english noseband and **buckles below the bit**, just snugly enough to keep the horse's mouth shut. You should be able to get **one finger under the chin strap**.

• Always undo a dropped noseband to put on and take off the bridle.

A **standing martingale** should **never be attached to a dropped noseband**, as it would be too severe and too low on the nose.

DROPPED NOSEBAND

HACKAMORE

A hackamore is a **bitless bridle** that **works on the horse's nose and jaw** but not in his mouth.

They are used in training young horses and for horses with injured or tender mouths.

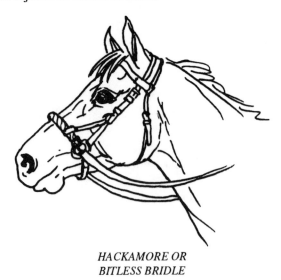

*HACKAMORE OR
BITLESS BRIDLE*

MECHANICAL HACKAMORE

A mechanical hackamore is a **leverage type** of hackamore that acts like a curb bit.

It works on the **nose and chin** and can be severe.

MECHANICAL HACKAMORE

MARTINGALE AND TIE-DOWN

Martingales and tie-downs are used to **control the position of the horse's head** for training, speed riding and horses with bad habits like head tossing.

For horses that toss their head, make certain that the horse really needs this restraint. First eliminate all physical possibilities for head tossing such as lameness or ill-fitting tack.

STANDING MARTINGALE

A standing martingale is a strap which **attaches to the girth** and **runs between the front legs** and up **to the noseband**.
• A **small strap** runs **around the horse's neck** to keep the martingale strap in place.

It puts **pressure on the horse's nose** when he gets his head up too high.

The standing martingale should be adjusted so that it doesn't bother the horse when his head is in the proper position. To test the adjustment, have your horse's head in the proper position.
• You should **be able to push the martingale strap up until it touches the horse's throat**.

TIE-DOWN

A tie-down is a western version of a english standing martingale. It attaches to **a bosal or noseband** and **runs between the front legs to the cinch**.

The adjustment is the same as above.

RUNNING MARTINGALE

A running martingale is a strap that **attaches to the girth, runs up between the front legs** and **splits into two straps** with a **ring at the end** of each strap. The reins are run through the martingale rings.

• This martingale **pulls down on the reins and the bit** when the horse raises his head, so that it pulls on the mouth and can be severe.

• It must be **used only by riders with excellent hands** or it may hurt the horse's mouth.
• It should only be used with a snaffle bit.

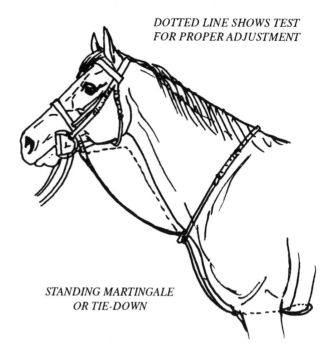

DOTTED LINE SHOWS TEST FOR PROPER ADJUSTMENT

STANDING MARTINGALE OR TIE-DOWN

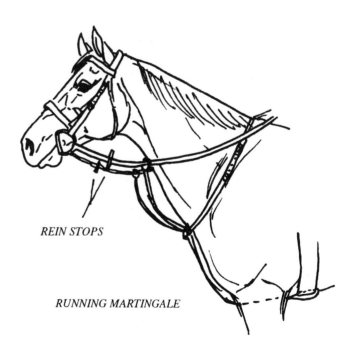

REIN STOPS

RUNNING MARTINGALE

17

BREASTPLATE AND BREAST COLLAR

Breastplates and breast collars are used to:
• **Keep the saddle from sliding back** on flat sided or very round horses.

WESTERN BREAST COLLARS

With western equipment, the breast collar may be decorative as well as useful. There are two styles of western breast collars.

They should **attach to the breast collar rings** at the front of the saddle or sometimes to the rigging rings.

• The breast collar must not be:
    • Too loose or it will not do its job or
    • Too tight as it will make the horse uncomfortable.

You should be able to **fit a fist between the breast collar and the horse's chest.**
• The **center ring** of the breast collar should come **about two inches above the horse's breastbone.**
• It should not press on his windpipe at the base of his neck or hang below the point of the shoulder.

ENGLISH BREAST COLLAR

The breast collar should **attach to the billet straps on the saddle.** A small strap runs over the horse's neck to help hold the breast collar in place.

• The breast collar must not be:
    • Too loose or it will not do its job or
    • Too tight as it will make the horse uncomfortable.

You should be able to **fit a fist between the breast collar and the horse's chest.**
• It should not press on his windpipe at the base of his neck or hang below the point of the shoulder.

ENGLISH HUNTING BREASTPLATE

An english version is the **hunting breastplate.**

This has a **strap which goes around the neck** and another **strap between the front legs that attaches to the girth.**
• The **neckstrap attaches to the dee-rings** at the front of the saddle.

Some breastplates also have a martingale attachment.

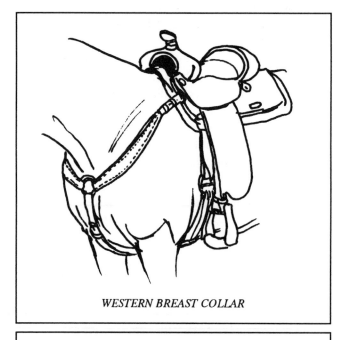

WESTERN BREAST COLLAR

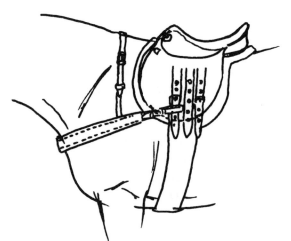

ENGLISH BREAST COLLAR
(2ND WESTERN BREAST COLLAR IS SIMULAR)

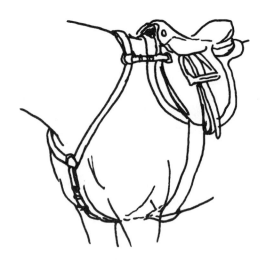

ENGLISH HUNTING BREASTPLATE

CARE OF EQUIPMENT

Good horse equipment or tack is an **investment** that can often **last a lifetime if it is well cared for**.
Yet the most expensive, highest quality equipment can be ruined quickly with poor care.

There are four words to remember in caring for your tack. They are:
PLACE, CLEAN, DRY and OIL

1) PLACE:

Put your tack away where it won't be **walked on, kicked over** or **rained on**.
Put it back in its place when you are through using it.
This simple step can save wear, tear and loss without much effort.

2) CLEAN:

There are two reasons for keeping your tack clean.
1. Both **leather and nylon equipment stays supple and strong much longer when it is kept clean** than when it is allowed to stay dirty.
2. **Clean equipment looks newer and nicer** and gives people a greater desire to take care of it.

For **nylon equipment, use soapy water and a sponge**.

For **leather equipment, use saddle soap** or a **leather cleaner and a rag**.

3) DRY:

It is important to keep your equipment dry.
Allowing it to **remain wet** for **long periods of time** will **cause it to mildew or rot** very quickly.

After riding a sweating horse:
1. **Wipe down the underside of your saddle** (*english saddle only*)
2. **Place your saddle so that air can easily get to its underside**.
2. Set your **pad or blanket, wet side out**, over a rail or rack to dry.

If you get caught in the rain, wipe all your wet equipment with a rag and set it someplace where
the air can dry it underneath as well as on top.
NOTE: Too much heat can dry out leather and cause it to crack. Don't put leather next to a heater.

4) OIL:

Although it is important to protect your tack from too much water, it is **harmful** if your **leather tack loses its
natural moisture**. This is not a problem with nylon equipment, but **leather equipment should be oiled once
or twice a year** according to the amount of hard use it gets.

Be sure to get the oil up underneath the several layers of leather on your saddle as well as
all the obvious leather parts.

If you are careful to remember, and put into practice these four words,
your equipment should remain useful for a long time.

HORSEMANSHIP

In Level 1 and 2, you were concerned with learning the basics of staying on, beginning control and riding at the walk, trot or jog, and lope or canter. Now you can begin to refine your horsemanship so that you can enjoy the challenge of riding a better trained horse with more control, comfort and understanding.

ARTIFICIAL AIDS

Artificial aids are those that **reinforce the natural aids** which are the legs, hands, weight and voice. They are sometimes used for correcting bad habits.

Artificial aids include **crops and whips, spurs and martingales**. Martingales have already been described under the Equipment section.

• **Artificial aids must be used with self control and judgement**, never with temper.

• Usually one or two taps will be sufficient. Repeated hitting will only make a horse angry and frantic.

• Artificial aids must never be used on or near the horse's head.

When using a crop, whip or spurs, remember the horse's short attention span.

• He can only **pay attention** to an aid or a correction for **about three seconds**. You must use a spur or crop **within three seconds** in order for him to connect it with whatever he has done wrong or failed to do.

• A light touch at the right time will teach him far more than a severe punishment too late.

SPURS

Spurs are used to **reinforce the leg aids** and to give a **more precise** and **delicate aid**.

They may be **used only by expert riders who have extremely good control over their legs**. If your legs move and bounce around, your spurs will jab the horse accidentally and he is likely to let you know about it!

A good rider gives a gentle or light leg aid, then supplies a touch of the spurs if the horse fails to respond.

• Misusing spurs can make a horse into a cranky, sour, tail-switcher or teach him to buck.

• **Western spurs** have rowels, which is a sort of wheel with blunt points.

• **English spurs** should be the *Prince of Wales* type, which is blunt without rowels or sharp points.

• Western spurs are worn low on the heel of the boot.
• English spurs are worn high along the seam, just below the ankle.

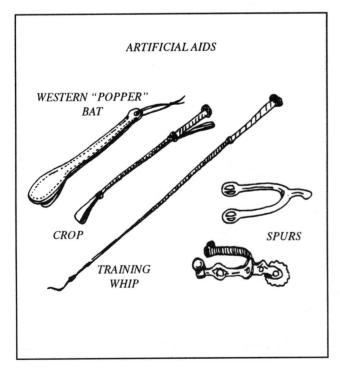

ARTIFICIAL AIDS

WESTERN "POPPER" BAT

CROP

TRAINING WHIP

SPURS

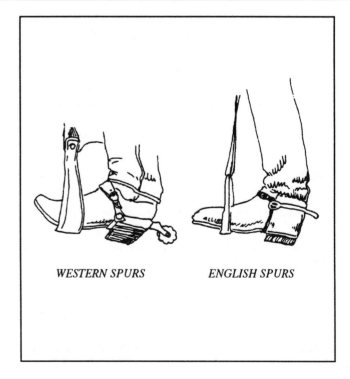

WESTERN SPURS　　*ENGLISH SPURS*

CROP OR BAT

A crop or bat is **short and stiff** about 18 to 24 inches long with a flat popper on the end.

• It is meant to make a loud noise rather than to really hurt your horse.

• A crop or bat should be used hard enough to make a noise, once or twice on the horse's side or hip.

• When you use a bat or crop behind the saddle, you must not keep hold of the rein in the hand that holds the bat or you will jerk the horse's mouth as you hit him.

Here is how to use a crop or bat:

◯ Put both reins in one hand and put the bat in the other hand.
◯ Reach back and tap the horse's side without looking back or pulling on the reins.
◯ Replace your hand on the reins.

• When you carry a crop or bat, hold it with the butt end up and the stick pointing down along with the rein.

Don't wave the crop around or threaten the horse with it. He should not notice that you have a crop until you have to use it.

USIE A BAT OR CROP ON THE HORSE'S SIDE OR HIP

TRAINING OR DRESSAGE WHIP

This is a **long thin whip** about 36 to 39 inches long.

It is used in training or dressage because the rider can tap the horse's side just behind his leg without taking his hand off the reins.

• The training whip should be carried with the butt up and the long end resting down across the rider's thigh.

• To use it, tap your thigh lightly. The tip of the whip will tap against the horse's side just behind your leg.

A whip stings if it is used hard and can make some horses very jumpy, so it is only for expert riders who can use it quietly and tactfully.

USE A DRESSAGE WHIP JUST BEHIND RIDER'S LEG

21

PUTTING THE AIDS TO WORK

You already know that the natural aids are your legs, hands, weight and voice. Now you need to learn what each aid says to your horse, one at a time. When you understand each aid clearly, you can begin to use the aids as a language to **communicate** with any horse. The better trained a horse is, the more easily he understands and responds to the aids.

A rider that doesn't know what he is trying to say with his aids, or one who is crude and rough, will upset and **untrain** a fine horse. As your use of the aids gets better, you will find that horses seem easier to ride and cooperate more. This is because you can communicate with them better and it is easier for them to understand you.

REIN AIDS

LEADING REIN

This is the first rein aid english riders learn to use to turn a horse.

• To use a leading rein you bring your hand out to the side and **lead** your horse around in a turn.

• The other hand must give a little to let the horse turn his head.

This rein aid turns the horse without his slowing down. It works best on wide gentle turns and can be used over jumps because it doesn't pull back.

DIRECT REIN OF OPPOSITION

The direct rein **puts pressure on the bit**, directly back toward the rider. It works in opposition to the horse's forward motion.

• If you use both direct reins together, the horse will slow or stop.

• If you use only one direct rein, the horse turns in that direction.

The direct rein makes the horse shorten his stride for the turn, so it works best where you need more control or a tight turn.

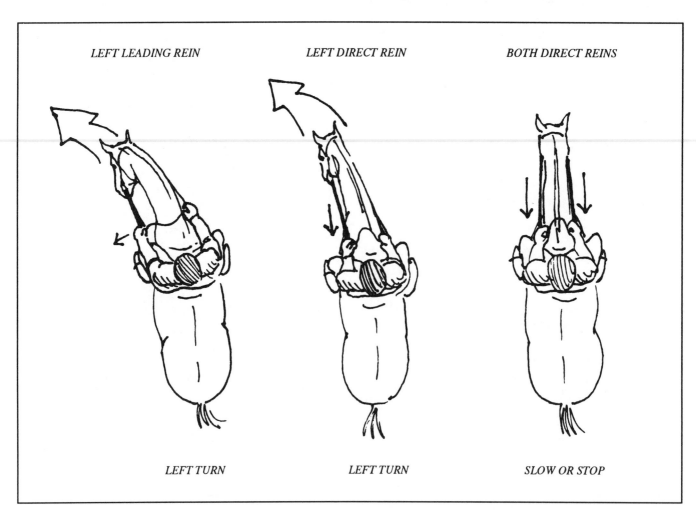

LEFT LEADING REIN   *LEFT DIRECT REIN*   *BOTH DIRECT REINS*

LEFT TURN   *LEFT TURN*   *SLOW OR STOP*

INDIRECT REIN

The indirect rein acts by **pressing slightly sideways** on **one side** of the horse's mouth.

• You do this by pressing the rein in toward the horse's neck, but not crossing your hands over the neck.
• This bends his head toward the rein but pushes him sideways away from the pressure.
• You will need to use a leg aid to assist the indirect rein aid.

An indirect rein can ask a horse to bend around a turn, or it can prevent him from cutting corners.

• If you pull backward, so that you **aim** the pressure at your opposite hip, it becomes an **indirect rein behind the withers**. This is a powerful backward and sideways rein which is used to correct a stubborn horse, or to move a horse sideways.

PULLEY REIN

PULLEY REIN

This is an **emergency rein aid** for disciplining a horse that bucks or gets his head down and refuses to stop with an ordinary rein aid. It can be severe, so it should not be used when a milder aid will do. All riders should know how to use a pulley rein in an emergency.

• To use a pulley rein, shorten the reins and hold one rein in each hand.
• Set one hand firmly on the crest of the horse's neck, then make a fist with the other and rock back in the saddle, lifting up and back sharply in a short jerk.
It may take several short upward pulls to bring the horse back to a stop. This rein aid twists the bit in the horse's mouth and lifts his head, making it a very powerful stopping rein aid.

NECK REIN AND BEARING REIN

A **neck rein** (western) applies **pressure on the side of the horse's neck** to tell the horse to move away from the pressure.

A **bearing rein** does the same, but it **also pulls sideways and backwards on the bit**.

• The neck rein is gentle; the bearing rein is powerful. For both rein aids, the horse must be trained to respond to neck pressure.
• Both should be used in short, light touches with a release or slack in between, never a long hard pull. That pull would make the horse open his mouth and perhaps throw his head around.

Because these rein aids can be given with both reins held in one hand, they are used in western riding, in polo and for any one-handed riding.

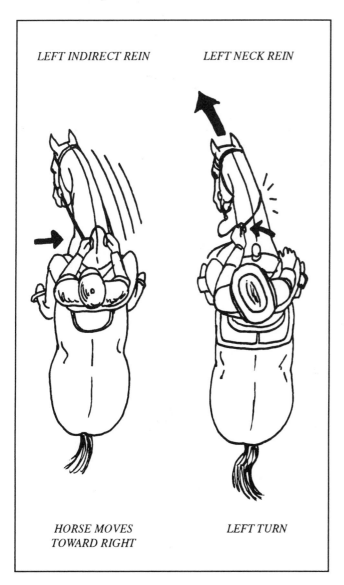

LEFT INDIRECT REIN   *LEFT NECK REIN*

HORSE MOVES TOWARD RIGHT   *LEFT TURN*

LEG AIDS

In order to give a proper leg aid, you first need to have a good leg position. If your leg is too far forward or back, or waving in the breeze, your horse will not understand your aid.

Leg aids should be given with the **big muscle of your calf**, not with your heel or ankle. This lets you give an invisible aid with the heels down.

○ **Both legs** used in the **normal position near the girth** tell the horse to wake up, to move ahead or to use his hind legs harder.

○ **One leg** (*usually the inside leg*) used in the **normal position near the girth** tells the horse to bend or **give** in his ribs and to move forward.

○ **One leg** used **three or four inches behind the girth** tells the horse to move his hind legs sideways away from the pressure. It can be used to **steer** or direct his rear end.

○ When **both legs** are used **in connection with proper voice and rein aids**, it will cue your horse to check his forward motion.

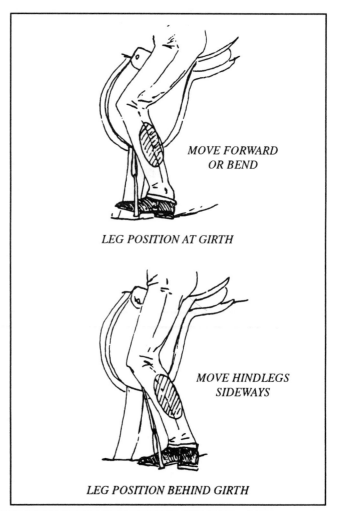

MOVE FORWARD OR BEND

LEG POSITION AT GIRTH

MOVE HINDLEGS SIDEWAYS

LEG POSITION BEHIND GIRTH

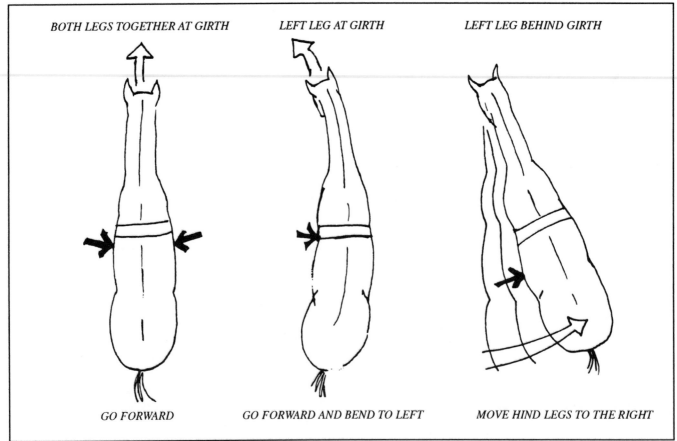

BOTH LEGS TOGETHER AT GIRTH

LEFT LEG AT GIRTH

LEFT LEG BEHIND GIRTH

GO FORWARD

GO FORWARD AND BEND TO LEFT

MOVE HIND LEGS TO THE RIGHT

SEAT AIDS (WEIGHT)

Seat aids are used to **strengthen or help the horse's movement from the hindquarters or rear**. Seat aids are essential for collection, stops and basically all advanced exercises and movements.

When you push your seat bones down and forward into the saddle, your weight change tells the horse:

- To wake up or to move forward
   OR
- To shift his weight back to his rear end and to prepare to stop or slow down.

- Pushing down and forward with **one seat bone** tells the horse to turn in that direction. Be careful not to lean with your shoulders, but simply shift the pressure on your seat bones.

When you use a seat aid, you must be careful not to let your legs slip forward. If you do, you will get out of balance and fall back on to the back of the saddle and probably pull on the reins. It takes a good position and careful use of your aids to avoid doing this when using a seat aid.

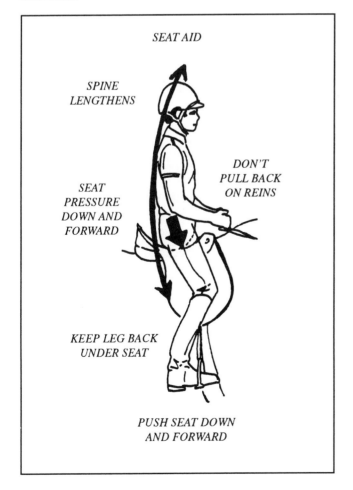

SEAT AID

SPINE
LENGTHENS

SEAT
PRESSURE
DOWN AND
FORWARD

DON'T
PULL BACK
ON REINS

KEEP LEG BACK
UNDER SEAT

PUSH SEAT DOWN
AND FORWARD

VOICE AIDS

Voice aids can be used as **verbal signals**, like telling a dog to sit or heel.

The horse must be trained to obey words such as **Walk, Trot,** or **Whoa**. Be sure that you always give the command in the same way that he is used to.

- You can use your voice to wake your horse up. This is usually done by giving a short, sharp clucking noise.

- Use your voice to soothe and calm your horse by speaking in long, low, drawn-out tone such as, *"E-e-e-e-a-s-y, boy"*.

The trouble with voice aids is that other horses may hear them and react to them.

If you use them a lot, the horse gets tired of hearing them and will stop paying attention.

It is better to use less and less voice aids as you become a better rider. However, don't forget to praise your horse when he has done well and you are pleased with him.

PUTTING THE AIDS TO WORK

Now that you know what each aid does, you can begin to use combinations of aids to get your horse to understand what you want and perform better.

When aids are used together, you must be careful to use them so that they cooperate, not clash.

Kicking to go, while pulling to stop, will make your horse confused and angry. Using just the right amount of leg aid, along with your rein and seat aids, will get you the results you want.

Start with the lightest possible aids and only make them stronger if you are sure that the horse knows what you want, but he doesn't want to obey.

WAYS OF USING THE REINS

There are several ways to handle your reins. Good riders can use all of them.

LOOSE REIN

LIGHT REIN

LOOSE-REIN RIDING

Loose reins give the horse freedom to move his head and stretch his neck. He feels **no pressure on the bit unless** the **rider pulls on the reins**.

Beginning riders should use loose reins so that they will not accidentally hurt the horse's mouth.

Western horses are usually ridden on a loose rein. Most western bits work better with a light touch and release. They are too severe for steady contact.

Loose reins are also good for relaxing a horse and cooling him out.

• When riding on loose reins, you should only give the horse enough slack to let him carry his head naturally with a sag in the reins, not a huge loop.

Too loose a rein gives you no control and is sloppy.

LIGHT REIN

Riding on a light rein means that there is a **little sag in the reins**, but the **rider can feel the horse's mouth by curling his wrist or fingers**.

It gives you finer control than a really loose rein, yet the horse still has quite a bit of freedom to carry his head naturally.

Most pleasure horses are ridden on a light rein. This rein is also used on western horses when the rider needs precise control.

• A light seat aid is necessary, otherwise the rein contact will check the forward motion.

A light rein asks the horse to pay more attention to the rider.

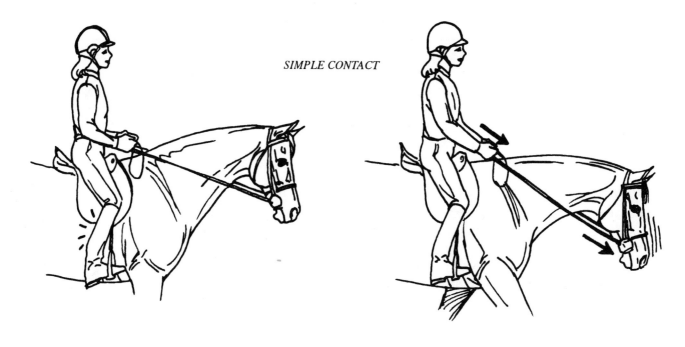

SIMPLE CONTACT

RIDING ON CONTACT

Riding on contact means that the rider **keeps a gentle feel on the horse's mouth at all times**, in all gaits and movements. The reins are important as your lines of direct communication with your horse.
• There should be no slack or sagging in the reins.
• The horse and rider should be able to feel contact with each other through the reins at all times.

When riding on contact, the **rein aids become almost invisible**. The rider can ask for a stop or turn by squeezing his fingers a little to change the pressure on the rein instead of pulling. This makes for very fine, invisible control and is easy on both horse and rider.

A rider cannot practice contact until his seat is steady and he is relaxed and supple. If the rider is not steady and relaxed, the horse may give him a jolt that will make his hand bounce and accidentally yank on the bit.

Contact is not done by pulling on the reins until you can feel the horse's mouth.
• There are **three stages** to maintaining contact.
First you use your seat, then legs and finally hands.

❍ The **first stage** is to **use your seat aids**. The seat aids are important to influence the horse.

❍ The **second stage** of contact **begins with the legs**. If a horse is sensitive and you tighten the reins and do not encourage him with your legs, he will want to stop. Your legs must squeeze the horse forward first.

• Move the horse out into an active stride (*a trot is the best gait for learning this*). He should be moving forward with energy.

❍ In the **third stage**, **gather up the reins** until you can **feel the horse's mouth**. This is like holding hands with another person.
• Your hands are quiet, gentle and steady, not pulling or bouncing. Do not pull back on the reins.
• The rider's hands move gently forward following the movements of the horse's head.

At the trot you may have to, at first, rest your fingertips on the horse's neck to keep your hands steady.

In the walk and the canter, the horse's head moves forward and back.
• Let him pull your arms forward, so that your elbows stretch out.
• Then bring them gently back, as if an invisible rubberband keeps pulling your arms back in place.

When you want to **slow down or stop**, keep your elbows still and stop following the movement of your horse's head.
• Squeeze your fingers on the reins. The horse will feel the extra pressure and will slow and eventually stop.

You are doing well when your reins stay straight from the bit to your hands and the contact feels light and steady all the time.

SHOCK ABSORBERS

When you were a beginner, you may have found the trot and canter very bouncy and hard to sit down to. Now you need to learn to use your natural **shock absorbers** to sit closer and deeper, even at bouncy gaits. This makes it easier on you and on your horse, too.

Your **ankles**, **knees** and **hip joints** act as shock absorber to absorb the bounces which come from the motion of your horse. The **muscles** of **your legs, back**, and **body** also help absorb shock.

• This helps you to ride smoothly with your horse instead of bouncing, and keep your arms, hands, and legs quiet, so you can give gentle, precise aids.

• Keep your back straight, tall, and relaxed.
• Poor back position can make you stiff, put you out of balance, and make you sore.
• You must be **relaxed** enough to **go with the horse's motion**, with enough **muscle control** to maintain a good balanced position.
• Stiff, tight muscles (*especially tightly gripping knees*) or being out of balance causes tension in your joints and muscles. This makes you bouncy.
• However, you must not be so loose and sloppy that you cannot keep a safe, correct balanced position.

Positions to avoid:
• Stiff, tense back, with tight muscles
• Over arched back
• Round, slumped back
• Tipping forward on the front of your seat
• Leaning back

BACKING

It is best to think of backing as a kind of forward movement, not as pulling your horse backward.

• To get him to back, you must tell him with your legs that he is to move.

• Then your seat and hands explain to him that he is to move backwards. Just pulling on the bit will hurt his mouth and make him confused and angry.

If he thinks that you are going to hurt him when you back, he may fight the bit, toss his head, refuse to back, or even rear.

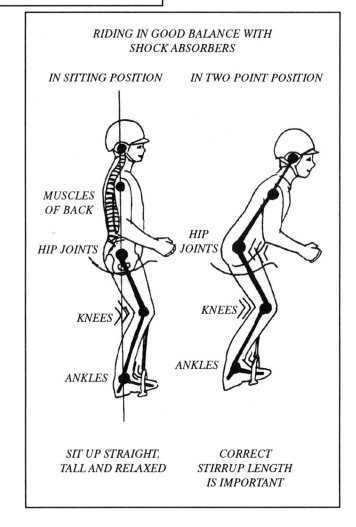

RIDING IN GOOD BALANCE WITH
SHOCK ABSORBERS

IN SITTING POSITION   IN TWO POINT POSITION

MUSCLES OF BACK

HIP JOINTS

HIP JOINTS

KNEES

KNEES

ANKLES

ANKLES

SIT UP STRAIGHT, TALL AND RELAXED   CORRECT STIRRUP LENGTH IS IMPORTANT

When backing well, the **horse tucks his chin, gives to the bit** and **backs straight** and easily with his **legs moving backwards in diagonal pairs**.

To ask your horse to back:
• First squeeze his sides with your legs as if you wanted him to walk.
• Before he can actually walk, relax your leg squeeze a little and increase your pressure on the reins a little. Some horses may need a check and release.
• You should feel him **give to the bit** and see him tuck his chin as he steps back.
• Give a slight release of the rein pressure, then repeat for another step back.
• Sit up tall and deep in the saddle.

• If your horse backs crooked, your legs can guide him. Slide your leg back a couple of inches on the side he is backing toward and squeeze with that leg to tell him to straighten out. If his hindquarters swing left, use the left leg. If they move to the right, use the right leg.

TROT

To learn to sit the trot better, start in a walk.

• Take a deep breath, hold it and then let it out slowly while you stretch your back up tall. (*Deep breathing helps you relax.*)

• As your horse walks, you may feel one side of your seat being lifted and dropped, then the other. This shows that your back and seat are relaxed.

When you can feel this happening, the next step is riding a slow, soft trot or jog.

• Try to stay tall, balanced and relaxed.
• See if you can still feel one hip and then the other being lifted and dropped. The horse's movement does this to you. You don't make it happen yourself.

When you can sit easily at a very slow trot, try a slightly faster one. Be careful not to grip with your legs to stay in position. This will make you stiffen up and bounce harder.

*INCORRECT POSITION CAN CAUSE
LOSS OF BALANCE, BOUNCING AND SORENESS*

TRANSITIONS

Transition means change. Transitions in riding are **changes from one gait to another**, or **changes of speed within a gait**. Good transitions should be smooth.
• They should look as if the rider just thought canter or halt and the horse did it.

To get good transitions:
• You should warn your horse with a **preparation signal** just before you want him to make the change of gait. This could be a squeeze of your legs to wake him up, a check and release or pressure on the reins, sitting taller and deeper in the saddle, or even a voice command.
• As you feel the horse pay attention to your preparation command, **follow** it with the **real command**. Sometimes he will need quite a while to prepare himself, so don't surprise him with a signal all at once.

In transitions, you have to **let your balance shift with your horse** or you may find yourself getting ahead or being left behind his motion.
• If you can keep a **good leg position**, keeping your balance is much easier.
• Try to let your **hips follow** the horse's back as he changes gaits. Coming down from a canter can be bouncy (*think of melting down into the saddle*).

If you have letters or markers in your ring, you can test your control by executing your transitions when your knee reaches the letter. Pick a letter and plan to trot there. You will learn just how far ahead you have to prepare your horse in order to make the change perfect.

STIFF, TENSE	*LOOKING DOWN*	*TIPPING FORWARD*	*LEANING BACK*
PINCHING KNEES	*LOOSE, ROUND BACK*	*TIGHT, ARCHED BACK*	*LEGS AHEAD*
STIFF HANDS	*HEELS UP*	*STIRRUPS TOO LONG*	*STIRRUPS TOO SHORT*

29

Sitting the canter or lope is a slightly different problem. The canter has a **forward dip and roll** to it. It doesn't bounce straight up like the trot or jog.

• To improve your seat in the canter, you need to **sit tall and straight** but **relaxed**. You also need to learn to **follow the rolling motion with your seat**.

The following is done from your waist down, so that your seat stays down in the saddle. Don't try to pump back and forth with your shoulders.
• Give a **little push down and forward** as you feel the dip in the canter. **Then relax** as the horse's back rolls back up. It may help to think of the way you use your seat to **pump a swing**, or to pretend that you have saddle soap on the seat of your pants and that you are polishing the seat of the saddle.

• Don't stiffen your legs and push against the stirrups or it will make you fly out of the saddle and bounce at every stride.
• Pinching tightly with your knees or legs will also make you bounce and is uncomfortable for your legs.
• Your legs should not grab your horse's side but rest on the horse and saddle.

When your horse canters, lopes, or gallops, he is either on a left lead or a right lead.

When you start the lope or canter, look up straight ahead and concentrate on **giving a good, clear signal**. Using the proper aids for the lope or canter tells the horse to take the correct lead. (*see Level 2 on the aids for the canter or lope*)

• You can ride **large circles** one direction, then come back to a walk or trot and reverse. Practice the circles the other way.
• This gives your horse practice on both leads and develops his cantering muscles on both sides.

He should always be **on the lead which is on the inside of the ring, turn or circle**. If he is on the wrong lead, he could cross his legs and trip or fall.

Make it a practice to check your lead every time you start a canter or lope.

To be sure he takes his leads correctly, you must be able to tell which lead he is on.

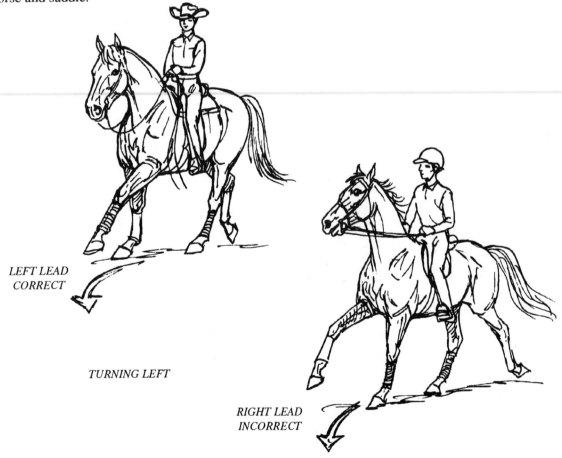

LEFT LEAD
CORRECT

TURNING LEFT

RIGHT LEAD
INCORRECT

HOW TO IDENTIFY LEAD

There are two ways to identify the lead your horse is on; by **sight** and by **feeling**. Sight is easier for most people at first. As you gain more experience, you can feel if the lead is correct or wrong.

On the left lead, the horse's legs hit the ground in the following order:

- Right hind, left hind and right fore together, left fore
- The left hind and left fore are the leading legs
- They move second and appear to travel farther than the outside legs.

When watching a horse canter from the ground, it may help to put colored leg wraps on his left legs and watch him canter.

From the saddle, you can't see the leg wraps, but you can see the inside front leg coming out in front of the left shoulder.

- If you look at both shoulders, you can see that the right moves first, then the left moves second and further forward.

Once he is in the lope or canter and it feels like he will keep going, glance down at the inside shoulder and see if you can see his inside front fore coming out ahead as he canters.

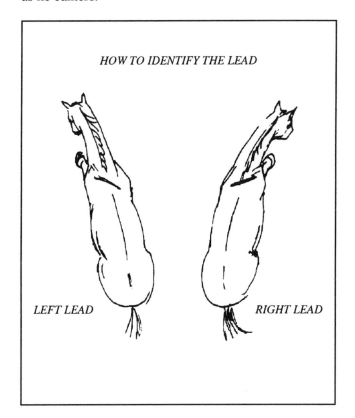

HOW TO IDENTIFY THE LEAD

LEFT LEAD   *RIGHT LEAD*

WRONG LEAD

If you can't see his inside front fore coming out ahead, check the other shoulder. If you see the other foot leading, he's on the wrong lead.

- If so, bring him back to a slow trot and start over, giving an extra clear aid for the proper lead.

If you look down or lean over while beginning the canter, you might put the horse off balance and cause him to take a wrong lead.

Don't punish a horse for taking a wrong lead.
- Often it is a mistake of the rider, not the horse.
- It may be that the horse is stiff and finds it hard to take that lead. He needs more practice, not punishment.

STIFF AND ONE SIDED

Horses that are not worked on both leads will become stiff on one side and have trouble with that lead, just as you find it hard to write with your left hand if you're right handed.

By doing extra practice circles at the trot on his stiff side, you may be able to improve a one sided horse.

CROSS CANTER

Sometimes you may feel a very awkward, sideways roll to the canter, even when you think the horse is on the correct lead with his front leg.

He may be in a cross canter, which means he is **on one lead in his front legs** and the **other lead in his hind legs.**

- The cross canter is very clumsy and uncomfortable for both the horse and rider.
- A horse can easily slip and fall if he tries to turn sharply in a cross canter.

If a cross canter should happen:

- Just bring the horse back to a slow trot and put him into a canter again.

CIRCLES

Circles should be round, not oval or pear-shaped.
• To make a good circle, pick out a starting and finishing point, a quarter point, a halfway point and a three-quarter point.
• Look about a quarter of the way ahead as you ride through the circle.
• Try to hit each of the points and be sure that you finish by returning to your start/finish point.
• Ask your horse to bend evenly around the circle and keep your speed even.

Don't ask for too small a circle as it may be difficult for your horse unless he is very balanced.

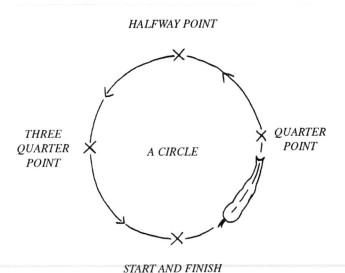

HALFWAY POINT

THREE QUARTER POINT   *A CIRCLE*   *QUARTER POINT*

START AND FINISH

HALF CIRCLE

The half circle is similar to the reverse you learned as a beginner.
• To ride a half circle, begin a medium-sized circle along the rail of the ring.
• When you are halfway through the circle you will be near the center of the ring. Instead of completing your circle, aim your horse back toward the rail on a short diagonal line.
• When he returns to the rail, you will have turned around and changed your direction.

Don't make your half circle too small for your horse to bend comfortably.

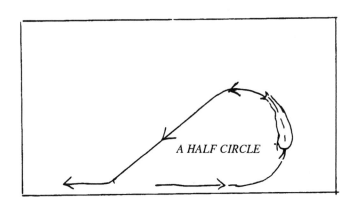

A HALF CIRCLE

SERPENTINE

A serpentine is a snakelike figure that includes half circles to the left and to the right.
• To start a serpentine, begin on the short end of the ring (*for example, tracking to the left*).
• Ride a medium-sized half circle to the left, and then ride straight across the center of the ring for a few strides. Then, ride a matching half circle to the right.
• Go straight across the center, then ride another half circle to the left, and so on, for as long as you have space.

Your horse will want to cut the turns and to zigzag instead of going straight across the center, so this exercise is good practice for your aids and his obedience.

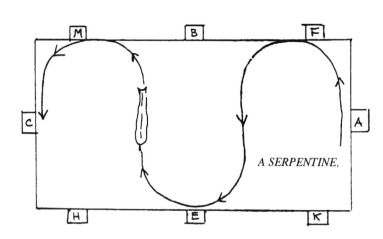

A SERPENTINE,

FIGURE 8

A figure 8 is made with two large circles touching. It is **not a lazy 8** which looks like two teardrops touching.

• Start by riding straight to the center of the ring and pick a center point for your start and finish point.
• Make a circle to the left that takes up half of the ring returning to the center point.
• Now go straight for a couple of strides, and then make a matching circle to the right, returning to the center point to finish.

If the ring is big enough, you can make a large figure 8 by crossing the ring in the center. A small figure 8 is made by starting down the center line.

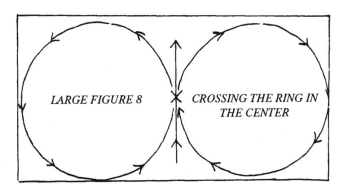

LARGE FIGURE 8   *CROSSING THE RING IN THE CENTER*

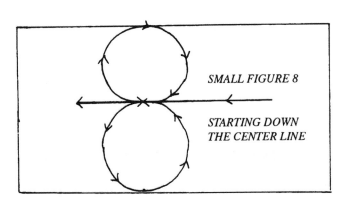

SMALL FIGURE 8

STARTING DOWN THE CENTER LINE

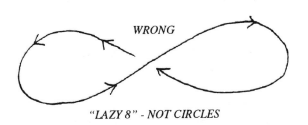

WRONG

"LAZY 8" - NOT CIRCLES

CHANGE OF DIRECTION

ON THE DIAGONAL

Sometimes this is also called *"changing the rein"* or *"changing hands."* To change direction on the diagonal, it is helpful if your ring has letters or markers as in the ring test.

• Ride through the short end of the ring (*for example, tracking to the left*).
• Just after you turn the corner, continue your turn and aim your horse diagonally toward the opposite corner of the ring.
• You should ride straight on the diagonal line until you reach the opposite rail of the ring, just before the corner.
• At the corner, you will simply turn right and follow the rail around in the new direction.

This way of reversing directions lets you keep going at a faster gait or lets a class *follow the leader* while changing directions.

Don't let your horse cut the corners or he will spoil your change of direction on the diagonal. At the trot, change diagonals at X (the center).

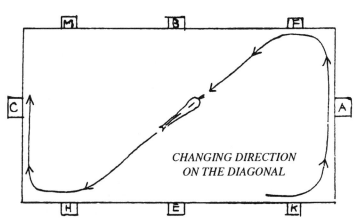

CHANGING DIRECTION ON THE DIAGONAL

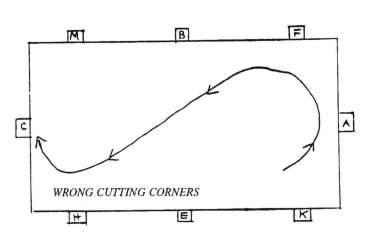

WRONG CUTTING CORNERS

33

EXERCISE

A turnback can be an effective western exercise to help some horses learn (*with minimal use of the reins*):

- To balance on their hocks
- To collect themselves
- To turn on their haunchs

Balance, relaxation and the **correctness** of this exercise is **more important** than a mere quick reversal of direction. The exercise is best **used for horses that run off or are heavy on the forehand.**

- It may not be the best exercise for horses early in their training. Other exercises may be more effective if your mount is easily excited or very young.

There are four stages to execute a turnback effectively.

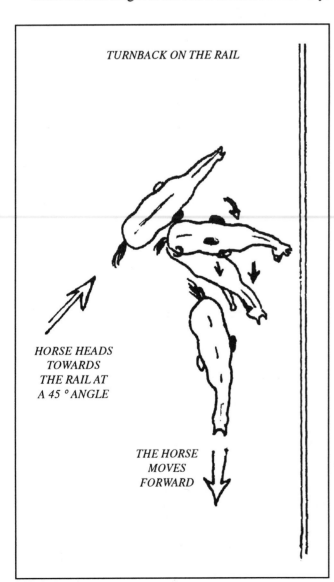

TURNBACK ON THE RAIL

HORSE HEADS TOWARDS THE RAIL AT A 45 ° ANGLE

THE HORSE MOVES FORWARD

FIRST STAGE

The first stage is preparation.

In the preparation stage the **horse should be relaxed, circling** either in a arena or along a fence.

- The horse should demonstrate a relaxed body, bending to the inside of the circle. The rider being able to see the corner of the inside eye and sense that his horse is bent appropriately for the turn.

- The aids used for this would be those necessary to keep a horse properly in a circle.
- The rider is sitting up straight. The legs are used to motivate his horse to go forward and maintain the circle.

SECOND STAGE

The second stage is alerting your horse to an upcoming change.

At this point the horse and rider are **heading toward the rail** at about a **45 degree angle.**

- When the horse and rider are 15 to 20 feet away from the fence, the rider **shifts his weight so that he is sitting balanced evenly.** The horse continues straight toward the fence.

If the horse and rider are too parallel to the rail:
- The horse will tend to run on through or fight the bit

If the horse approaches the fence too directly:
- He may tend to slow down and stop
- Turn on his forehand or
- Anticipate the turn and
- Attempt to duck out in either direction

This is critical as:
- The horse must have enough forward motion so that he feels like he can continue in a circle.
- Enough angle toward the fence that he will be forced to make a change of direction.

The fence is to be used as an aid in turning rather than a using a heavy hand.

At this stage:
- The horse is ridden **straight forward**
- The rider is **sitting on both seat bones evenly**

THIRD STAGE

The third stage is turning.

Within 10 to 15 feet the rider **turns the horse to the outside** (*towards the fence*) using either a neck rein or direct rein if using the trainer's hand hold.

In reining the horse it is important for the **hand to make contact** and gently but firmly **direct the horse around** about **180 degrees** without *snatching* or *jerking* the horse's mouth.

• **Prior to reining:**
   • The rider should give a **verbal command** (*one that is often used is a Shhhhh sound*)
   • Simultaneously **shift weight to the inside** (*the outside has now become the inside*)

The rider's weight should always be **on the inside of the turn, over the pivot leg.**

FOURTH STAGE

The fourth stage is following through.

As the horse begins to consistently turn toward the fence and pivot on his new inside hind leg, the rider should be careful to **continue rein contact until the horse turns a complete 180 degrees.**

• The **riders weight**, on the inside of the turn, should be **placed well back over the pivot leg** to maintain the horse's balance.

• As the horse begins to complete the 180 degree turn, the rider should release the rein and **squeeze with both legs to encourage the horse forward.**

If done correctly, the horse should come out of the turnback with the opposite lead (*if cantering*) to the one in which he entered the turnback.

At first, the turnbacks are best learned at a trot so as to have enough forward motion without excessive speed.

The horse should be quieter and lighter upon successful completion of a turnback.

BENEFITS

The significant **benefits of a turnback** are:

• The horse remains light on the mouth
• He is better able to balance on his haunches
• He is more attentive to the shift of his riders weight and verbal commands

The turnback can be an excellent preparation for more advance maneuvers.

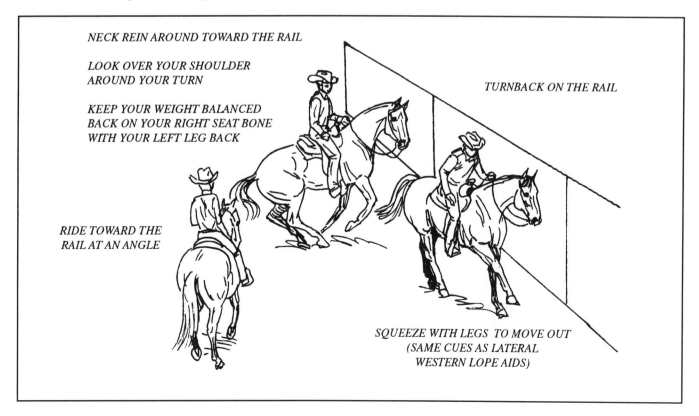

NECK REIN AROUND TOWARD THE RAIL

LOOK OVER YOUR SHOULDER AROUND YOUR TURN

KEEP YOUR WEIGHT BALANCED BACK ON YOUR RIGHT SEAT BONE WITH YOUR LEFT LEG BACK

RIDE TOWARD THE RAIL AT AN ANGLE

TURNBACK ON THE RAIL

SQUEEZE WITH LEGS TO MOVE OUT (SAME CUES AS LATERAL WESTERN LOPE AIDS)

JUMPING

In Level 2, you learned the basics of jumping. Now you can build on those basics to jump new and different fences. The height is not very important at this stage (**too high is hard for** *many* **horses** *and can even* **be dangerous for riders**). You can practice your basics and put them to work for you in many new and interesting ways.

Before you continue on with new jumping, you should review your basics by riding over ground poles or cavaletti, and by trotting over a low crossrail. This is a good jumping warm-up used even by advanced riders to be sure that everything is ready for more difficult work.

LINES OF FENCES

When you can jump one fence easily at the trot, you can move on to riding two fences in a line.

• The first fence should be **low and easy** and the second should be no larger than you are used to jumping.

• They should be about 48 feet apart, which allows you room to recover from the first jump and be ready for the next.

• Trot both fences, aiming your eyes at a **target** (*which could be a tree branch or a spot on the fence or wall*) in the center of and beyond the second fence.

• After the second fence, ride straight to the target and stop, correcting your horse if he has drifted sideways.

In jumping more than one fence, **control after the fence** becomes **important**.

• For this exercise, you should remain in jumping position from before the first fence until your horse has taken several strides after the second fence. Don't sit down between fences.

CANTERING FENCES

When you can trot a line of two fences easily, you can start cantering.

• A good way to do this is to **trot the first fence** at a fairly **lively trot**, then squeeze your legs and cluck to your horse as he lands and encourage him to canter over the second.

• Stay in the jumping position and let him rock your heels down as he canters. The jump may feel a little bigger and smoother in the canter.

• Be sure to **stay up in jumping position until after your horse has landed**. Don't forget to release him correctly so that you don't hurt him.

When you are getting nice jumps trotting the first and cantering the second fence, you can begin your canter early and canter into the first fence as well.

TURNS TO FENCES

Many fences require you to ride around a turn in order to line up with them.

• If you can turn well, you will come into the jump straight. If you make a poor turn, the horse may come in crooked and won't have a fair chance to jump the fence.

• Most horses will try to cut corners instead of turning properly unless you direct them well.

To make a good turn to a fence, you must **use your eyes** to look for your turning point and to decide where you want to start to line up with the fence.

• Look directly over the center of the fence and look at something high at your eye level, never at the ground **Aim for your target**, which could be a tree branch or a spot on a wall, and try to line your horse up with it.

Don't let him **cut corners** or **turn** right **after** the jump or he may get into the habit of turning quickly which can unseat you if he does it unexpectedly after a jump.

If he tries to drift sideways, weave, or cut corners, use the exercise of jumping a fence straight, then stopping on a straight line with the target to correct him.

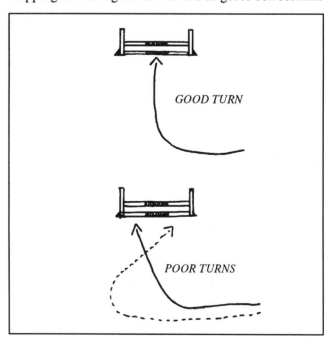

GOOD TURN

POOR TURNS

A course of fences is **two or more lines of fences** put together with turns. Often it will have a variety of fences.

When you can jump single fences, lines, and do turns correctly at the trot and the canter, you can put them all together in a simple course.

Before you begin a course, it is a good idea to **make a preparatory circle**.
• This circle lets your horse see the jumps and gets him prepared to trot, canter and jump.
• The circle should be comfortably wide, and part of the circle should line up with your first fence.

Start with a posting trot, then sit down and ask for a canter on the proper lead.
• Canter around the corner and on to your first fence, aiming for your **target** at the end of your first line.

After your second fence, think about where you will turn and about not cutting the corner, then look for your next line of fences.
• After the last fence, finish with a circle as you come back to a posting trot.

Don't take extra circles when beginning your course or in between fences. In show ring competition, these circles are counted as **technical refusals**.

If you have three refusals or runouts, you would be eliminated in a show class.

Your instructor can put together easy but interesting courses for you to practice on at this level.
Remember, you should be able to:

• Jump many different kinds of low fences about two feet high

• Make excellent turns and lines before you try to jump higher fences

Your position, control, and riding form should be nearly perfect before the rails go an inch higher.

If you don't have many low fences to practice on, perhaps you would enjoy helping your instructor build and paint some new jumps for your program.

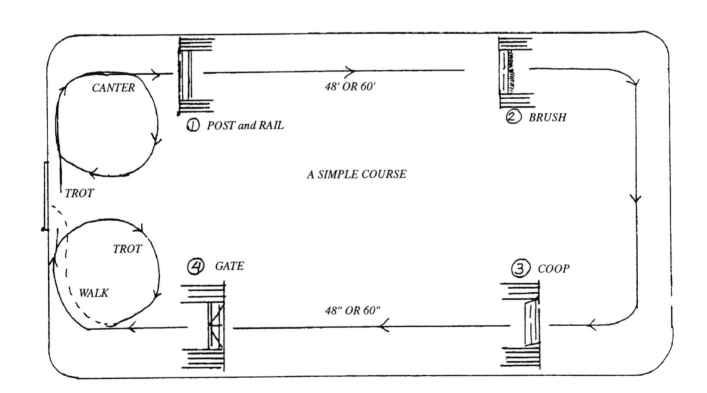

A SIMPLE COURSE

REFUSALS AND RUNOUTS

When a horse **refuses** a fence, he **stops in front of it**. A horse **running by or away** from the fence is called a **runout**.

Horses refuse or runout because they do not want to jump. Ask yourself why?

- *Has the horse been hurt in the mouth or back by a rider?*
- *Is he tired or sore?*
- *Is the fence too big or too difficult?*
- *Did the rider clearly tell him to go straight over the fence?*
- *Was he prepared to jump?*

You must not punish a horse for something that was not his fault, but if you fail to correct a refusal or runout, he will quickly learn to do this instead of jumping.

REFUSALS

To correct a refusal, remember that you are on a balky horse (*a stopper*).

- First, keep him right in front of the fence and make him look where he should have gone, straight over the middle of the fence.
- Next, turn him away from the fence and while you are circling around to re-jump the fence, apply a stronger leg and possibly a tap of the whip to back up the leg aid that he originally didn't listen to. Let him get a little stronger in his gait; then bring him back to the pace you want.

- As you approach the fence for a second time, apply a stronger leg aid, adjust your weight back to drive him on, and if you feel him suck back (hesitate), add a tap with the whip behind your leg and cluck with your voice, reminding him with your leg and a cluck that he is not to stop this time.
- It may be necessary to lower the jump the first time to get him over it.

REFUSAL

RUNOUTS

To correct a runout, remember that he is running away. Whipping him will only make him run out faster.

- Bring him to a full stop, using a pulley rein if necessary. Try to not let him go past the jump. Now ask yourself, "*to which side did he disobey and run out?*"
- **Turn him the other way** and march him back to where he should have gone, right in front of the fence.
- Put your whip on the side he ran out to and use your leg on that side to make him **move over** a step or two and **give** to your leg.
- Then, turn him around, away from his **bad** side and repeat the jump. Let the whip stay close to the shoulder of the bad side. It can be used as a "wall".

- Have enough impulsion that he won't stop but not too much as he may run out again.
- Be prepared to steer him straight with a leading rein as soon as you feel him wanting to possibly run out again and apply a strong leg on the opposite side of your leading rein. Sometimes this can be quite a few strides out from the fence.

When you have to correct a refusal or runout, you must remember to keep your temper and to do what is right for the horse.

- Hitting a horse once or twice might teach him not to try again. More hits may relieve the rider's temper, but not help the horse's training.

Don't pat or praise your horse after a misbehavior, even if it was your fault. **If you don't correct him, he may learn a bad habit. Be firm, but be fair.**

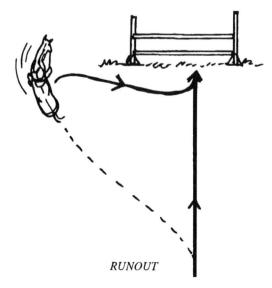

RUNOUT

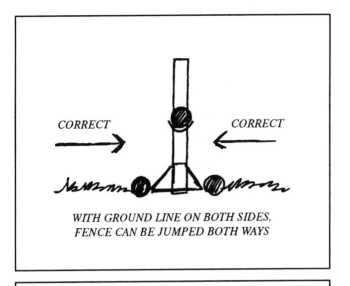

CORRECT → ← *CORRECT*

*WITH GROUND LINE ON BOTH SIDES,
FENCE CAN BE JUMPED BOTH WAYS*

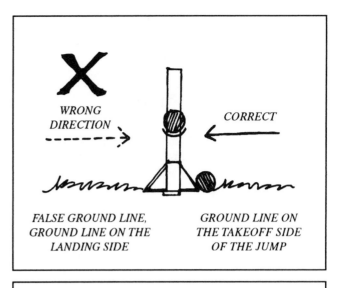

*WRONG
DIRECTION* ⇢ ← *CORRECT*

*FALSE GROUND LINE,
GROUND LINE ON THE
LANDING SIDE*　　　*GROUND LINE ON
THE TAKEOFF SIDE
OF THE JUMP*

GROUND LINE

A ground line is **not a jump but a pole on the ground, set at the base of a jump** so that horses can see and judge the jump better. It is important to always have a ground line with a vertical fence.

- It must always be on the takeoff side
- It must never be on the landing side

NEW FENCES

When you are jumping ordinary crossrails and post and rails well, you can move on to jumping a variety of low but different fences.

Many horses will be reluctant to jump a strange new fence at first and you will have to use your legs firmly and keep your horse straight.

If a horse is very spooky, he may need a chance to walk up and take a close look at a new fence before he jumps it.

There are numerous kinds of jumps. The most common jumps that are used in the ring are:

- Post and Rail
- Vertical
- Panel
- Spread Fence
- Gate
- Coop
- Brush Box
- Wall

FALSE GROUND LINE

A false ground line is:

- A ground line on the landing side
- A jump that slants toward the landing
- A shadow that makes the jump look different

A false ground line is dangerous. They can trick a horse into taking off incorrectly.

This is why **you should never jump fences backward** unless they have been set up to be jumped in both directions. **It is dangerous**.

POST AND RAIL JUMP

Here are a few examples.

VERTICAL

Verticals are fences that are built straight up and down without spread. Most beginning fences like post and rails are low verticals.

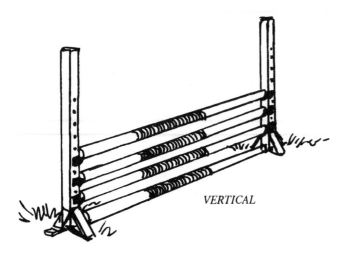

VERTICAL

PANEL

A panel is a solid piece, like a narrow door, which is usually slanted or propped up against a rail. The solid look and slant tend to make the horse take off at the right place. Panels are often brightly painted.

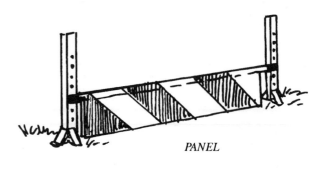

PANEL

SPREAD

Spread fences are fences with some width. The front (*takeoff side*) should be lower than the back on beginning spreads. The back should only be one rail since this rail is the one most likely to be hit if the horse makes a mistake. Spreads tend to make the horse jump longer and stay up in the air longer.

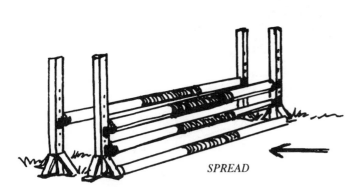

SPREAD

GATE

A gate is usually made of planks or pickets, often painted white. Horses jump it very much like a panel, although horses sometimes are spooky about things painted white. The spaces should not be wide enough to let a horse get a leg caught.

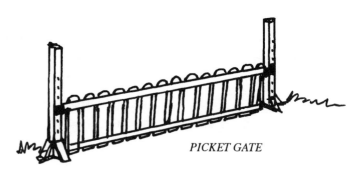

PICKET GATE

COOP

A coop is two panels attached to each other solidly, back to back. It looks like a triangle from the side. Just like a panel, it helps a horse to take off properly. Coops should always be solid, never made with a hinge at the top, which can be dangerous.

BRUSH BOX

The brush box is a low box, usually made of white planks, which can be stuffed with greenery to look like a low hedge. Most horses find a brush box easy to jump and often brush their legs through the evergreen which sticks up.

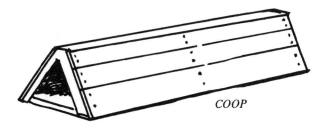

COOP

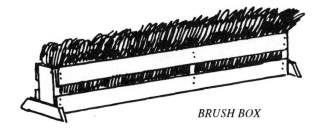

BRUSH BOX

WALL

A wall is an oblong jump, usually made of plywood and painted to look like brick or stone. It may be slanted slightly on one side, which makes it easier to jump.

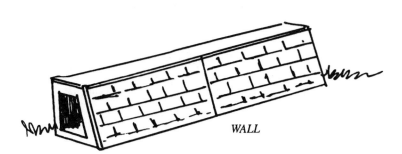

WALL

41

GAMES

COMMAND CLASS

A command class is a game that **tests your control and transitions**. It's fun!

• Your instructor calls out commands for any gait or movement: walk, trot or jog, canter or lope, halt, reverse, or circle.
• Anyone who breaks his gait, takes too long to execute the command, or makes a mistake like a wrong lead is called to the center.
• The last one left on the rail is the winner.

• Besides performance errors, your instructor may call you in on **horsemanship** if you are caught in a horsemanship error, like posting on the wrong diagonal or being rough with your horse to get quick obedience.

This game also teaches you to steer smoothly around other riders and not to get caught in a bunch.

RIDE-A-BUCK GAME

When you have learned to sit down well at various gaits, you might like to play the Ride-A-Buck game.

• In this game, each rider is given a slip of paper representing a dollar bill (*buck*) which is placed under his seat or leg.

• He is then asked to perform the different gaits, walk, trot or jog, and canter or lope.
• As a rider loses his dollar or paper, he is eliminated.

• The winner is the last one left with his dollar or paper under his seat or leg.

Some horse shows hold this class bareback, but it can be played with saddles just as easily.

RIDING BAREBACK

Riding bareback can be fun for riders who have learned to sit relaxed and secure. It puts you closer to the horse. You almost feel like you are part of each other.

However, **bareback riding has to be done right or it can lead to trouble and a very sore seat!**

If possible, the horse you ride bareback should have a rather **flat back**, or at least he should not have a very high, sharp backbone.

You may also use a bareback pad strapped onto the horse to cushion his back if you choose to.
• This pad should **never be used with stirrups**.
• You should not hold onto the pad, as it doesn't have a tree as a saddle does. The pad could slide around underneath your horse.

When you ride bareback, you will have to **sit up tall** and keep your **weight** more **toward the back of your seat bones** (*back where you have more natural padding*).

If you tilt forward, it will make you lose your balance and become very uncomfortable.
• If you feel as if you need to hold on to something, hold the horse's mane.
• Don't grab his sides with your heels.

Practice at the walk until you are comfortable.
• When you first trot, it should be a slow, soft jog trot that is easy to sit.
• Your back is your shock absorber when riding bareback just as in sitting the trot.

It is possible to **post** when riding bareback, just like posting without stirrups, but it is very tiring.

Don't try a canter until you are very good at sitting the trot, both slow and fast. Your horse might trot fast instead of cantering or loping or when you ask him to start, and you must be able to sit securely.

Riding bareback is fun:

• For games like walk tag
• For practicing turns and circles
• For relaxing, *just-for-fun* riding

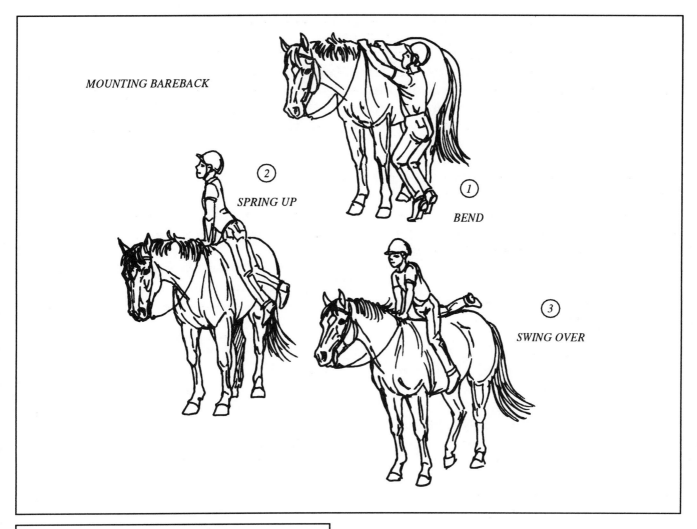

MOUNTING BAREBACK

② SPRING UP

① BEND

③ SWING OVER

MOUNTING BAREBACK

To mount bareback, you will need a fairly small horse and plenty of spring in your legs.

• Stand facing the horse's left side, right where the saddle would be.
• Put your left hand, holding the reins, on the horse's neck near the withers.
• Put your right hand on his back where the back of the saddle would be.
• Bend your knees and sink down, then spring up and try to land with your belly against the horse's back.
• Your arms should straighten out and hold your weight.
• Arch your back and swing your right leg over his back and settle down into riding position.
• Be careful not to kick the horse or bang into him as you jump up.

If you have tried two or three jumps and you can't make it, ask your instructor for a leg up. Too many tries will only make your horse angry, especially if you bump into him each time.

Don't try to climb onto your horse from a fence or some other object. He might move away while you are trying to get on.

*RIDING BAREBACK YOU NEED
TO SIT UP TALL AND KEEP YOUR WEIGHT MORE
TOWARD THE BACK OF YOUR SEAT BONES*

43

TRAIL RIDING

As you become a better rider, you can enjoy the challenge of Level 3 trail riding.

When you have demonstrated a good seat and control in the ring, you can begin loping or cantering on trails. You can now ride longer and more difficult trails and might take part in a long ride with a picnic stop.

As you learn more about trail riding, you should know how to preserve the environment and how to keep good trails available to all trail riders.

PREPARING FOR A TRAIL RIDE

Check your equipment carefully before you start. A dirty or pinching girth or cinch can make a sore on a long ride, and a loose shoe or a slipping saddle pad could spoil your ride.

• It is a good idea to carry a hoof pick clipped to your belt or attached to your saddle.

• Take bug repellent for yourself, and use fly spray or fly wipe on the horse before you leave.

• Be sure to carry a long sleeved shirt or jacket in case the weather changes or in case you are pestered by bugs.

• You may want a canteen (*clean, small bleach bottles make good canteens*).

• You should wear a hat for protection from the sun.

Anything you carry like cameras, lunch, or snacks should be attached securely so that it won't drop on the ground or bang into the horse.

• Put your gear in a saddlebag or roll it up in your jacket. Tie the jacket or saddlebag securely across the back of the saddle.

Your horse should wear a halter under his bridle and you should carry a tie rope if you plan to tie him up for a lunch or rest stop.

Someone, probably your lead rider or rear guard rider, should carry a compact first aid kit.

Before you mount, check your horse's shoes, tack and equipment for proper fit.

HERE IS A CHECKLIST

Feet:
Clean the feet with a hoof pick.
Shoes should be tight.

Saddle pad:
Clean, set well forward and pulled up into the gullet of saddle to make an air space.

Saddle:
Fits the horse without pressing on the spine, with the girth smooth, clean and tight.

Bridle:
Adjusted properly with no pinching or loose straps. All leather in good condition.

Halter:
Worn under bridle; fits horse.

Lead rope:
Around the horse's neck or coiled and fastened to the saddle.

Horse:
Groomed clean, especially on back, elbows, belly and wherever tack will touch him.
Protected with fly spray or wipe.

TRAIL GAITS

On long rides, encourage your horse to move out in a long striding walk which is easy to ride and develops the horse's muscles.

He should be warmed up at a walk for the first 15 minutes of any ride.

If he is a slow walker, use your legs in **alternating leg aids**, left leg, right leg, left leg, right leg, as if you were walking with him. This tells him to stretch his legs and walk with longer, not quicker, strides.

An **easy jog** is a **good trail gait**. The horse must be relaxed and steady or the jog will be uncomfortable to ride. Jogging covers ground faster than walking and yet the horse can do it for a long time without tiring.
• If you get sore, try standing in your stirrups for a while to ease your seat.
• Never sit crooked in the saddle (*sitting off to one side*), even if you are sore because this can wear a sore in your horse's back.

Long distance trail riders use a **long trot** to cover ground at speed.
• They usually ride standing up and balancing, but you can post if you like.
• Let the horse stretch his neck, and give him a loose rein to pick his way.
• Don't let him crowd the horse ahead.
• Trotting with long strides covers the most ground in the shortest time.

Remember that your horse will need a rest break from the trot every so often. Bring him back to a walk for awhile, before trotting again.

A GOOD LONG DISTANCE TRAIL TROT RIDER IN 2 POINT

CANTERING OR LOPING ON TRAILS

When you **first** try a **lope or canter outside the ring**, it should be **in a situation where you can control your horse easily**. Never canter back toward the barn since this encourages horses to run away to get home.

• Don't ever let a horse get the idea that you are racing with another.
• Passing fast or riding fast in a big group excites some horses so much that they give in to their herd instinct and run out of control. One rider charging past a group can start a chain reaction.

Even if it is fun for some riders, running is terrifying for someone who can't handle his horse and is the worst possible horsemanship.

The best way to try a lope or canter for the first time is **behind a reliable leader going up a gentle slope away from home**.
• The leader can set the pace with a fast trot.
• Anyone who can lope or canter and stay in line may do so.

To canter, you will have to restrain your horse from trotting fast.
• Keep him in a slow jog.
• Give the proper canter signal.
• Don't let him try to pass, get out of line or crowd the horse ahead.
• Pull him up with checks and releases before this happens on the trail.

When the leader slows down and stops, all the other horses will want to stop, too.

Cantering and loping is smooth and pleasant for the rider, but **tires the horse more** than other trail gaits. Hence, long distance riders seldom canter, except for a brief change of pace.

Don't canter downhill. This is harder for your horse to balance and he could stumble or get out of control.

HORSE TIED SAFELY TO OVERHEAD BRANCH FOR LUNCH STOP

PASSING AND BEING PASSED SAFELY

Up to this point, you have been riding in single file. You should not pass other horses unless asked to do so by your instructor or trail guide.

When you pass:
• Ask the rider you want to pass first
• Pass widely (*giving the rider plenty of room*)
• Never surprise another horse or rider

When you are being passed:
• Turn your horse's head toward the passing rider
• Keep your horse's rump turned away so he won't be tempted to kick

REST STOPS AND LUNCH STOPS

On every long ride you should make a **check stop after the first 10 or 15 minutes**. This is important to check for girths or cinches that have loosened or anything that needs fixing.

It's a good idea to have a rest stop for about **ten minutes out of every hour on long rides**.
• Dismount and loosen your horse's girth or cinch and lift up the back of the saddle and pad so that air can get to his back and cool it.
• If you want to let your horse eat, slip his bridle off and hang it on the saddle.
• Use the lead rope to hold him.

• Don't forget to tighten your girth or cinch. Be sure and recheck your equipment before you get going again.

It is all right to let horses drink at any streams you come across, but if the horses are hot, they should keep on walking afterwards.
• If there is water where you stop to rest or eat, take advantage of it and let the horses drink.

TYING YOUR HORSE

When you must tie your horse up for a meal or rest stop, he should be **tied with the halter rope**.

• The knot should be level with his back or higher.
• He may be just able to reach the ground with his nose, but he shouldn't be able to get a foot over the rope if he paws.
• The best thing to tie to is a strong branch overhead that will give a little if he pulls on it.
• Tie him with a **quick release knot** (*see Level 2*) that can be pulled loose if a horse gets into trouble but that he can't untie by himself.

Your instructor, lead rider or rear guard rider can demonstrate the proper knot and should check to be sure that your horse is tied safely.

If you are **riding english**, don't forget to **run your stirrups up whenever you dismount**. If left down they can bang your horse or catch on things.

Trail riders, like everyone who goes out in the wilderness, have a responsibility to keep the environment safe and beautiful. In addition, they must not abuse the privilege of riding on private land or public land. A rude or careless trail rider can make land owners close their land to all trail riders in the future.

NINE IMPORTANT TRAIL COURTESY RULES

1) **Never trespass or ride on someone's land without permission.**
   This is illegal.

2) **Keep horses away from where they aren't wanted.**
   Nobody wants horse manure on his sidewalk or hoofprints on his lawn!

3) **Never leave trash behind you.**
   If you find trash where you stop, pack it out with you.

4) **Trail riders should never smoke while riding.**
   A lighted cigarette dropped because a horse acts up could start a fire and destroy a wilderness.

5) **On farm land, leave livestock alone.**
   Leave all gates just as you found them, open or shut.
   If in doubt, shut the gate.

6) **Don't let horses injure the environment.**
   Hoofprints chopping up fragile ground cover can start erosion.
   In fragile areas, stay on trails and don't take short cuts.
   When you stop, tie horses so they can't strip the bark from trees.
   Spread horses out so they won't make a trampled, muddy mess of the area.
   Rake, scatter or bury manure before leaving.

7) **Observe fire regulations and be sure that any fire you make is completely out, drowned, and scattered before leaving.**

8) **Don't let horses foul the water near a camping spot.**
   Keep horses away from areas and places where manure will bring flies and be a nuisance.

9) **Be polite and friendly to hikers, bikers, farmers, or other people you meet on the trail.**
   Slow down and move off the trail for hikers. Nobody wants to be run down by a group of horses.

We all have to share the environment, so be pleasant to others who use it.

LEVEL 3 REQUIREMENTS

To complete Level 3 you must be able to pass each of the following requirements. This can be done by performing the Level 3 Ring Test, which includes all the movements in it (or an alternate test made up by your instructor), or by having your CHA instructor check off each requirement as you pass it. This can be done in regular riding lessons, as a group or individual test.

RIDING REQUIREMENTS

_____ 1. Ride with good position, balance and control for Level 3 at the:
    ___ a. The walk, with and without stirrups or bareback.
    ___ b. Sitting trot or jog, with and without stirrups or bareback.
    ___ c. Posting trot on correct diagonal, demonstrating change of diagonals. *(optional western)*
    ___ d. Jumping position *(english)* or standing *(western)*
    ___ e. Canter or lope in both directions on the correct lead, identifying lead.
_____ 2. Demonstrate the following aids and explain what they ask the horse to do.
    ___ a. Leading rein
    ___ b. Direct rein of opposition
    ___ c. Indirect rein *(optional western)*
    ___ d. Neck rein or bearing rein *(optional english)*
    ___ e. Pulley rein
    ___ f. Both leg aids used in normal position near the girth
    ___ g. One leg aid used in normal position near the girth
    ___ h. One leg aid used three or four inches behind the girth
    ___ i. Seat aid (weight aid)
_____ 3. Show Level 3 form and control while riding through the following movements.
    ___ a. Circle at sitting trot or jog
    ___ b. Figure 8, large or small
    ___ c. Smooth transitions
        __ 1. Walk to trot or jog
        __ 2. Walk to canter or lope
        __ 3. Trot or jog to stop
        __ 4. Canter or lope to walk
    ___ d. Serpentine or alternate riding pattern
    ___ e. Change of direction on the diagonal *(optional western)*
    ___ f. Turnback on the rail *(western only)*

GENERAL REQUIREMENTS

_____ 1. Identify the type of bit used by your horse and explain how it works.
_____ 2. Check the adjustment of your horse's bridle and saddle and correct any problems.
_____ 3. Clean a saddle and a bridle.
_____ 4. Identify two kinds of roughage and four kinds of concentrates and assist with feeding horses.
_____ 5. Pass written test.

_____ 1. Check out your horse, tack and equipment before a trail ride.

_____ 2. Demonstrate good trail gaits at a:

___ a. Long striding walk

___ b. Jog trot

___ c. Long striding trot

___ d. Canter

_____ 3. Demonstrate how to pass another rider and how to handle your horse when being passed.

_____ 4. Give 5 rules for being a responsible trail rider.

JUMPING REQUIREMENTS

Jumping is NOT required to pass any CHA level.

It is recommended that riders pass the Level 3 Jumping Test before beginning Level 4 jumping.

(You may wish to give a special award for passing Level 3 Jumping requirements.)

A CHA badge is available picturing a jumping rider.

_____ 1. Demonstrate a secure jumping position with heels down,

body in balance, eyes up and a correct release in elementary jumping exercises by

___ a. Trotting over cross-rails and a trotting grid.

___ b. Cantering over a line of fences *(crossrails or fences approximately 12" high)*

___ c. Cantering over a single fence *(not to exceed 2' high)*

_____ 2. Demonstrate ability to turn horse accurately and line up with a single fence or line of fences.

(not to exceed 2' high)

_____ 3. Ride over a simple course at a trot or canter with good form and control.

_____ 4. Jump a fence that varies from simple post and rails (brush, coop, panel or any other type of fence).

(not to exceed 2' high)

_____ 5. Demonstrate or tell how to handle a refusal and a runout.

NOTES TO INSTRUCTORS ON TESTING

The goals of Level 3 are to continue to **improve on the use of the aids and control**.

Level 1, 2 and 3 tests must be passed before a rider may take the Level 4 tests.

Requirements for Level 3 may be tested:

• individually

• in a group

• or by checking off as the rider passes each requirement

Students should be scored on their technique and safety rather than on the performance of the horse.

The Ring Test is not a requirement in itself, but one way of testing the rider.

Alternate tests such as group tests are also acceptable.

MULTIPLE CHOICE (select the best answer)

1. When a horse lays his ears flat back against his neck:
   a) He is feeling sleepy
   b) He is feeling angry
   c) He is interested in something behind him

2. Bits are used to communicate and control horses by:
   a) Pressure
   b) Pain
   c) Shutting off the horse's wind

3. If you use the inside leg aid in the normal position near the girth, the horse should:
   a) Move straight forward
   b) Swing his hindquarters to the right
   c) Move forward and bend

4. When using a direct rein of opposition with the left hand only, the horse should respond by:
   a) Turning left
   b) Slowing down and stopping
   c) Moving sideways to the right

5. To change direction or rein on the diagonal means:
   a) Ride directly down the center line of the ring changing rein at X
   b) Ride from corner to corner changing rein at X
   c) Ride directly across the center line from where you are changing rein at X

6. When the rider keeps a steady, even feel of the horse's mouth with his hands, he is:
   a) Riding on loose rein
   b) Riding on simple contact
   c) Pulling on the horse's mouth

7. To get a left lead, you should:
   a) Lean to the left and kick on the right
   b) Sit up and use your inside leg at the girth and your outside leg behind the girth
   c) Lean forward and use both legs

8. Horses focus their eyes on faraway objects:
   a) By lowering their heads
   b) By raising their heads
   c) By opening their eyelids wider
   d) Just the same way people do

9. Smooth transitions are achieved by:
   a) Using the aids to prepare the horse
   b) Using a whip or spurs
   c) Using an indirect rein

10. A martingale is used to:
    a) Keep the horse's mouth shut
    b) Keep the saddle from sliding back
    c) Prevent the horse from raising his head too high

SHORT ANSWERS (fill in the missing word)

1. Curb bits multiply the pressure the rider puts on the reins. They are called _____ bits.

2. Snaffle bits that put the same amount of pressure on the mouth as the rider uses on the reins are called _____ bits.

3. When a horse is on one lead in his front legs and on the other lead in his hind legs, he is said to be _____.

4. A rein aid that is used for discipline or emergency stops is the _____ rein.

5. If a horse does the same thing two or three times in a row, he is learning a _____.

6. A device that works on the horse's nose and chin instead of his mouth is a _____.

7. The four words to remember about caring for tack are:
   1. _____
   2. _____
   3. _____
   4. _____

8. Horses lose water and _____ when they sweat in hot weather.

9. Hay and pasture are _____ feeds. Grain and supplements are _____.

10. A change of gait is called a _____.

MATCHING (2 points each)

__ 1. A horse that is on top of the pecking order is a ...

__ 2. A horse mimics other horses because of ...

__ 3. The horse's ears are the key to his ...

__ 4. A horse should walk returning to the stable because of ...

__ 5. Horses that are trained fairly and consistently are ...

__ 6. To run in time of danger is one of the horse's natural ...

__ 7. Touch, scent, taste and hearing are ...

__ 8. Horses's eyesight is geared to finding ...

__ 9. All horse groups have a system of rank called ...

__ 10. A horse that has heart has ...

A. Horse senses

B. Herd instinct

C. Danger

D. Strong homing instinct

E. Standing up to foes

F. Courage

G. Pecking order

H. Emotions

I. Defenses

J. Easy to handle

K. Boss horse

TRUE OR FALSE

__ 1. A horse should canter with the inside leg leading on a turn or circle.

__ 2. A leg aid used 3 or 4 inches behind the girth tells the horse to go forward.

__ 3. A horse should not be fed grain when he is hot and tired.

__ 4. Bit shouldn't touch the corners of the horse's mouth.

__ 5. Horses should be fed on a regular schedule.

__ 6 All snaffle bits are mild bits.

__ 7. A bit with shanks, a curb strap and a jointed mouthpiece is a snaffle bit.

__ 8. Horses have very good memories.

__ 9. It is not normal for a horse to try to boss or pick on other horses.

__ 10. To back a horse all you need do is to pull back on the reins.

LEVEL 3 RING TEST • SCORE SHEET

(Based on 5 points each, a total of 100 points)

Name: _____ **Place** _____ **Date** _____

		POINTS	COMMENT
1. Walk. Halt A to X	(5 pts.)		
2. Sitting trot, X to M	(5 pts.)		
3. Jog/trot circle, M through X	(5 pts.)		
4. Posting left diagonal	(5 pts.)		
5. Left circle, X through K	(5 pts.)		
6. Posting, right diagonal	(5 pts.)		
7. Canter/lope, left lead A through C	(5 pts.)		
8. Circle at canter/lope	(5 pts.)		
9. Transition to sitting trot, C to X	(5 pts.)		
10. Halt from trot/jog at X	(5 pts.)		
11. Transition from halt to trot/jog, X to A	(5 pts.)		
12. Canter/lope, right lead A through C	(5 pts.)		
13. Circle at canter/lope at E	(5 pts.)		
14. Sitting trot at C	(5 pts.)		
15. Serpentine, C to M to E to F to A	(5 pts.)		
16. Halt from trot at X	(5 pts.)		
17. Walk, X to A through C and B	(5 pts.)		
18. Overall accuracy of pattern	(5 pts.)		
19. Overall control	(5 pts.)		
20. Overall equitation	(5 pts.)		
Possible 100 points Passing score 70%	TOTAL SCORE		

Scoring: 1 = Not performed   2 = Unsatisfactory   3 = Sufficient, fair   4 = Good   5 = Outstanding

PASSING: _____ Yes _____ No _____ Instructor's signature _____

(Based on 10 points each, a total of 100 points)

Name: _____ **Place** _____ **Date** _____

Letter	Directions	You are scored on		Points	Comment
1. A	Enter at walk	Position, seat			
X	Halt, pause 5 seconds	Aids & control			
	Continue at sitting trot or jog	Halt without roughness			
C	Track to the right	Ability to sit trot	(10 pts.)		
2. M	*Posting trot on correct diagonal	Correct diagonal			
	*Western balance position at jog	Position and seat			
B	Turn right across ring	Accurate turn and circle			
X	Circle right, width of ring	Not breaking gait			
	(Posting trot on correct diagonal)		(10 pts.)		
3. X	Circle left, width of ring	Position and seat			
	(change diagonals)	Diagonal change			
E	Turn left along rail	Accurate circle	(10 pts.)		
4. K	Sitting trot or jog	Aids for transition			
A	Canter or lope, left lead	Correct lead	(10 pts.)		
5. B	Circle width of ring at canter or lope	Correct lead			
	Left lead	Not breaking gait			
	Continue along rail to C	Seat in canter, aids	(10 pts.)		
6. C	Sitting trot or jog	Seat and aids while sitting the trot			
H-X-F	Change directions on the diagonal	Accuracy of change of direction			
X	Halt. Pause 5 seconds	Not breaking gait			
	Continue at sitting trot or jog	Halt without roughness	(10 pts.)		
7. A	Canter or lope, right lead	Aids for lope or canter			
		Correct lead	(10 pts.)		
8. E	Circle width of ring at canter or lope	Seat in canter or lope			
	Right lead	Correct lead, not breaking gait			
	Continue along rail to C	Accurate circle	(10 pts.)		
9. C-A	3 loop serpentine	Seat and aids in trot			
	Sitting trot or jog	Accurate turns,			
		Not cutting corners	(10 pts.)		
10. A	Turn down center line	Accurate turn			
X	Halt, pause 5 seconds	Halt with control, without roughness			
	Continue to walk on loose reins	Calmness and quietness of walk			
C	Track to right along rail	On loose rein			
	Walk along rail to exit at A	Seat and aids	(10 pts.)		

Total = 100 pts.   **TOTAL**

A score of 70% is considered passing.   **SCORE**

Scoring:

0 = Not performed		6 = Satisfactory	
1 = Very bad		7 = Fairly good	
2 = Unsatisfactory		8 = Good	
3 = Poor		9 = Very good	
4 = Insufficient, not good enough		10 = Outstanding	
5 = Sufficient, fair			

Passing scores are 5 and over. Note: **10 means outstanding, not perfect,** (10 is a possible score, though rare).

PASSING: _____ Yes _____ No _____ Instructor's signature _____

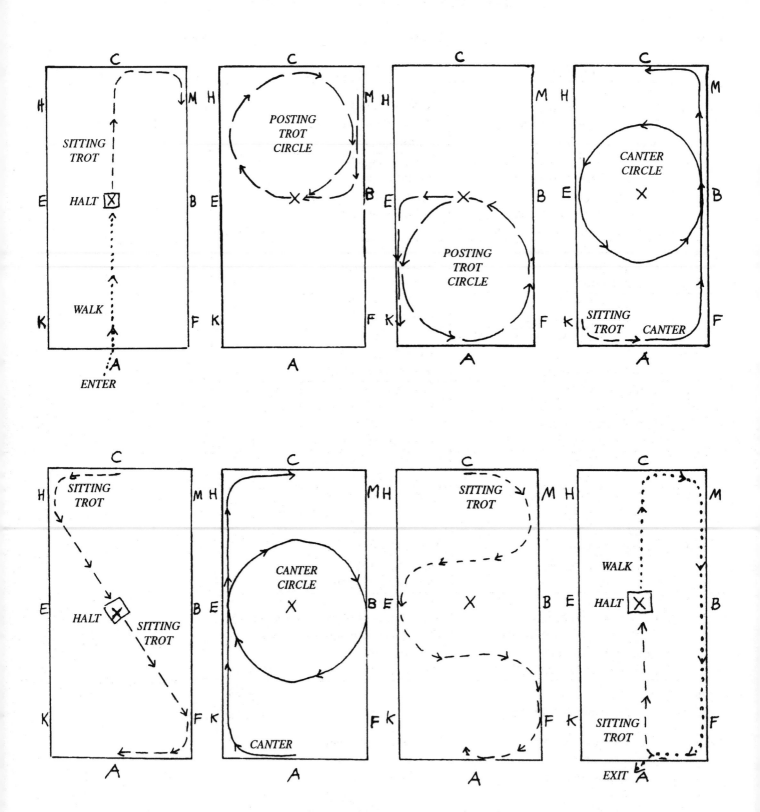

Certified Horsemanship Association

CHA LEVEL 4
HORSEMANSHIP
MANUAL

Certified Horsemanship Association

HORSEMANSHIP MANUAL

LEVEL 4

TABLE OF CONTENTS

Through Levels 1, 2 and 3, you have worked hard to become a good rider and horseman. You have learned a great deal about horses, riding, horse care and equipment. As you advance, you will discover that there is always more (*not less*) to learn.

You have developed a good seat and have learned to use the aids to communicate with your horse. Now you can put your hard work and knowledge to use to become a better rider. You will be able to enjoy riding a truly fine horse and to improve the horses you ride and handle.

The Level 4 manual will introduce you to more advanced performance skills, greater challenges in jumping, trail riding and knowledge that will help you to care for a horse of your own or help with stable management. As you advance, remember that **a true horseman never stops learning or becomes smug about how good a rider he is**.

There's always another challenge ahead.

GENERAL HORSE INFORMATION

HORSE BEHAVIOR PROBLEMS

Most horses do not have behavior problems.
These **bad habits or vices** are not inherited but learned responses.
Most are the **result of the wrong handling by people**.

NIPPING AND BITING

Horses learn to nip people by:
- Being teased about their food
- Someone playing with their lips and nose and encouraging them to nip and nuzzle

Feeding too many treats by hand can make a horse grabby and bossy toward people. He expects treats every time and acts like a spoiled brat when he gets none.

Prevent nipping by not:
- Spoiling horses with treats
- Playing with their mouths.

If a horse nips, **slap his shoulder hard**.

Do not slap his head. You may miss, and you will make him head shy if you hit his nose.

HORSES BUCK BECAUSE THEY ARE HURT OR ANNOYED

KICKING

Kicking is a **defense**.

- Horses kick other horses to keep them away.

- Some horses kick if threatened by people.

- If a horse is frightened, it is instinctive for him to kick, so have respect for his rear end.

If a horse bullies people by threatening to kick, he needs to be disciplined and made to obey.

The correction needs to be done by someone expert enough to discipline the horse just enough and not too much. Someone who can avoid getting hurt while he or she is giving the correction.

THIS IS A JOB FOR A PROFESSIONAL TRAINER.

BUCKING

Horses buck because they are **hurt** or **annoyed** by:
- Something around their middles
- Something on their backs
- Something near their rear ends

They sometimes buck just because:
- They are feeling frisky
- Having fun

He can't buck as well with his **head up** and **moving forward**.

If a horse tries to buck while you are riding:
- Straighten up
- Drive your seat bones into the saddle
- Lift his head up and
- Drive him strongly forward

Check to be sure the horse's **back** is **not sore**, as this may be the reason for bucking.

SHYING

Horses shy from things that **startle or scare them**.

Sometimes horses shy at little things just because the horses are full of energy and feeling frisky or to intimidate their riders.

When a horse shies, his **mind is on the thing he is shying from**.

- If he is **hit** or **jerked** in the mouth for shying, he will connect the punishment with that object and fear it more in the future.
- **Petting** and **indulging** him can make the shying attractive, as he has been rewarded for the action.

The best way to handle shying is to **put him back to work as soon as possible without any fuss**.

- Ride near the spooky object but not so close as to make him shy again, and let him get used to it.

- If he is very frightened by something, it sometimes helps to let him stand and look at it.

- Encourage him to move up to it and sniff it. Once he has examined it, it will not look so scary to him.

HORSES SHY AT THINGS THAT STARTLE OR SCARE THEM OR BECAUSE THEY ARE FULL OF ENERGY

RUNNING AWAY AND HARD TO STOP

A real runaway is **dangerous**, because he runs in panic, out of control, and is not looking out for himself. This is rare, however, and such horses belong in a trainer's hands.

- Most horses that run away are simply **hard to stop**.

Remember that it isn't hard to stay on at a gallop, so don't panic:
- Sit deep and tall
- Shorten your reins
- Use several hard pulley reins, switching from right to left

- If you have room, pull one rein and turn in a circle. Make the circle smaller until the horse has to stop.
- If possible, turn up a hill which will tire the horse out faster.

If you keep your head and steer, you can ride out most *runaways* and bring them back under control.

If a horse is **hard to stop**, his **bit** may be too mild, too severe or he may have been hurt by the bit until it was unbearable for him. He will need careful bitting and retraining.

BALKING

A horse that **stops** and **refuses to move** is a balker. This can range from being annoying to making him useless to ride.

- When you feel a horse starting to hesitate, send him directly forward. Sometimes pulling him to the side will make him move forward more easily.

Whipping a balky horse usually doesn't work. It makes him sulky and more stubborn.

- Sometimes the best way to deal with this problem is to make him **halt** and **stand** until he is completely bored and wants to go. Then, make him **wait** until the rider decides to let him move.

Horses that become *barn sour* sometimes balk when being ridden away from the barn. They need better riders and a lot of work away from the barn.

REARING IS DANGEROUS

REARING

Rearing is the **most dangerous habit** because a horse can fall over backwards.

It is foolish and dangerous to show off by teaching a horse to rear. Rearers are very difficult to cure and MUST BE SENT TO A TRAINER.

If a horse rears with you by accident:
- Lean forward and hold onto the mane.
- As he comes down, drive him forward.

Rearing often starts with balking and backing up. An unusually severe use of the bit is often to blame.

WEAVING

Weaving is a **nervous habit**. It is an **addiction**. A horse that is **bored** and has **energy to burn** may see another horse weaving and pick up the habit.

A weaver **sways** rhythmically back and forth, swinging his neck and shifting his weight from one front leg to the other.
- Some weavers are thin and do not eat well.
- Turning the horse out more helps.
- Also, he might settle down if he has a companion such as a dog or cat as a friend.

A weaver is an **unhappy** horse.

CRIBBING

Cribbing is a **stable vice**, a **habit** horses get addicted to like some people who bite their nails.

A cribber **braces his teeth** on something like a fence rail, **arches his neck** and **gulps in air**.
- The air he swallows hurts his digestion.
- Cribbing is not good for his teeth or for the stall.

The only way **to prevent** cribbing is to keep a tight strap buckled around his throat. This makes air swallowing impossible.

You cannot cure cribbing by yelling or hitting the horse. This would be unkind as well as ineffective.

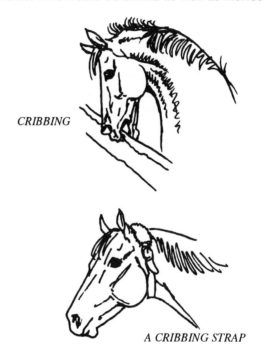

CRIBBING

A CRIBBING STRAP

WOOD CHEWING

Wood chewing is related to cribbing, but wood chewers **don't suck in air**. They just remodel every piece of wood they can reach.

- Horses may do this because they **lack salt** or some **essential mineral** in their diet, so be sure they have a balanced diet.
- They may also chew wood when they are **bored** and **hungry**.

Wood can be painted with bad tasting substances to discourage wood chewing.

5

HORSE CARE AND HANDLING

HOOF CARE

"*No foot, no horse*" is an old, but true horseman's saying.
A lame horse can't do the work you want him to and can become crippled permanently by neglect.
Good horsemen check their horses' feet daily and follow a hoof care program to prevent trouble.

A GOOD HOOF CARE PROGRAM INCLUDES THE FOLLOWING

○ **Daily Attention:**
- **Clean** horses' feet **daily** before riding and **check feet after work**.
- Hoof dressing may be used to keep feet conditioned.

○ **Shoeing:**
Trim or shoe on schedule
- Horses' feet **grow** an average of **3/8 inch per month**.
- Every horse needs his feet trimmed periodically to remove excess growth.
  This will keep his feet from growing at the wrong angle
  which can strain his bones and joints and make him stumble.
- Horses should be **trimmed** or have their **shoes reset** every **six to eight weeks** on the average.

Shoe as needed
- If a horse is worked hard or his feet aren't strong,
  they may break off and wear down until he is tender.
- Shoeing **gives protection** to tender feet and also lets the hoof **dig into the ground**
  more securely for better traction in some forms of riding.
- Some horses need special shoeing or trimming to **correct problems** in their feet or their way of going.
- Shoeing depends on:
  - The kind of work
  - The ground the horse works on
  - How hard he works
  - The needs of the individual horse

FOOT CORRECTLY SHOD	*NEEDS SHOEING*	*NEEDS RESETTING*

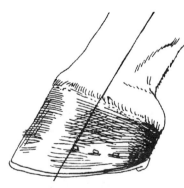  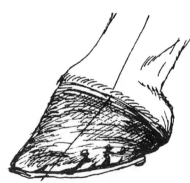

ANGLE OF HOOF MATCHES
ANGLE OF PASTERN
CLINCHES TIGHT
FOOT NOT RASPED EXCESSIVELY

HOOF WORN AND BROKEN
TOE TOO SHORT
ANGLE OF HOOF AND
PASTERN BROKEN

TOES TOO LONG
CLINCHES RISEN FROM WALL
WALL BREAKING UP
HEELS TOO LOW
ANGLE OF HOOF AND PASTERN BROKEN

FOOT PROBLEMS

THRUSH
WET, GRAYISH OR BLACK DISCHARGE
VERY FOUL ORDOR

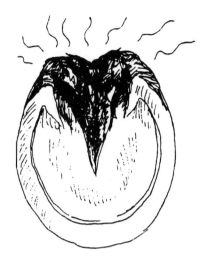

THRUSH

Thrush is an **infection found in the frog** of horses.

It may be found in horses that are neglected and allowed to stand in dirty stalls without having their feet cleaned daily.

Some horses have a very deep cleft in the frog and are susceptible to this problem even if not neglected.

• Thrush is recognized by a **wet, grayish or black discharge,** and by a **very foul odor**.

It doesn't make the horse lame until it is very advanced. When it has become advanced, it is hard to cure and will take a long time.

IF YOU FIND SIGNS OF THRUSH
• Keep the stall very clean.
• Pack the cleft with clean cotton and saturate it
 with liquid bleach or a commercial thrush remedy.

The farrier may have to cut away the diseased portion of the frog and help you treat the foot.

SCRATCHES OR MUD CRACKS

Horses that stand in muddy conditions may get a **chapped, cracked**, and **oozing condition** on the backs of their pasterns called mud cracks.

• They must be kept out of mud and wet conditions to cure it.
• The scabs should be gently soaked off and patted dry, and the area treated with a protective ointment.

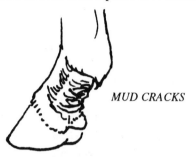

MUD CRACKS

This condition gets progressively worse if not treated and can make the horse too lame to work, so it should be treated promptly until fully healed.

FOUNDER OR LAMINITIS

Laminitis is a crippling condition that occurs in the horse's feet. The **blood vessels inside the foot become engorged with blood**. The horse becomes **very lame**.

The inner structure of the foot begins to tear away from the wall of the hoof at the laminae. This tearing can be mild or so severe as to cripple. It can even kill the horse because he can't walk.

FOUNDERED FOOT

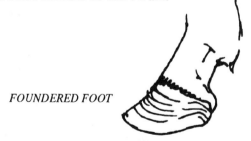

A horse crippled by laminitis is said to be foundered.

Laminitis can be caused by many kinds of stress:
 • Overeating grain or lush grass is one of
  the most common ways
 • Severe overwork on hard ground
 • Chilling a hot horse by letting him gorge on
  cold water before he is cooled down.
 • Certain diseases and drug reactions

Even if a horse recovers, he is usually left with some damage to his feet.

PREVENTIVE HEALTH CARE

Many common horse diseases and problems can be prevented by a good health care program. Your veterinarian can tell you which inoculations he recommends for your horse and when he should have them. Horses should receive **yearly vaccinations** against the most common and dangerous diseases, especially those listed below.

- **Tetanus (lockjaw)** is a serious disease which is especially common to horses because tetanus germs live in the horse's gut and are present in manure.

- **Equine encephalomyelitis (sleeping sickness)** is carried by migrating birds and transmitted by biting flies and mosquitoes.

- **Influenza** is an upper respiratory infection that is common where large numbers of horses gather, like at shows and sales.

- **Rhinopneumonitis** is an acute virus infection which causes abortion in mares and can also cause side effects in other horses.

- **Strangles or distemper** is a bacterial infection which affects glands beneath the jaw and is often found at shows, sales and large gatherings of horses.

HORSE PARASITE PROBLEMS

Parasites live on or in another creature and feed upon the creature. **Internal parasites or worms live part of their life cycle in the horse's digestive tract**, sapping his strength and damaging his health.

Too many parasites can kill a horse.

Even a few can do permanent damage that can make him thin, weak, and unhealthy. All horses are exposed to horse parasites, so all horses need to be **dewormed** periodically to remove these parasites.

Horses may have symptoms such as those described below, but even an apparently healthy horse may carry a load of parasites.

The only way to tell for sure is a microscopic **fecal exam** for worm eggs.

Here is a list of conditions that may indicate that your horse may have worms:

- Thin horse, especially if also potbellied
- Poor hair coat
- Colic, especially in repeated episodes
- Worms in your horse's manure
- Tail rubbing, or a gray discharge under the tail

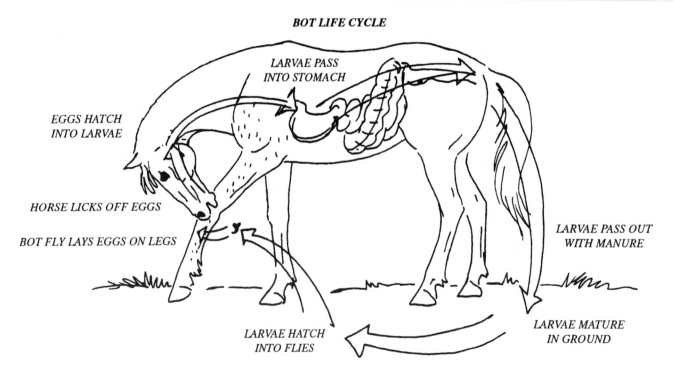

BOT LIFE CYCLE

LARVAE PASS INTO STOMACH

EGGS HATCH INTO LARVAE

HORSE LICKS OFF EGGS

BOT FLY LAYS EGGS ON LEGS

LARVAE PASS OUT WITH MANURE

LARVAE HATCH INTO FLIES

LARVAE MATURE IN GROUND

TYPES OF PARASITES

○ **Bots** are **flying insects** that lay **small yellow eggs** on hair. The horse licks the eggs off and larvae enter his mouth. They grow to bots in the horse's stomach and **attach to the stomach lining**. Later, the larvae leave the body in manure and hatch into flies.
  • You should scrape the eggs off your horse.

○ **Strongyles** (*bloodworms*) are **worms** whose **larvae** are eaten with grass, then **migrate through intestinal walls into blood vessels**, where the larvae do severe damage, often causing colic. The eggs **are passed out** with the manure. Horses are then infected by grazing where manure has been.
  • This is the **most dangerous parasite**.

○ **Ascarids** (*roundworms*) are **worms** that have a life cycle much like that of strongyles, but these live in the **intestines**.
  • Ascarids are most serious in young horses.

○ **Pinworms** are the least harmful **worms**. They live in the **end of the intestinal tract** and cause irritation and tail rubbing.

CONTROLLING PARASITES

All horses should be **dewormed periodically** by administering worming preparations by mouth paste, powder or pellets in the feed, or by a stomach tube handled by a veterinarian.

Horses need **deworming** about every **three months**, depending on how severe the parasite problem is where they are kept.

The type of deworming preparation must be changed frequently or parasites may develop a resistance to it.

You can **prevent parasite problems from getting out of hand by the following:**

• Pastures should be mowed and dragged to break up manure and kill parasite eggs.

• Cleaning up manure and not overcrowding pastures will help.

• Every new horse should be dewormed before they are turned out on pasture.

STRONGYLE LIFE CYCLE

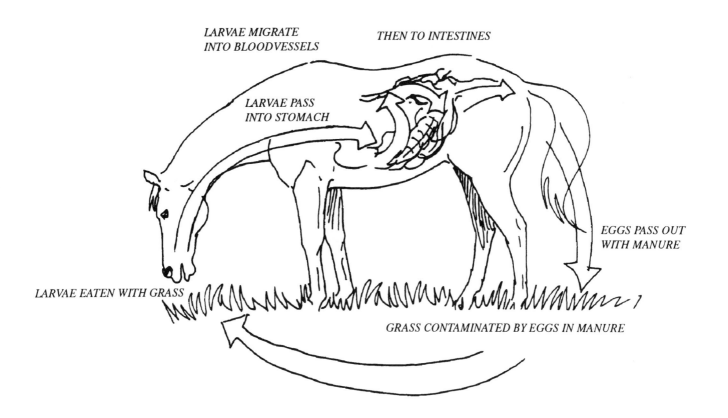

LARVAE MIGRATE INTO BLOODVESSELS

THEN TO INTESTINES

LARVAE PASS INTO STOMACH

EGGS PASS OUT WITH MANURE

LARVAE EATEN WITH GRASS

GRASS CONTAMINATED BY EGGS IN MANURE

SIGNS OF HEALTH AND SICKNESS

Everyone working around horses should know what shows that a horse is healthy or sick. It's important to know your horse's normal vital signs when he is healthy, so that you will notice any major change that may point to illness.

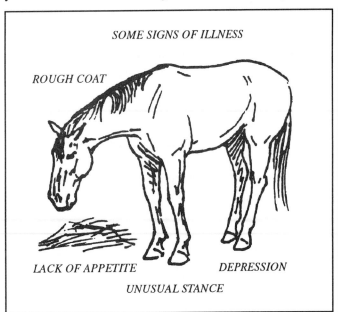

SOME SIGNS OF ILLNESS

ROUGH COAT

LACK OF APPETITE   DEPRESSION

UNUSUAL STANCE

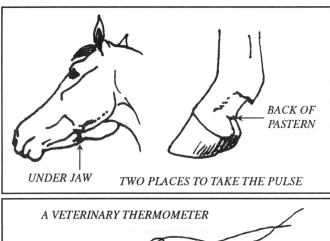

BACK OF PASTERN

UNDER JAW   TWO PLACES TO TAKE THE PULSE

A VETERINARY THERMOMETER

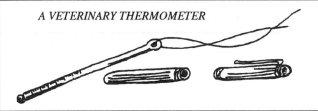

THESE ARE THE HORSE'S MAJOR VITAL SIGNS.

○ **Appearance and Attitude** • A healthy horse is **alert, bright-eyed** and has a **glossy coat**.
If your horse is dull and unwilling to move, or unusually nervous and jumpy, he may be sick.
A dull rumpled looking coat can indicate sickness, especially if the hair is usually shiny.
Horses will sometimes lie down to rest.
A normal healthy horse will get up but a sick horse may not be able to.

○ **Appetite** • Losing the desire to eat, change in eating habit, or eating unusual things
like dirt or hair can be a sign of illness or a dietary deficiency.

○ **Temperature** • The normal rectal temperature of a horse is **between 99° and 101°**.
This can vary according to the time of day and exercise.

○ **Respiration** • A normal horse breathes evenly about **8 to 16 respirations per minute** when he is not exercising.
Breathing hard or coughing can signify that your horse may have an illness.

○ **Pulse** • The pulse is taken at the artery inside and underneath the jawbone or in the digital artery at the back
of the pastern. The pulse is normally about **30 to 40 beats per minute**.
This varies with the size of the horse and can go very high with exercise or excitement.
A high pulse can indicate pain and stress.

○ **Excretions** • The manure should look normal. A change in the manure can indicate digestive upsets.
A discharge from the nose or eyes may indicate an illness.

○ **Posture and actions** • Often a sick horse *just doesn't look right*. He behaves in a different way than normally.
Horses often rest a hind foot, but resting a front foot may indicate lameness.
Standing stiffly and not wanting to move or eat can mean that something is wrong.
Rolling, getting up and down repeatedly, looking at the belly, kicking, and sweating are all signs of pain.

SADDLE SORES AND GALLS

Sores start with **dirt, friction**, and **pressure from improperly fitted tack**, especially in soft horses that are not toughened up yet.

• If you see a rubbed place, clean it and change the equipment before the area becomes raw.

• If it is already raw, it must be treated as an open wound and allowed to heal completely, before that place can tolerate pressure again. This may mean switching to a different saddle or not using the horse.

Placing padding over an open sore will not keep it from hurting the horse. The sore can become so severe that the horse will be out of work for weeks if not treated correctly and promptly.

LAMENESS

Every rider should know how to tell if a horse is lame and what to do about it.
• Lameness **indicates pain** in a leg or foot.
• Horses do not *fake* lameness, but some lamenesses come and go. Some lameness are more severe than others. It is unkind to work a lame horse as work may make him worse.

When a horse is lame, he tries to keep from using that leg as much as the good ones.
If a front leg hurts:
• He will lift his head up as the sore leg hits the ground and will drop his head down as the good leg hits.
If a hind leg is lame:
• He may hitch the hip higher on the lame side, trying not to let the hurt foot hit the ground as hard.

• He will usually take a **shorter step** with the **sore leg**, and the pastern may not sink as low.
• A very lame horse might even hobble on three legs.

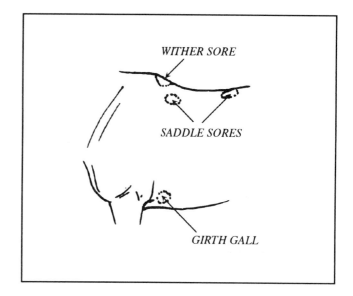

Lameness shows most at the trot.

If you notice that your horse is lame, **stop and check** his feet. He may have picked up a stone which you can remove to give him relief.

• Clean the foot and wash it out with water. The foreign object might be a nail or stone stuck into the frog or sole of the foot.
• Perhaps you will see a cut or an obvious swelling on the sore leg.
• If your horse goes lame out on the trail, he should be ridden back at a walk, or if very lame, led back slowly.

There are so many possible causes of lameness, that it may take some detective work to uncover the cause. An experienced horse person can examine the horse and perform various tests to determine which leg is lame and why. A farrier's or a veterinarian's opinion may be needed to determine the cause.

Lameness can be caused by injury, riding over rough ground, incorrect shoeing, certain illnesses, arthritis, or conditions due to old age.

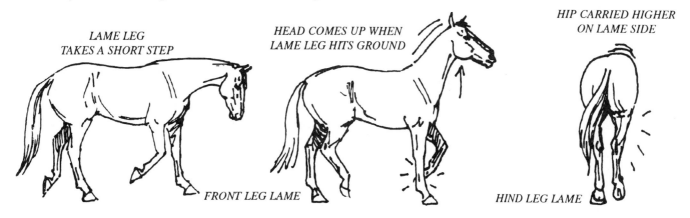

LAME LEG TAKES A SHORT STEP

HEAD COMES UP WHEN LAME LEG HITS GROUND

FRONT LEG LAME

HIP CARRIED HIGHER ON LAME SIDE

HIND LEG LAME

COLIC

Colic means **pain in the belly**. It is the number one killer of horses, so colic should always be taken seriously.

• A stomach ache is serious in horses because their digestive systems are sensitive, and because horses cannot vomit to get rid of something they have eaten that causes the problem.

Colic is a pain in the belly that can come from **gas**, **cramps**, **spasms**, a **blockage**, or even a **twisted intestine**.

The signs of abdominal pain are:
  • Uneasiness and sweating
  • Trying to lie down and get up repeatedly
  • Looking and kicking at the belly
  • Pawing
  • Stretching
  • Trying to urinate
The signs may be mild or very severe.

Remove the horse's feed, and keep him from getting chilled if it's cool. Walk him slowly or let him stand quietly but don't let him roll or hurt himself while waiting for the veterinarian to arrive.

Colic has many causes such as:
  • Overeating grain
  • Gulping cold water while he is hot
  • Eating unsuitable feed or spoiled feed
  • Having a change of diet
Veterinarians believe that most colics are at least partly caused by parasite damage to the horse's digestive system. A good parasite control program and good feeding practices will do much to prevent colic.

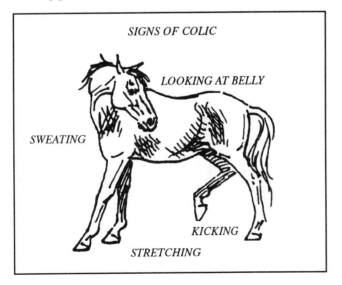

SIGNS OF COLIC

LOOKING AT BELLY

SWEATING

KICKING

STRETCHING

COLDS AND VIRUS INFECTIONS

Horses can get a cold or a runny nose, usually from contact with another horse that has the infection.
  The signs are:
    • A runny nose
    • Coughing
    • Swollen glands under the jaw
    • Fever and dullness
Most colds are caused by a virus. Some are more severe than others.

A sick horse should be **isolated**. His bucket and equipment should not be used by other horses, or they may get his virus. Usually, the disease will run its course in a few days. Sometimes, the veterinarian will prescribe medication to prevent complications from developing.

Horses can be inoculated against certain virus diseases such as influenza and rhinopneumonitis, but the inoculation must be done in time to let the horse build up his immunity before he is exposed to the disease.

New horses entering a herd such as a new purchase or horses shipped in from a sale or large show may bring a new virus in and give it to others.

HEAVES OR EMPHYSEMA

Just like people, horses can get emphysema which leaves them **short of breath**.

• In horses, it is usually due to breathing dust or pollen, or to having an allergy like hay fever.

• This disease causes a cough and breaks down lung tissue, making the horse flare his nostrils and give a *double respiration*, an extra push to breathe out.

Heavey horses sometimes can do easy work, but usually can't stand dust, pollen, or dusty hay.

• Some horses need medication to control the cough.
• Their hay should be dampened to keep down the dust. Instead of feeding hay, you may need to feed a substitute roughage such as beet pulp which does not affect their allergy.

The condition is permanent, but some horses can live with it quite well.

IF YOUR HORSE IS HURT

A sick or injured horse needs help to get well. He is a powerful animal that can hurt you unintentionally when he is frightened and in pain. An animal that needs first aid should be handled by the most experienced horse person present.

You can help most by **staying calm** and doing the useful things that you can. It might be aiding the horse, getting skilled help, keeping others out of trouble, or staying out of the way and fetching whatever is needed.

Every stable should have a **horse first aid kit**, but only those who have the required knowledge and experience should be allowed to use it.

MINOR WOUNDS

Most nicks, cuts and scrapes will not require you to call a veterinarian.

• They should be **thoroughly cleaned and gently patted dry**. Running water over them for ten minutes is a good method.
• Use only a mild ointment (*like A & D ointment*) or antibiotic ointment. Never use strong remedies that can irritate healing tissue.
• Clip the hair from around the wound to keep the hair from irritating the wound.
• Keep the wound clean.

A bandage may be advisable on lower leg wounds, but a bandage must be evenly and correctly applied or it will do more harm than good.
• Most wounds do better if left unbandaged and if not over medicated.

PUNCTURE WOUNDS

Puncture wounds are **dangerous** because they are apt to **become infected** and they carry the danger of tetanus or lockjaw.
• Horses should have **tetanus shots yearly** to protect against tetanus, but a puncture wound may require a tetanus booster shot.

• The wound should be **allowed to bleed for thorough cleaning**. It must **heal from the inside out**, rather than seal over with bacteria trapped inside.

SERIOUS WOUNDS

If a wound is bleeding severely or a horse is badly hurt, he must first be **kept under control**. You may need to put a bridle on him or a chain over his nose to make him stand still. Stay away from wire or fencing or anything he could get hurt on.

If a horse is caught in wire, you will need skilled, sensible help to get him free without getting entangled and hurting yourself.

Control serious bleeding with pressure directly on the wound, preferably using a pad of clean cloth.
• Keep the pressure on the wound, and add more padding if it becomes soaked.
• A tight bandage may be used over the pad to hold it in place and keep pressure on the wound until the veterinarian arrives, but **do not apply a tourniquet**.
• Bleeding is alarming, but because a horse is so much larger he can lose a lot more blood than a person can without danger.

If a wound looks serious, the best thing to do is **keep the horse quiet** and **prevent further injury** while you **send for the veterinarian**.
• Moving the horse, applying home remedies, or trying to treat it yourself may make his job harder.

If a wound needs stitching, this should be done as soon as possible after the injury for the best chance of healing. It is also important that you do not apply anything to the area except water.

LAMENESS

Since lameness can have **many causes**, there is no single first aid which is right for all.

Most bruises, sprains, and strains benefit from **soaking or hosing with cold water for 20 minutes** several times a day for the first few days or until the leg is no longer hot and swollen.
• The **cold packs** can be **alternated** with **hot packs**. To make a hot pack, dip a towel in a bucket of warm water, wring out and wrap around the leg, covering it with a dry towel to hold in the heat.

If lameness is severe at first or if it persists after a day or so of cold and hot packing, call the veterinarian.

SELECTING A GOOD HORSE

The more you know about horses, the better you will become at choosing a good horse to own or work with, and at judging horses in competition.

A horse is only as good as he is useful, so form, or how he looks, is based on function, or what he does.
• A good horse is suitable for his job and rider.
• He has the temperament, balance and movement to be good at his job.
• He also has the strength and durability to hold up under hard work without breaking down.

SUITABILITY

Suitability means that a **horse fits his job and rider**.

Some horses, because of their build or talent, will specialize in one field or another. A horse that would make a good roping horse would not have what it takes to be a high stepping saddle horse, or vise versa.

There are three main types of horses: stock, saddle, and hunter type.

• **Stock type** horses are built for quick starts and stops. This horse can "*turn a cow inside out*". They have large, well-developed hindquarters and forearm muscles and are compact, short coupled, and agile. Stock horses are not usually very tall or long legged. They should be alert but calm.

• **Saddle types** are smooth, showy, and pleasant horses to ride. They should have brilliant gaits and a refined, elegant appearance. They often have small heads which are carried high with the neck arched, a flat back and croup, and a high-set tail. Saddle horses will often have high action.

• **Hunter types** are horses with long legs and muscles that enable them to move with long, low strides for speed, smoothness, and jumping. They tend to carry their heads lower than do the saddle horse type and move with lower action, yet they are taller and lighter than most stock horses. Hunter type horses need a deep chest for endurance, a good neck and shoulders for galloping and strong hindquarters for jumping.

Suitability to the rider means that:
• The horse is a **reasonable size for the rider** and that the horse has a **good temperament** and the **right training** for the rider's ability.
• A horse that is too big, too small, too high-strung or sluggish, or not well trained may not be the right horse for one person while he might suit someone else.

CONFORMATION

Conformation is **the way the horse is put together**, his physique. Good conformation is beautiful, but more important, it makes a horse able to work well and stay sound even with hard work.

Conformation defects can make a horse weak in a particular part or they can just make him less handsome.

No horse is perfect, but you should look for good **functional** conformation and good **working parts**. It's nice to have some beauty, too.

The major points of good and poor conformation are described on the conformation diagram. (*page 16-17*)

Pay attention to the conformation of the feet and legs, as these are the horse's *running gear*.
• If the feet and legs are weak, the horse may be pretty but not an athlete.

Look at a horse you are judging from the side, at a distance. Then look at him from the front, the rear, and both sides close up. This way you will see all sides and miss nothing.

SOUNDNESS

A sound horse is one that **has no defects** that will impair his ability to live a normal life and to do his work.

• An **unsoundness** is a serious condition that affects a horse's usefulness.

• A **blemish** is a defect that hurts his appearance but doesn't hurt his working ability, like a scar.

Every horseman wants a sound horse, so he must learn to recognize unsoundness and serious conformation problems. It is important to know which things are a blemish and which are an unsoundness.

GOOD LEGS MEAN GOOD MOVEMENT

A horse is only as good as his legs. If he has good leg conformation, he should be strong, sound, and able to move well. Poor leg conformation means weak legs that may break down under hard work.

• It's important to notice whether or not a horse moves straight.
• If he has crooked legs, he may interfere or strike one leg with the opposite foot as he moves, hurting his legs.
• Besides straight legs, good proportions and conformation of the leg bones means smoother, more powerful gaits.

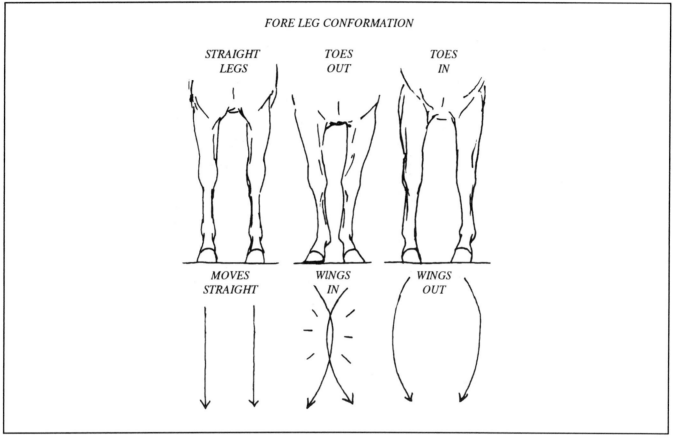

FORE LEG CONFORMATION

STRAIGHT LEGS   TOES OUT   TOES IN

MOVES STRAIGHT   WINGS IN   WINGS OUT

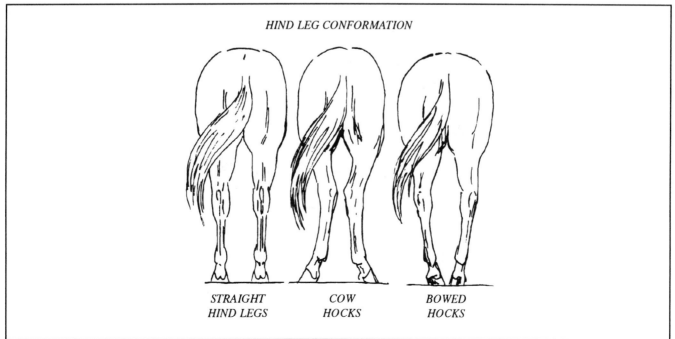

HIND LEG CONFORMATION

STRAIGHT HIND LEGS   COW HOCKS   BOWED HOCKS

GOOD CONFORMATION POINTS

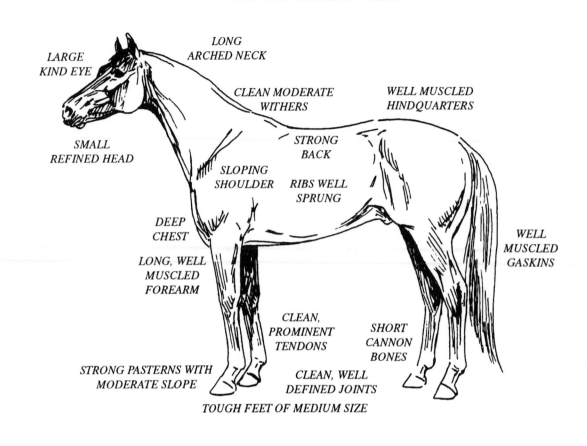

LARGE
KIND EYE

LONG
ARCHED NECK

CLEAN MODERATE
WITHERS

WELL MUSCLED
HINDQUARTERS

SMALL
REFINED HEAD

STRONG
BACK

SLOPING
SHOULDER

RIBS WELL
SPRUNG

DEEP
CHEST

WELL
MUSCLED
GASKINS

LONG, WELL
MUSCLED
FOREARM

CLEAN,
PROMINENT
TENDONS

SHORT
CANNON
BONES

STRONG PASTERNS WITH
MODERATE SLOPE

CLEAN, WELL
DEFINED JOINTS

TOUGH FEET OF MEDIUM SIZE

BETTER SHOULDER AND FORELEG CONFORMATION
MEANS BETTER GAITS

LONG SLOPING SHOULDER

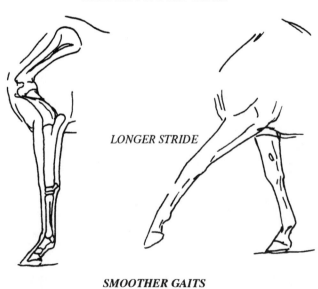

LONGER STRIDE

SMOOTHER GAITS

POOR CONFORMATION

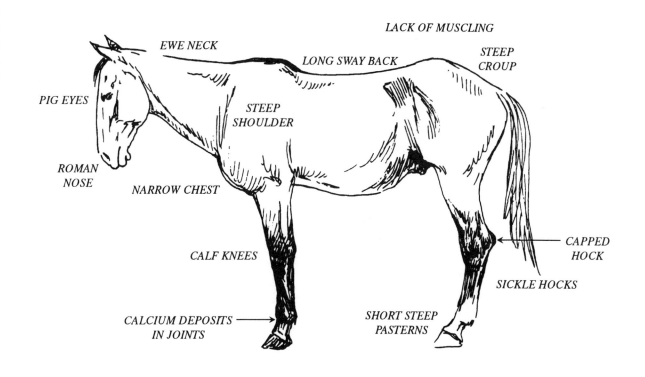

LACK OF MUSCLING

EWE NECK

STEEP CROUP

PIG EYES

LONG SWAY BACK

STEEP SHOULDER

ROMAN NOSE

NARROW CHEST

CALF KNEES

CAPPED HOCK

SICKLE HOCKS

SHORT STEEP PASTERNS

CALCIUM DEPOSITS IN JOINTS

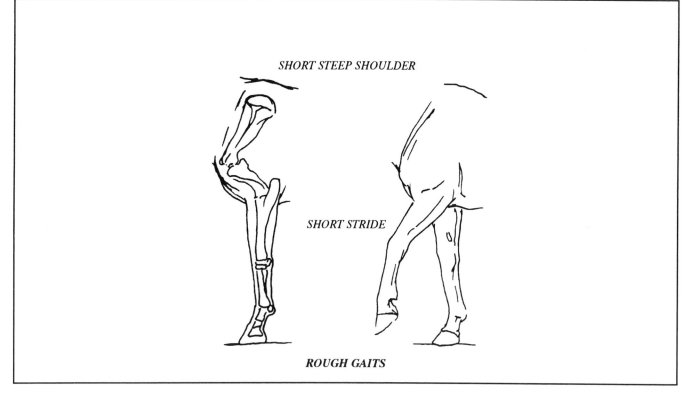

SHORT STEEP SHOULDER

SHORT STRIDE

ROUGH GAITS

UNSOUNDNESS

○ **Bowed Tendon** is caused by injury to the flexor tendon and to the tendon sheath, it is usually in the front legs. Scar tissue in tendons causes a thickening and a **bowed** appearance. This is an unsoundness.

○ **Bone Spavin** is arthritis in the bones of the hock. There may be a swelling on the lower inside of the hock. This is a **serious** unsoundness.

○ **Contracted heels** are pinched, narrow heels and a shrunken frog due to the lack of normal hoof expansion. This can lead to unsoundness.

○ **Foundered foot** is a hoof crippled by **laminitis**. The hoof has irregular growth rings and may have a dropped sole. The wall may separate from the sole at the white line. Often the feet are tender or the horse is lame. This is an unsoundness.

○ **Fistula** is a deep infection of the withers. It can extend down into the shoulder muscles. It is usually caused by the neglect of a saddle sore. It is an unsoundness until it heals.

○ **Gravel** is an infection beneath the white line. It may break and drain at the coronary band and cause severe lameness until it has healed.

○ **Interference marks** are small cuts or callouses on the inside of the ankles which indicate where the opposite foot strikes the ankle during movement.
    They may not cause immediate lameness, but indicate faulty movement and potential for unsoundness. Interference marks may be caused by bad shoeing or crooked legs.

○ **Navicular** disease is a crippling change in the navicular bone within the hoof. It is caused by hard work, bad conformation, or poor shoeing. It is incurable and a progressive unsoundness that is inevitable with continued abuse.

○ **Quarter crack** is a split in the side of the foot extending upward from the ground. If the crack is deep, it can cause lameness and unsoundness.

○ **Ringbone** is a form of arthritis in the bones of the pastern. This unsoundness causes progressive lameness.

○ **Stifled** refers to a condition in which the stifle joint accidentally locks due to a loose ligament and poor conformation. The stifle joint may need corrective surgery to correct this. It is an unsoundness.

BLEMISH

○ **Big Knee** is a swelling on the front of the knee caused by an injury and is common in jumpers. It may cause soreness at first, later it may be a blemish.

○ **Bog Spavin** is a swelling of the joint capsule of the hock due to strain. It is usually a blemish.

○ **Capped hock** is a permanent swelling on the point of the hock due to a direct blow to the hock. It is only a blemish.

○ **Capped elbow** is a permanent swelling on the point of the elbow caused by pressure of the shoe when lying down. It is a blemish.

○ **Windpuffs** are firm, fluid swellings on or near the ankles due to the joint capsule being stretched with extra joint fluid. Windpuffs are a sign of stress or of previous hard work. They are blemishes and not an unsoundness. They do not cause lameness.

UNSOUNDNESS AND BLEMISH

○ **Curb** is a thickening of the ligament which runs along the back of the hock. A Curb is due to strain. It may be an unsoundness or blemish, depending on the severity of the curb.

○ **Sidebone** is a condition in which the collateral cartilage of the hoof turns to bone. At first, sidebone causes lameness. Later it is a blemish.

○ **Splint** is a calcified lump that cements the splint bone to the cannon bone. Splints are often found in young horses. Splints cause lameness when new but later become blemishes.

UNSOUNDNESS AND BLEMISHES

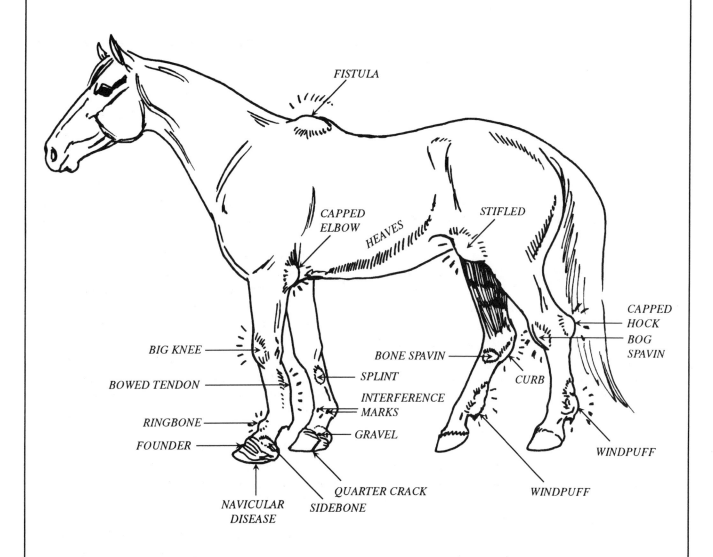

FISTULA

CAPPED ELBOW

HEAVES

STIFLED

CAPPED HOCK

BOG SPAVIN

BIG KNEE

BONE SPAVIN

CURB

BOWED TENDON

SPLINT

INTERFERENCE MARKS

RINGBONE

GRAVEL

FOUNDER

WINDPUFF

NAVICULAR DISEASE

QUARTER CRACK

SIDEBONE

WINDPUFF

HORSEMANSHIP

You have now reached a point in your riding in which you can stay in a good position without too much trouble and can control your horse fairly accurately. To move up to Level 4 you will have to learn to ride with *automatic* good form and balance while you concentrate on refining your aids and asking your horse to listen more closely to your signals.

When an advanced rider rides a well-trained horse, either english or western, his aids and signals are so light as to be nearly invisible to anyone watching. It looks like the rider *thinks the command and the horse performs it easily, smoothly and in perfect balance*. **Horse and rider seem to become one.**
  • All Level 4 riding, whether english or western, requires lightness, coordination, balance, relaxation, and rhythm.

LIGHTNESS

Your aids should be as **light** as you can use them and still get the horse to respond. He can feel a fly on his skin, so he can feel a very light signal.

If he doesn't respond to a light aid:
  • You may have given an incorrect aid
  • The horse may not have been paying attention
  • He may need to be taught to respond more promptly

If you persist in using a stronger aid, you will make him dependent on stronger and stronger aids instead of improving and getting lighter with your aids.

A light aid is easier on both horse and rider. It is the goal of every good rider.

COORDINATION OF THE AIDS

Your aids must **cooperate**, not clash.

If you pull back on the reins while legging the horse to go forward, he will become confused and frustrated.

Sometimes the aids are used in cooperation.

  • A leg aid may be used to wake up or activate the horse at the same time as a rein aid is used to restrain or direct him.
  • At this time, it is important to use just enough leg and rein aid to get the result you want and no more.

It is impossible to avoid clashing your aids and disturbing your horse by accident when you bounce or lose your position if your seat isn't entirely secure or if you are out of balance.

SUPPLENESS

A horse is an athlete and like any good athlete, he should be **supple**. This means that he is **relaxed, flexible** and **can bend and turn easily**.

Stiff horses feel awkward and clumsy to ride, especially in tight turns or intricate patterns. Horses may have trouble picking up one lead if they are very stiff.

To make your horse supple:
  • He first needs a gentle warm-up at slow gaits.
  • Then he should be worked on circles and turns which bend and stretch his muscles. Start with large easy circles and work down to tighter and more difficult ones.

Don't try to make him bend too much or bend more in his neck than he can in his body, or he may discover that it is easier to **cheat** by just bending in his neck. This is called *rubbernecking* and is very hard to cure.

All horses have one side that is more supple than the other, just like people are right-handed or left-handed. Horses will need **more work** on their **stiff side** to become supple.

  • They should be worked in both directions, on both leads, and on both diagonals when posting in order to avoid developing the muscles on one side more than on the other.
  • If your horse is very stiff on one side and cannot take that lead, practice many circles at the trot or jog on his stiff side. When he becomes more supple, the lead problem usually disappears.

In order to supple a horse, the rider must understand rhythm, relaxation and the aids for bending (*see English section page 42-43*).

CALMNESS AND RELAXATION

In order for you and your horse to perform at your best, you must both be relaxed and work calmly. This does not mean being lazy or sloppy.

Horses and people do not perform well when they are tense and stiff. If your horse is tense, it may be because you are making him upset or uncomfortable in some way.

• If he is confused, scared, or hurting, he will naturally tense up and can't work well for you.

It may also be that some other rider has hurt his mouth or frightened him. He is tensing up at the memory of this bad experience.

Slow, quiet work at a steady rhythm such as a posting trot or jog can help to relax a tense horse.

While allowing your horse to relax, check to be sure that your seat is correct and that you are not causing the trouble yourself in some way.

Horses can feel your nervousness through your hands and seat. Very often, tension in the horse comes from a tense, stiff rider or from overuse of the bit.

RHYTHM

To move well and be comfortable to ride your horse must move with a consistent steady rhythm in each gait.

If he speeds up, slows down, and constantly changes his stride and balance, he'll be hard to ride.
• These things can put you out of balance with him.

To help your horse get and keep his rhythm, try counting steadily to the beat of the gait.
• For example, in the trot count one, two, one, two.

If the horse:
• Begins to **trot slower** than **your rhythm:**
• Squeeze your legs in the rhythm you want until he picks up the trot again.

• **Speeds up** and **gets quicker:**
• Squeeze and release your hands on the reins until he settles back to the rhythm you want.

• When you are riding western, use a check and release on the bit.

• When a horse moves with a very steady, noticeable beat, his gait is said to be *cadenced* .

IT IS IMPORTANT TO BE RELAXED AND WORK CALMLY

21

BALANCE

Before giving your horse an aid or signal, you must ask yourself
if your horse is in the proper balance to obey your aids.

If he is moving along half asleep with too much weight on his front legs, or if he's tense, stiff or crooked, he will be clumsy and awkward even if he wants to obey.

When your horse is properly balanced for the movement you are performing, he will feel as though he can do it easily and comfortably without leaning, tripping, breaking his gait or rhythm, or feeling like he might fall.

He should be balanced right for the job he is doing, neither too collected nor too extended.

Often a horse's balance problems begin with a rider who sits a little out of balance and handicaps his horse without knowing it. There are several types of balance.

TYPES OF BALANCE

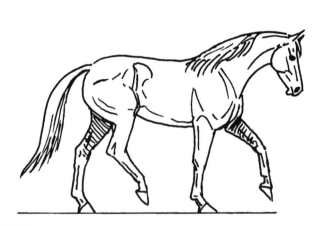

WORKING TROT

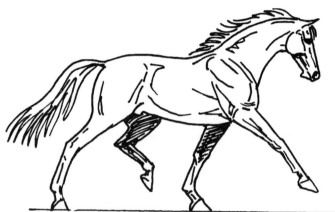

EXTENDED TROT

WORKING BALANCE

Working gaits are slightly more collected than ordinary gaits, but not to the extreme of full collection.

Working gaits have the balance in which a horse can best carry his rider easily and alertly. They are used for most training exercises.

• In working gaits, the horse's **hind legs** are still working and must be **lively** and **carrying weight**.

• It is important that the legs do not slow down nor take short lazy steps. In a working gait, the horse should feel **relaxed but at attention**.

EXTENSION

Extension means:
  • A lengthening of the horse's stride
  • Covering more ground at each step
  • Pushing off with a powerful stride that makes the horse appear to glide over the ground

In extension, the horse's neck, spine, and outline appear to stretch and become longer, and the legs stretch farther with each step.

Going faster with short steps is not extension!

COLLECTED CANTER

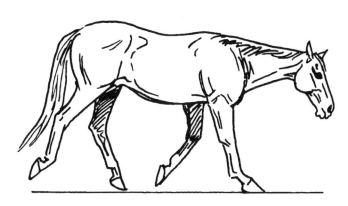

ON THE FOREHAND

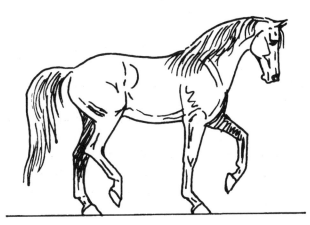

COLLECTED TROT

COLLECTION

In collection, your horse's **balance is farther back** than in ordinary balance.

His weight is carried more over his hind legs.
• When his weight is shifted to the rear, his back works like a lever and lifts his front end higher.
• To help do this, his neck rises and flexes at the poll, bringing his nose in closer to vertical.

His steps are shorter but lively, and he is alert and gathered to move out, turn, or stop quickly.

When he collects himself, a horse may appear to be **sitting on his hocks**.

Collection is used when slowing down, turning, preparing for changes of gait, and also when you want the horse to move slowly but with controlled energy.

ON THE FOREHAND

A horse is said to be on the forehand when he **moves with his head low and forward**, keeping **most** of his **weight on his front legs**.

Calm horses, lazy horses, and tired horses usually move on the forehand.
• This can make them clumsy and awkward if they are asked for fast turns or changes of gait and balance when they are on the forehand.

It is normal and natural for a walking horse to be on the forehand when he is relaxing or cooling out.

HORSE'S BALANCE

To help your horse balance, you must first have a good position and not need to hang on to the reins to keep your seat.

• Your legs signal the horse to bring his hind legs more under him when your legs squeeze in their normal place near the girth.
• When you sit up tall, your balance can tell the horse to collect or balance back.
• When you sit forward your balance may encourage him to shift his balance forward.
• Your hands can ask him to raise and flex his neck and head when you check and release, shorten the reins or increase pressure on the reins.

Riding medium sized circles gives a horse practice in improving his balance at the walk, trot, canter or lope.

Good western horsemanship means a natural, easy, and balanced seat, a light rein and smooth, quick control.

As you advance, you will be able to get the most out of your western horse by improving your aids and by working in balance and harmony with him. You may be working toward western shows, speed events, ranch work, training horses, or just enjoying the wonder of riding a really fine horse performing at his best.

AIDS AND CUES

By the time your performance can be called advanced, your aids and cues should be light, effective and easily understood by both you and your horse. Here are some specific points to work on.

REIN HANDLING

A highly trained western horse responds to a light neck rein, without needing to be pulled or forced.

• This response comes from the proper balance and head position, and also from the rider's light and correct use of the reins. A heavy-handed rider can never make a horse light to the reins.

Advanced western riders may **use either of two standard rein holds:**
  • The split rein style
  • The California style

These styles are used for horses that respond properly to a light neck rein.

For training and practice, the rider may also use:
  • The two hand rein hold or
  • The one-handed trainer's hold

The two hand hold is excellent for schooling and some types of showing. The one hand hold is for schooling and corrections only. It is not permitted in the show ring.

If your horse does not respond promptly to a light neck rein, you should switch to one of the training styles to correct him instead of pulling harder and harder with a one handed rein hold. This could make him *hard to the rein* and can spoil his head set and response to a light neck rein.

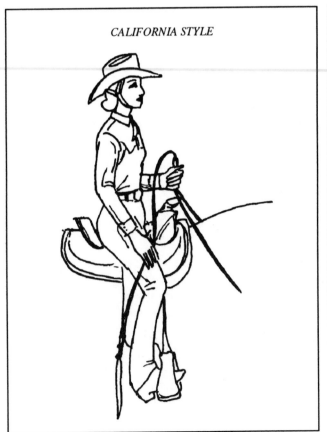

CALIFORNIA STYLE

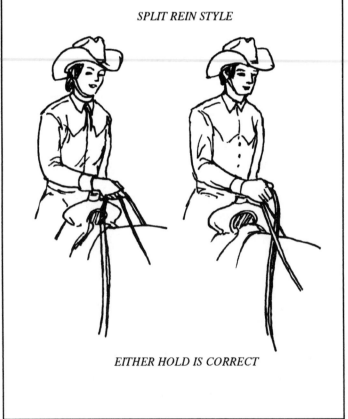

SPLIT REIN STYLE

EITHER HOLD IS CORRECT

NECK REINING

TWO HAND REIN HOLD

The two-hand rein hold is used when **starting young horses in neck reining** and when **schooling older horses**. It works best with a loose-jawed or direct pressure bit or bosal, but it can be used with any bit.

• The hands should be kept low, near the level of the withers, to avoid getting the horse's head high.
• Give a light neck rein with one hand.
• Then if the horse does not respond promptly, you might use the other rein in a quick leading rein to pull him the way he ought to have gone, or use a direct rein.

Don't use both reins at once. Give a neck rein, and then a quick correction if needed.

ONE HAND TRAINER'S HOLD

As the horse begins to respond better to the neck rein, you may switch to the one hand trainer's hold as a **transition between two hands** and the **proper show style rein hold**.

• In the trainer's hold, all your fingers are between the reins.
• You can give a neck rein, and then use your index finger or your little finger to *cheat* and give a little pull sideways if the horse forgets to respond.

This rein hold is so effective that it is illegal in the show ring. It can make a horse look as if he neck reins better than he actually does.

When he is responding well to the neck rein and no longer needs even small finger corrections, you may switch your reins to the split rein style or California style.

Remember, it is not good training to try to force a horse to turn with a long, hard neck rein pull if he doesn't respond to a light pull.

• Long hard pulls on the neck will:
  • Force his head up and sideways
  • Make him open his mouth, and
  • Make him ignore a light, correct neck rein signal

A very sluggish horse may need a slap or a touch of a spur to make him wake up and pay attention so that he can respond to any aid or cue promptly.

TWO HAND REIN HOLD

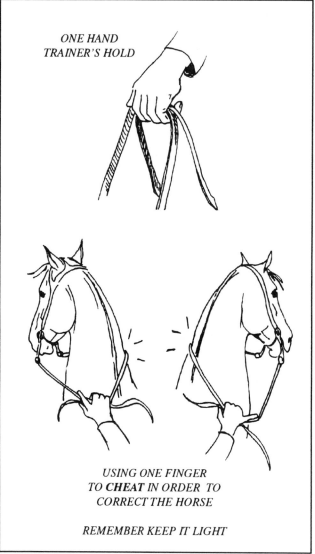

ONE HAND TRAINER'S HOLD

*USING ONE FINGER TO **CHEAT** IN ORDER TO CORRECT THE HORSE*

REMEMBER KEEP IT LIGHT

HEAD POSITION AND COLLECTION

Head set or position and collection are not the same thing, but they are often talked about together.

A western horse must be able to collect himself quickly for western performance movements like quick stops, pivots, and rollbacks. Sometimes we want him to move in a collected lope or jog.

• **Collection** refers to the balance of the whole horse when he is gathered for action with his weight shifted to the rear and his hocks under him.

• **Head set or position** refers to the position your horse carries his head when he responds to the bit.

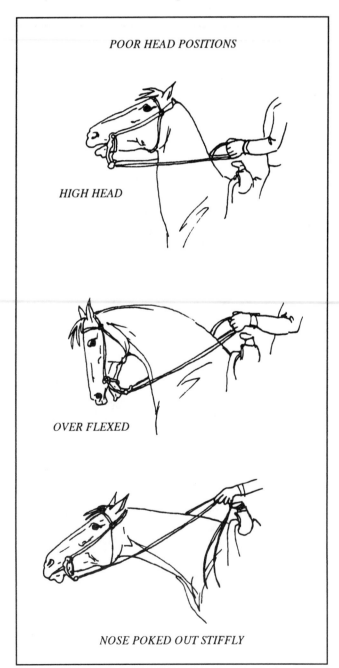

POOR HEAD POSITIONS

HIGH HEAD

OVER FLEXED

NOSE POKED OUT STIFFLY

COLLECTION

A collected horse has a **nearly vertical** head position and responds to bit pressure by **flexing at the poll** and **relaxing his jaw**. Judges look at the horse's head position to see if he is properly balanced and responding nicely to the reins. A high, stiff, or overly extended head position indicates problems.

Just getting the horse's face vertical isn't enough. He must also be **light** and **relaxed in his jaw**, **responsive to the bit**, and **balanced correctly** or he is *faking* instead of truly collecting himself.

• A horse can have a perfect but *faked* head position and be poorly balanced.

In order to achieve true collection (*more than just a head set*):

• The rider must use his legs to get the horse's hind legs under him. This will take sensitivity and good coordination of the hands, legs, and balance.

HEAD POSITION

When working on a horse's head position, you must teach him how to **flex his jaw** and **give to the bit** first.

• Take up your reins in two hands, short enough to feel a little pressure on the bit. Place both your hands low, about level with the horse's withers.

• Now *flutter* your fingers on the reins, gently closing and relaxing your fingers on the reins as if you were tickling the horse's mouth with the bit. Eventually you should feel your horse relax his jaw and lighten the pressure on the bit.

• He may tuck his chin or drop his nose a little. When he does, reward him instantly by keeping your fingers still and relaxed. With practice, he should learn to relax his mouth and tuck his chin a little as soon as he feels light rein pressure.

• When he will do this easily, you may switch back to a one-hand rein hold and repeat the exercise.

It is important for the horse to find that he is rewarded with a light and comfortable feeling as soon as he puts his head in the right position and relaxes his mouth.

When your horse will place his head and give to the bit nicely, you should ask him to do this whenever you prepare for a new gait or movement, or whenever you need to get him to balance himself better.

IMPROVING HEAD POSITION

*USE GENTLE GIVE AND
TAKE WITH BOTH HANDS*

*RELAX PRESSURE
WHEN HE DROPS HIS HEAD
AND GIVES TO THE BIT*

WEIGHT AIDS

In western riding, you must often shift your weight to give a cue or signal to tell your horse to move, turn, or stop.

• These weight shifts should be **done in the hips and seat** and should be subtle so that you and the horse can feel it but someone watching cannot see your actions.

• If you lean over with your shoulders, you will spoil your balance and may throw your horse off balance.

Your **back** should **stay tall and straight** when you give any seat aids.

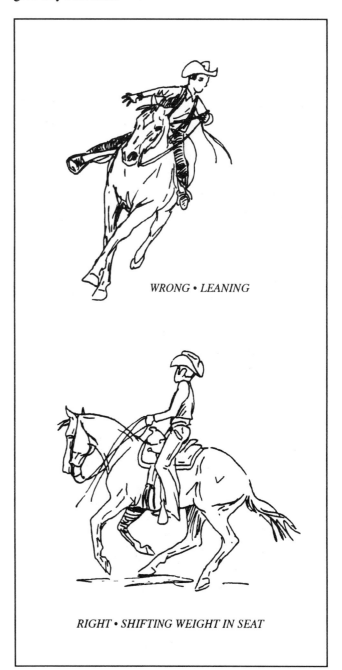

WRONG • LEANING

RIGHT • SHIFTING WEIGHT IN SEAT

A western horse that is stiff and clumsy is hard to ride. He will be slow and awkward in turning and will have trouble with ordinary performance movements. He isn't ready for advanced movements until he is **supple**.

Start by teaching the horse to **give his head easily to either side**. This is easiest to do with a snaffle, loose-jointed bit or bosal.

• Keep the reins in two hands and ask the horse to flex his neck and relax his jaw.
• Then give little *flutters* with just one hand until he bends his neck and looks toward that side.
• Ease up on the other rein to let him turn his head, then repeat on the other side of the mouth. He should eventually be able to bend his neck until he almost touches his nose to your foot.

He must never be pulled to make him do this. He has to learn to do it from a light, gentle touch on the reins.

You can also teach your horse to **respond to a leg aid near the girth**.
• Use just one leg and relax the other.
• When he feels pressure with the left leg on his side, he should move forward and also drift a little to the right. It should feel as if his ribs soften as he moves away from the left leg.
• If he just moves straight ahead without *giving* in the ribs, stop him and try again with a stronger leg aid.

Eventually you can use a squeeze of the inside leg to move the horse out into the corners or to keep him from cutting in on a turn.

A western horse should **follow his head in a turn**. This means that his nose will be slightly to the inside of a turn so that he is looking in the direction he is going.

If he is stiff and resisting you, he may carry his head to the outside and his hindquarters to the inside of a turn. This makes him clumsy and hard to control in turns, especially in fast turns. **More suppling is needed to cure this problem** .

STIFF
RESISTING TURN

SUPPLE
FOLLOWING HIS
HEAD IN A TURN

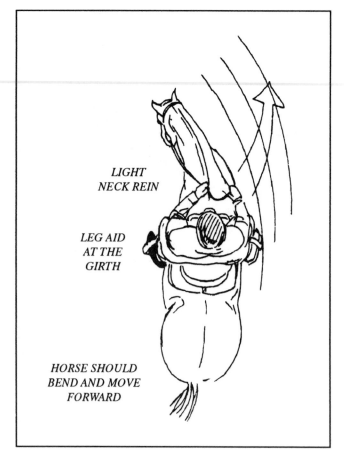

LIGHT
NECK REIN

LEG AID
AT THE
GIRTH

HORSE SHOULD
BEND AND MOVE
FORWARD

TEACHING THE HORSE
TO SUPPLE HIS NECK

LEG AIDS

The same leg aids are used in western riding as in english riding.

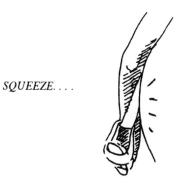

SQUEEZE. . . .

You learned the three basic leg aids in Level 3:
1) Both legs to wake up or move out,
2) One leg near the girth
   to bend or ask the horse to move out,
3) One leg stretched back behind the girth
   to move the horse's hind legs sideways.

• When you give a leg aid, be sure that you use the side of your calf against the horse's side.

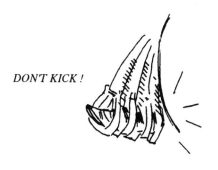

DON'T KICK !

• Do not raise your heel to kick up and back. Raising your heel loosens your seat and spoils your balance. It also makes some horses angry.

If a horse is not responsive to correctly given leg aids, he may need to be schooled to obey a lighter leg aid by reinforcing the leg aid with a training whip or a spur. *(See the section on artificial aids in Level 3 page 21.)*

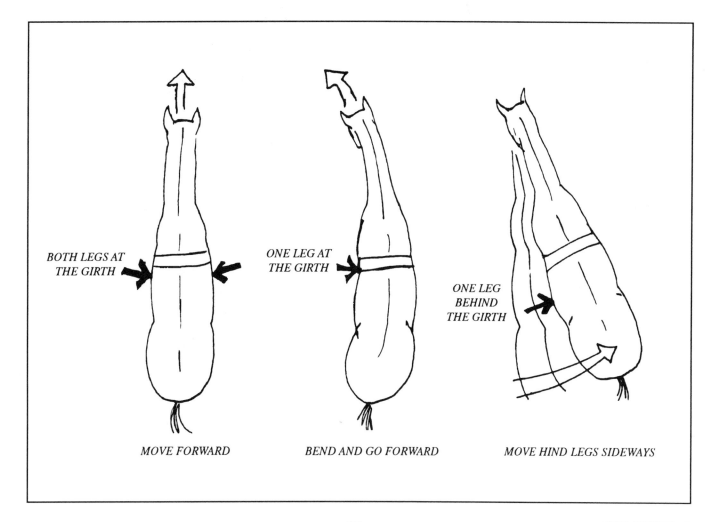

BOTH LEGS AT THE GIRTH

ONE LEG AT THE GIRTH

ONE LEG BEHIND THE GIRTH

MOVE FORWARD   *BEND AND GO FORWARD*   *MOVE HIND LEGS SIDEWAYS*

29

LATERAL LEG AIDS

Lateral means sideways. Lateral leg aids tell the horse to position himself or to **move his hind legs sideways** on command.

• **To give a lateral leg aid:**
• You must stretch your leg back to a position three or four inches behind the normal leg position.
• Keep your heel stretched down and give the leg aid with a squeeze of your calf, not by kicking up and back into the horse's side.

Your horse has to be **trained to understand what lateral leg pressure means**. You can begin this training on the ground.

• Use your fist or the end of a brush to push against your horse's side where your leg aid will touch him.
• Give repeated pushes until he takes a step sideways with his hind legs to get away from the pressure on his side.
• When he takes even one tiny step, immediately stop the pressure and reward him with a pat and praise.

With practice, you can teach him that a touch in that spot means to move his hind legs one step sideways. Teach him on both sides before you try it mounted.

TURN ON THE FOREHAND

The turn on the forehand is the **first** basic **lateral leg aid exercise**. Once your horse understands that he is to step sideways from pressure three or four inches behind the girth while you stand beside him, you may give the leg aid in the same spot from the saddle.

• Start with a quiet halt with your horse's attention on you. Don't pull on the reins, but be ready to use them to stop him if your horse tries to walk off instead of stepping over.
• Sit up tall and stretch your leg back into position. Give several squeezes to ask your horse to step over with his hind legs.
• As he takes a step, relax your leg aid and pat him.
• Then you may repeat the aid for the next step over.

This exercise can be used to move the horse over, to turn around, or to open and close gates while mounted.

TURN ON THE FOREHAND TO OPEN A GATE

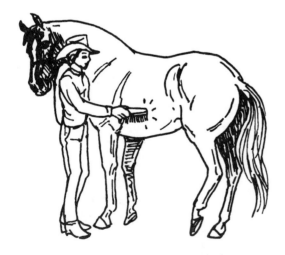

TEACHING A HORSE TO STEP AWAY FROM A LEG AID BEHIND THE GIRTH

THE TURN ON THE FOREHAND

SIDE PASS

The side pass is a useful movement in which your horse goes **straight sideways**.

The horse's **outside leg** should **cross over in front of the supporting leg**. This movement has a slight degree of forward motion.

- Side passing lets you move your horse over to open and close gates easily when mounted.

- Side passing also helps in suppling and in preparing for flying changes.

Before your horse can side pass, he must be good at the turn on the forehand. You will cue him with your lateral leg aid, your reins, and your seat.

THE SIDE PASS

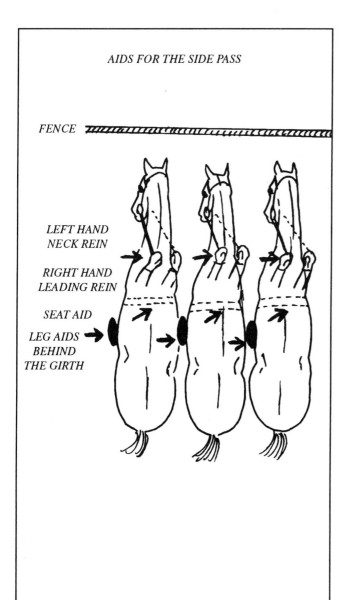

AIDS FOR THE SIDE PASS

FENCE

LEFT HAND
NECK REIN

RIGHT HAND
LEADING REIN

SEAT AID

LEG AIDS
BEHIND
THE GIRTH

To side pass to the right, ride your horse up to a fence so that he cannot go forward.

- Sit tall and deep in the saddle. It helps to hold the reins in two hands at first. Later you can switch to a one-handed hold.
- Stretch your left leg back three or four inches behind the girth and give a lateral leg aid to move your horse's hind legs sideways.
- At the same time give a little push with your seat bones sideways, pushing your horse to the right.
- Give a little neck rein to send your horse's front legs to the right.
- His head may turn a little bit to the left at first, but his neck and body should stay straight as he steps over.
- These aids must be repeated for each side step.

To side pass to the left, reverse the aids.

It is easier to teach a horse to sidepass if you use two hands and a snaffle bridle. Very well trained horses may side pass from a neck rein, with a curb bit.

PERFORMANCE SKILLS

Advanced western performance skills help you get the most out of your horse's speed, quick responses, and athletic ability. Quick stops, pivots, rollbacks and lead changes are needed for cattle work, reining, gymkhana classes and advanced equitation. Be sure you and your horse start slowly and work in harmony.

Rushing and roughness can ruin any horse. The better you ride, the better your horse can perform for you.

STOPS FROM THE LOPE

STOP

A good stop is not necessarily a sliding stop.

• A **good stop** is a **balanced, smoothly executed** stop with the **horse's hindquarters well under his body** to balance his weight.
• His forehand, neck and head are kept light.

The horse should be balanced and ready to do whatever is required next, whether it is to settle and stand, move on ahead, pivot, roll back, or take off in another direction.

TIMING

Timing is very **important** when **asking for a stop**, especially from a lope.

• There is a time in the lope, when the horse's hind feet are off the ground, when it is easy for your horse to get ready to stop.
• Once his hind feet have landed it is hard for him to stop well.

You should use a **preliminary cue** to alert your horse that a stop is coming. The cue will allow him time to adjust his balance. This cue can be a voice command like *whoa*, a light touch of your reins and squeeze of the legs, or even a light touch on the top of the neck.

The preliminary cue should be **given just a second before applying the full stop signal**. Don't wait too long to give the full stop cue, or the horse will no longer be ready to stop.

QUICK STOP

To cue for a quick stop, you will need to take the following actions.

O **Squeeze with your legs** to get your horse to bring his hind legs under his body to balance for a stop.

O Give a **firm** but flexible **series of pulls** (*give and take*) on the **reins in rhythm** with the horse's strides.
• If using two hands, use one rein and then the other, not both at once.
• Try to use your reins as the horse's leading foreleg hits the ground. This is the moment when the horse's hind legs are off the ground and he can prepare to stop.

O As you feel your horse responding to the first two aids, **sit more erect** and **settle** your seat into the saddle. **Sit down** as you feel your horse sit down into his stop.
• Push down on your heels and keep your thighs close to the saddle to help absorb shock and to stay balanced over your feet.

Don't get into the bad habit of thrusting your feet forward, throwing your weight back, and hauling back on the reins!

Some western riders may prefer to rise up a bit, balancing on their legs with their seat clear of the saddle as the horse prepares to stop. This lets the horse round his back and bring his hind legs under him.

Other riders do not stand up but sit lightly balanced in the saddle at this point. Both riders should sit down as the horse sinks into his stop. It helps to think of *tucking* your seat under you as the horse stops.

Practice stopping with the above cues at a walk, then a jog, and finally at a slow lope.
• This gives you and your horse time to learn the cues and perfect your timing at slower gaits before trying the more difficult lope.
• Get the rhythm and feel of your horse and keep your rein cues light and soft whenever you stop.

When practicing stopping, make your horse **stop completely and stand**, preferably on a slack rein.
• If he fails to stop properly or tries to walk off, back him a step or two, and then require him to stand still.
• It is wise to vary the time he must stand still so that he will not anticipate a short stand and move off without being told to do so.

LEG SQUEEZE

CHECK WITH REINS

SIT DOWN WITH THE HORSE

Don't rush your horse's schooling. You are making progress when you feel the horse's hindquarters sink under you slightly when you stop.

• Keep working for light response, and don't overdo the number of times you ask for stops.
• Vary the places you stop so the horse will not always expect to stop in the same place.

LEAD CHANGES

Whenever you make a change of direction at the lope your horse will have to change his lead.

There are two ways to do this:
1) The **simple change**, in which he is brought back to the trot or walk and restarted into the new lead.

2) The **flying change**, in which he changes leads without breaking his lope.

Before you or the horse can expect to change leads, you must be able to take the correct lead consistently by using the correct aids.

• You must also be able to tell when your horse is loping on the correct lead.
• Your horse must be well balanced and responding nicely to all of your aids or he won't be able to do as you ask.

CROSS CANTER

Rushing prematurely into a flying change will probably cause him to **cross canter**, in which he is **on one lead with the front legs and the other lead with the hind legs**.

This is a very clumsy gait and can cause him to fall. It is even more awkward than not changing leads at all and being on the wrong lead.

Cross cantering often **results from** a rider trying to force a horse to switch leads by **leaning over** and using a **hard neck rein**, changing the lead only in front.

If you try to force a flying change, you can teach a horse to do this awkward and dangerous gait instead.

• If you are cross cantering, come back to a trot and rebalance the horse before asking him to pick up the correct lead again.

33

Always **begin with the simple change of leads**. This tests your horse's response to and understanding of your aids and cues. If he can't handle the easier change, he will have trouble trying to perform the more difficult flying change.

To perform a simple change of leads:

❍ Begin by **loping along the rail** on the left lead, tracking to the left.

❍ Ride around the end of the ring and begin a **change of direction on the diagonal**.

❍ Before you reach the center of the ring, bring him **back to a jog for five or six strides**.

❍ Then give the **aids** for a right **lead** lope just before reaching the rail. Your horse should pick up the right lead and lope around the end of the ring.

To change from right to left lead, repeat the process from the other direction.

With practice, you will be able to lope straight and shorten the trotting steps in the center until you are only breaking gait for two or three steps before you pick up the new lead.

❍ At this point, you may bring your horse down to a walk for a couple of steps to make the change. Keep the simple change straight, controlled and quiet.

Don't get into the bad habits of leaning forward or sideways, throwing your body around, or twisting your horse sideways as you change leads.

❍ When you can make good simple changes on the diagonal, you can progress to a **large figure 8 pattern**. This gives you less time and room to make the change of leads.

• The horse should make two circles touching with a few straight strides between the circles, not a lazy *8* which looks like two teardrops touching (*see diagram in Level 3 page 33*).

• He should always be on the inside lead on each of the circles.

• He will have to change leads at the center point as he changes circles.

• This should be done on a straight line.

• Don't lean over or throw your body around.

When you are making good, short, trotting changes, you may reach a point where your horse can lope, break to a trot for only half a stride or so, and then pick up the new lead. This is building toward a flying change.

It is very important that he keeps picking up the correct lead in trotting changes in both the front and hind legs.

*LEFT LEAD
LOPE*

JOG

*RIGHT LEAD
LOPE*

SIMPLE CHANGE OF LEADS

FLYING CHANGE OF LEADS

When the horse is **ready to do flying changes**, he will **usually switch of his own accord** by accident when you are asking for a quick simple change. If he changes front and hind leads together, wonderful! If he only changes in front, go back to simple changes.

The aids for a change of leads are the same in both a simple change and a flying change. The difference is that a flying change requires split second timing and more agility of both the horse and rider. There is more of a margin for error in a simple change.

Use these aids for a flying change.

○ **Pick up a lope** on the **correct** (*inside*) **lead** with your outside leg behind the girth, using a slight neck rein in the direction of the lead you want, using your inside leg at the girth to keep the horse out. Ride this lead long enough to be sure that it is correct and that you are in balance with your horse.

○ **Straighten your horse out.** Make sure that both your hips are even and that neither leg is farther back. Lope straight ahead. This should be done at the middle of the diagonal line or the center of the figure 8.

○ Give the **aid for the new lead** by shifting the new outside leg back behind the girth, looking in the new direction and giving a slight neck rein in the direction of the new lead.

For example, if you are changing from left to right, you will switch to a left leg behind the girth and neck rein to the right to ask for the right lead.

• Sitting up straight and keeping your weight slightly on the outside hip will enable your horse to shift more smoothly to the new lead.

In a flying change, it is **necessary to time the aids** so that they are **given** when the **horse's hind legs are off the ground** and when he can switch hind leads as well as front leads.

He has to **make a sort of sideways step with his hind legs in order to switch.** Practicing side passing at the walk and trot can help prepare him to make the switch with his hind legs.

• Giving a little sideways push with the hips can also help *shove* the hind legs over and help the horse make the change behind.

Flying changes are **necessary** when a horse must make **sudden changes of direction at fast speeds**. This happens in barrel racing, pole bending, in cattle work and other speed work.

Riders should not ask their horses to make sudden turns at speed until both horse and rider are advanced enough to perform flying changes if necessary.

FLYING CHANGE OF LEADS

LEFT LEAD

FRONT AND HIND LEGS SWITCH IN AIR

RIGHT LEAD LOPE

35

PIVOTS

Pivots are **developed from the turnback on the rail** that you learned in Level 3. In this kind of turn, your horse **sits on his hocks** and **brings his front end around without moving his hind feet except to pivot in a small circle**. This kind of turn makes him light and handy.

• He can turn around in a small space and be ready to move out, halt and stand, or pivot the other way.

• He must pivot mostly on the inside hind leg, which is called the pivot leg.

To make a pivot:

• You will first have to halt and collect your horse. He should feel like he *rocks back* on his hind end. Your horse should not actually back up.

• You will have to sit in balance with him as he turns with his weight on the pivot leg. You must give him an aid he understands to bring his front end around.

• Finally, you must make sure his hind legs don't skid or move around sideways. This unbalances your horse and leaves him unable to turn or move out quickly.

Pivots require a calm but alert and responsive horse.

The aids for a pivot on the hindquarters to the right are as follows:

○ **Halt** and **squeeze your legs** to bring the horse's hind legs under him. Rock him back by sitting taller and using a give and take on the reins until he feels collected under you.

○ **Sit on the pivot leg** (*the inside hind leg*) by shifting your weight back over your right seat bone.
• It is important not to lean forward!

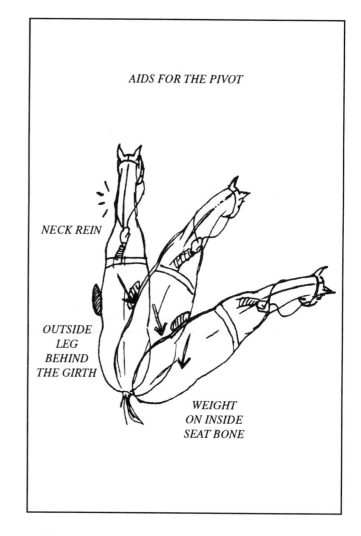

AIDS FOR THE PIVOT

NECK REIN

OUTSIDE
LEG
BEHIND
THE GIRTH

WEIGHT
ON INSIDE
SEAT BONE

○ Hold the hindquarters and prevent *skidding* by stretching your **left leg back behind the girth** three or four inches.

○ **Rein** him around **to the right** with short, light neck reins. If he is slow to respond, use a voice aid as you did in the turnback on the rail like a hissing sound to remind him.

SQUEEZE YOUR LEG
ROCK BACK

LEG BACK AND
NECK REIN

SIT OVER PIVOT LEG

LEFT LEAD LOPE

BALANCED STOP

ROLLBACKS

A rollback is a **series of movements** that blend together so smoothly into each other that they look like one movement. The rollback incorporates a run or lope, a balanced stop, a fast, smooth 180° pivot, and a fast break out of the rollback into a run or lope on the proper lead. It originated in ranch work where a good cowhorse would have to run, stop, and pivot in either direction to head off a cow.

The rollback is a fast, smooth and beautiful movement to ride or to watch when done well.

To perform a rollback:

Your horse must first be good at stops from the lope, turn-backs on the rail, and pivots. He must take both leads easily when given the correct aids. You must be in balance with him and must understand the aids and cues for what you are asking him to do.

When you ask for a rollback, you will start in, for example, the left lead.

○ **Lope** down to a smooth, balanced stop and hesitate just long enough to feel that your horse has regained his balance under you.

○ Next, you will **shift your weight** and give the **aids** for a **pivot** to the right. **Sit** on the right **seat bone**, using the left **leg behind the girth** and neck rein to the right.

○ As your horse makes the pivot, **squeeze** the left **leg behind the girth** and send him forward out of the pivot in a right lead lope.

If he starts in the left lead, he should rollback to the right and come out in the right lead. If he begins in the right lead, he should rollback to the left and finish in the left lead. A reining pattern will specify the direction a horse must rollback.

When learning the rollback, it is easiest if you perform it like a turnback on the rail.

180° PIVOT RIGHT

RIGHT LEAD LOPE

Be sure to make a balanced stop on the hindquarters and leave the horse room to roll back toward the rail without bumping his nose. Don't try to make him pivot while he is still sliding or stopping or else he will slip.

Get forward with him as he jumps out in the lope or run as he completes the pivot.

• It is especially important to keep the outside leg back to keep the horse's hindquarters from *skidding*, as this is very likely to happen when a horse tries to turn fast. Skidding slows him down and can make him clumsy, and it will spoil the rollback.

• If your horse isn't responding quickly, use a voice aid like *whoa* to prepare for the stop and the voice aid or hissing noise to signal him to come around quickly in the rollback.

37

Old-time cowboys tested their horses' ability in everyday cattle work, but many modern western riders use competition patterns to test and demonstrate their horses' performance and handling skills.

Remember, it is not how fast or how hard you stop or turn that counts, it is **how smoothly and skillfully you and your horse work in balance and harmony**. This is especially important for riders who are interested in speed games like barrel racing, pole bending, and other gymkhana events.

Good horsemanship will pay off in a smoother working horse and faster times, but rough, sloppy riding will quickly ruin even a talented horse.

WESTERN RIDING PATTERN

The Western Riding Pattern is not a race, or a stunt but a test of an easy handling ranch horse and his ability to move at ordinary gaits and get his rider around on the usual ranch chores.

Horses are scored on their smoothness, reining, balance, ease of movement, and attitude. They must be obedient and accurate in performance.

If your horse doesn't perform good flying changes, you can set the pattern extra wide and make short simple changes instead. Flying changes are expected in open horse show competition.

The Western Riding Pattern is explained in the pattern diagram. Working the gate is optional.

Western Riding Pattern:

1. Open and close gate, mounted (*optional*)
2. Walk over log
3. Jog to end of ring
4. Lope. Weave through markers, changing leads between markers
5. Serpentine, changing leads in center
6. Lope down center line and stop
7. Back in a straight line

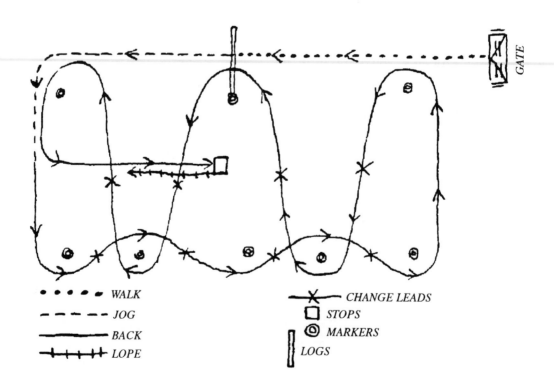

WESTERN RIDING PATTERN

WESTERN REINING PATTERN

A Reining Pattern is a demonstration of a western horse's balance, responsiveness, attitude, and ability to perform all the western movements.

There are several standard patterns which may be used in horse shows. The pattern described here is one of the simplest and must be followed exactly. Making a wrong turn or going off pattern disqualifies a competitor.

• Reining horses are faulted for errors like missing a lead, failing to change leads, poor balance, high head, open mouth, hard to rein, or attitude problems like hesitating, bucking or switching the tail when cued.

• The rider may not touch the horse with his free hand or change hands on the reins in competition.
• He also may never spur or hit his horse forward of the cinch.

The movements of the reining pattern are explained in the diagram.

Reining Pattern:
I. Run with speed past center of ring
2. Stop
3. Back to center of ring in a straight line
4. Lope small figure 8, beginning to right
   Change leads in center
5. Lope larger figure 8 faster, beginning to the right
   Change leads in center
6. Run to end of ring, roll back to left
7. Run to other end of ring, roll back to the right
8. Lope to center and stop
9. Pivot 90° one way, 180° the other way,
   then 90° back to center

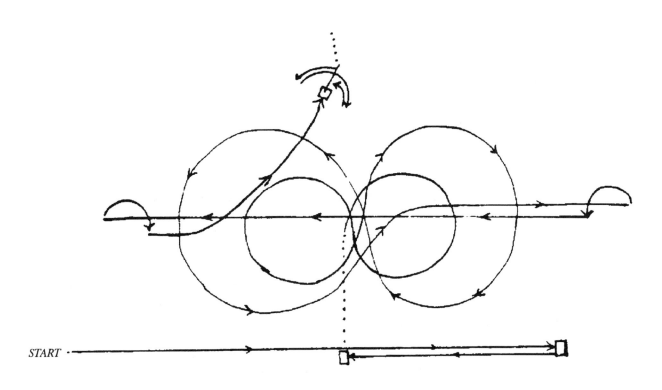

WESTERN REINING PATTERN

Going off course, using two hands on the reins or striking and/or spurring the horse
in front of the cinch disqualifies the entry in either of the patterns.

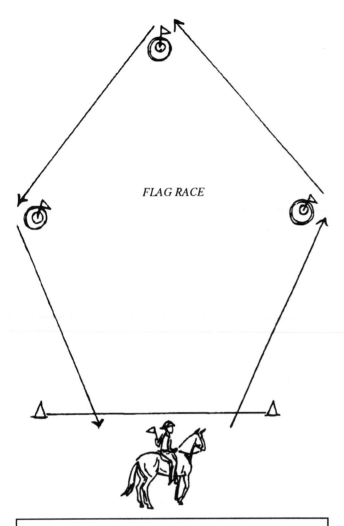

FLAG RACE

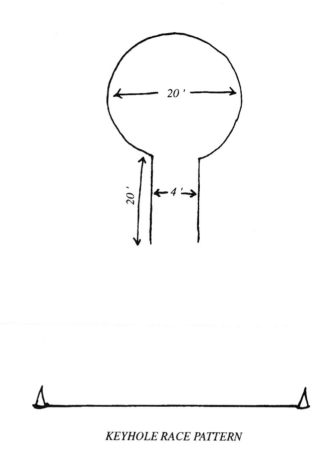

KEYHOLE RACE PATTERN

FLAG RACE BARREL

FLAG RACE

This race tests the rider's ability to make accurate stops from the lope.

• Three barrels are set up around the ring.
• On top of each barrel is a can of sand containing a flag. The rider has a flag in his hand.
• He leaves the starting line and runs to the first barrel, stops and changes flags, then runs on to the next barrel and changes flags, and so on.
• Finally he crosses the finish line.
Dropping a flag or tipping over a barrel disqualifies him. Missing a change of flags means that he must go back and make the change again.
• The rider with the best time wins.

KEYHOLE RACE PATTERN

The Keyhole Race is a speed event that tests a horse's ability to make an accurate stop and rollback.

• A circle 20 feet in diameter is made with lime, with an entrance four feet wide and twenty feet long.
• The horse leaves the starting line and runs into the keyhole, stops, rolls back, and exits without touching the line of the circle or the sides of the entrance.

He is disqualified for putting a foot outside the keyhole or entrance, or for stepping on the lime line.
• The fastest time wins.

OTHER PATTERNS

You may also run the Cloverleaf Barrel Race Pattern and the Pole Bending Pattern at faster gaits.

Don't push a horse that is not able to do flying changes into trying to make fast turns at speed. This requires advanced skills and good balance. To see a diagram of these patterns look in your Level 2 manual.

ENGLISH HORSEMANSHIP

To advance your riding, you need to apply your aids and your knowledge to improve your horse's performance. A beginning rider needs a horse that will put up with his mistakes and take care of him. An intermediate rider can ride the average horse without upsetting it. It takes an advanced rider to improve a horse's performance or to ride a really fine horse. Here are some performance skills used by advanced english riders.

LENGTHENING AND SHORTENING

The ability to lengthen and shorten your horse's stride gives you precise control over his speed and gait. One member of the Olympic team could do this so well that he could make his horse put its left front foot on a quarter dropped on the ground without missing a beat of the canter.

LENGTHENING STRIDE

To make your horse take longer strides, you must **squeeze with your legs in rhythm with his strides**.

• In a trot, squeeze your legs when you sit and relax them as you rise.
• In the canter, squeeze with your inside leg as you feel yourself sit deeper into the canter at each stride.

Your hands must be light and flexible enough to let the horse stretch out his neck and to let his stride get longer. If you don't keep a steady contact, he will probably just speed up with little fast steps instead of taking longer strides or he might break into a faster gait.

SHORTENING STRIDE

To shorten your horse's strides, you must **shift your balance back** a little and ask your **horse to shift his balance back** also.

• Squeeze your hands on the reins in short squeezes in rhythm with his gait as you sit taller, and use a little leg aid to keep him awake so he doesn't simply stop.
• Use several half halts, one right after the other.

When you shorten your horse properly, you will feel as if he is restrained but awake and **sitting on his hocks**, not like he is about to fall on his nose. As he shortens up, his rhythm should stay the same, not get slower.
He should not break down to a slower gait.

THE THREE TROT EXERCISE

This exercise is good practice in lengthening and shortening your horse.
• Start with an ordinary medium speed posting trot.
• Near the end of the ring, shorten your horse's stride to a working trot and ride this to the next corner.
• Then on the long side lengthen to a medium trot.
• At the corner, shorten back to a working sitting trot.
• On the next long side, lengthen to a strong trot.
• At the next corner, shorten back to a medium posting trot again.
During this exercise the **rhythm should stay the same**. If your horse just trots faster and slower, he isn't really shortening and lengthening stride.

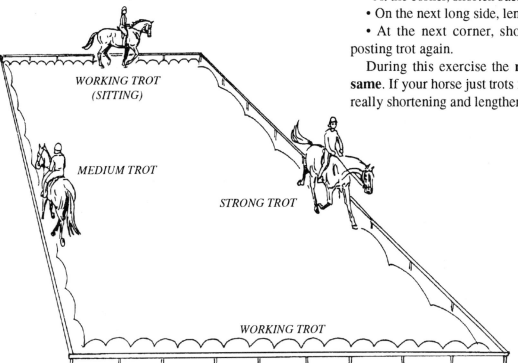

WORKING TROT (SITTING)

MEDIUM TROT

STRONG TROT

WORKING TROT

41

Flexion means bending; to flex something is to bend it. There are two kinds of flexion in riding.

DIRECT OR LONGITUDINAL FLEXION

Direct flexion or longitudinal flexion is **flexion the long way**. This means flexion from the **hind legs all the way to the head**.

When the horse collects himself:
• His hind legs flex more as they carry more of his weight, making his steps light and springy.
• His neck also flexes, especially at the poll. This brings his head up and in so that his face comes close to the vertical.
• He also flexes in the jaw, chewing the bit lightly and relaxing his mouth. This gives you a light, responsive feeling through the reins.

To ask a horse to flex:
• You must use your leg aids to tell him to bring his hind legs under him more while you are restraining him with gentle rein pressure.
• Your hands must hold, not pull, or he won't relax his mouth and flex properly.
• If you try to force a horse to flex, he may try to get away from the pressure by over flexing, tucking his chin too much and keeping his jaw stiff, *faking* flexion. This makes a horse very difficult to control once he has learned the habit from a heavy handed rider. It is a hard habit to cure.

Flexion requires cooperation, correct aids, time and patience not force.

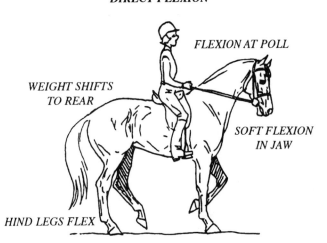

DIRECT FLEXION

FLEXION AT POLL

WEIGHT SHIFTS TO REAR

SOFT FLEXION IN JAW

HIND LEGS FLEX

LATERAL FLEXION OR BENDING

Lateral flexion or bending, is what a horse should do around a turn or a circle.

He **bends his spine** so that **his hind feet** can **follow in the tracks of his front feet** around the curve, with his **neck bent** in the **same curve** as his **backbone**.

This means that he looks in the direction in which he is going and *stands up* instead of having to lean over to make the turn. When a horse bends properly, he feels nicely balanced and comfortable to ride in a turn.

• The rider can just see the inside of his eyelashes, not the whole side of his head.
• He should not bend more in his neck than in the rest of his body. Some horses do this instead of bending correctly. This is called *rubbernecking* or faking and makes them quite difficult to control in turns.

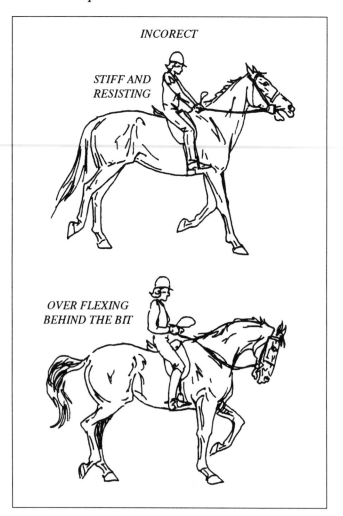

INCORECT

STIFF AND RESISTING

OVER FLEXING BEHIND THE BIT

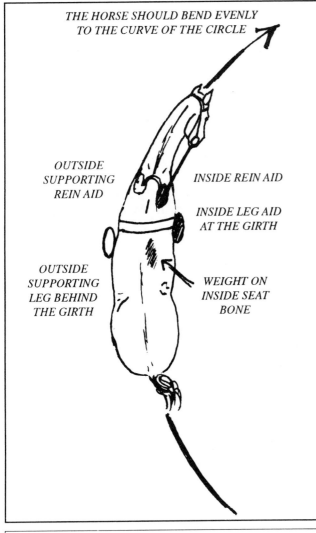

THE HORSE SHOULD BEND EVENLY
TO THE CURVE OF THE CIRCLE

OUTSIDE
SUPPORTING
REIN AID

INSIDE REIN AID

INSIDE LEG AID
AT THE GIRTH

OUTSIDE
SUPPORTING
LEG BEHIND
THE GIRTH

WEIGHT ON
INSIDE SEAT
BONE

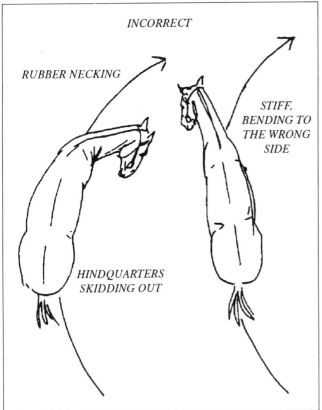

INCORRECT

RUBBER NECKING

STIFF,
BENDING TO
THE WRONG
SIDE

HINDQUARTERS
SKIDDING OUT

AIDS FOR BENDING

To ask your horse to bend:
• You should use your inside leg aid in the normal position near the girth, squeezing and relaxing in time with his strides.
• Shift your weight slightly onto your inside seat bone. Don't overdo it or lean with your shoulders.
• Keep your outside leg stretched back about three or four inches behind the girth to keep the horse from slipping sideways instead of bending.
• Squeeze your inside hand softly on the rein. You may need to use a little indirect rein on some horses. Maintain a gentle but even contact on the outside rein.

Practice bending your horse around each corner in the riding ring and all the way around large and medium sized circles. (*A horse finds it very difficult to bend well in small circles.*) You can practice changing the bend on a large figure 8, a serpentine, in half circles, or reverses.

HALF HALTS

The half halt is a signal to the horse that is very much like the signal to halt. It tells him to wake up, to come to attention, and to get his hind legs under him. It is used to collect him and prepare him for a new movement.

In a half halt, the horse should not actually halt or even break down to a slower gait. He should feel like he has *come together* for a moment and is ready for action.

To make a half halt:
• You first sit deep in the saddle, give a leg squeeze, and push with your seat bones.
• In the next instant, before the horse has time to go faster, your hands restrain him and ask him to flex instead. It is almost like asking him to go and then changing your mind.
• Be very careful not to clash your aids. If you squeeze to go while you pull to stop when making a half halt, your horse will become frustrated and confused.

Doing too many half halts will make some horses upset and fretful. If this is the case, it's better to omit the half halts.

You can use several half halts, one right after the other, to shorten his stride or bring your horse down to a slower gait. Half halts can be used to ask him to balance himself, to get ready for any new movement, or to stay collected.

43

To change leads at the canter, most riders use the **simple change** of leads in which the horse is **brought back to a walk or trot** for a **few strides** and then **restarted** into the **canter on the new lead**.

The **flying change** in which the horse **changes leads without interrupting the canter**, is too advanced for many school or camp horses.

To learn to do a simple change of leads:
You must be sure of your aids for both leads of the canter. You also need to know how to ride a change of direction on the diagonal.

◯ Start with a left lead **canter**.

◯ Ride around to the end of the ring, and begin to **change directions on the diagonal**.

◯ **Shorten the canter strides** until you can easily bring your horse **back to a sitting trot** before reaching the center of the ring.

◯ Ride the trot for **two or three strides** in a **straight line**, then give the **aids** for a right lead **canter**.

Your horse should take the right lead canter just before reaching the rail and canter around the end of the ring on the right lead.

With practice, you can shorten the trot in the center to two or three strides. Then you can try coming down to a walk and going back into the canter.

It is important to sit tall and quiet in the saddle while making the change from the canter down to the trot or the walk and back to the canter again.
• If you lean, kick, or try to *throw* the horse into the lead, you'll lose precision and control and will make him upset.
• During transitions, keep you and your horse as straight as possible.

Your canter should be somewhat short and collected. It is hard to change leads if your horse is going too fast or all stretched out.

When you can do good simple changes of lead, you can practice them on a large figure 8 or in a serpentine.

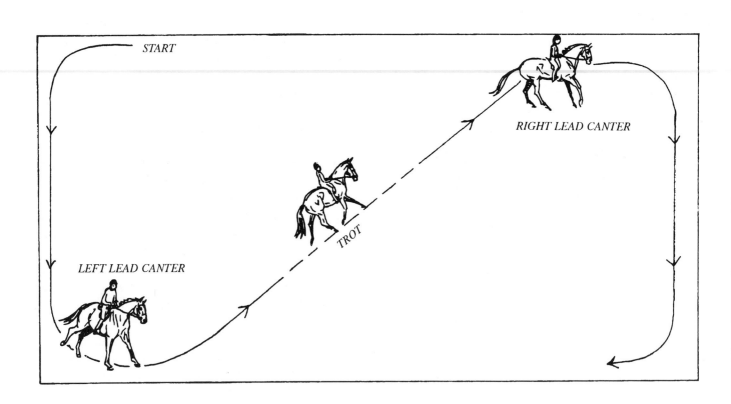

START

RIGHT LEAD CANTER

TROT

LEFT LEAD CANTER

When you are able to make good short trotting simple changes, you will reach a point where your horse will be able to canter, trot for half a stride or so, and canter on, in the new lead. This is building toward a flying change of leads.

All of the work you have done up until now, should have helped you to establish clear communication and excellent responsiveness from the horses you ride.

It is important that you can do the following well before attempting to try flying change of leads:
• Turns on forehand and haunches
• Suppling
• Bending
• Half halts
• Smooth transitions
• Balanced canter departs
• Combined with lateral work like:
  • Leg yielding
  • Half pass

○ The aids for a flying change are the same as for a simple change, except the **timing** is more important.

• The **half halt** will help **balance** the horse under you. The change of lead needs to **occur** when **both of the horse's back feet** are **off the ground.**

• This is because the **sequence of footfalls for the new lead must begin with the correct hind leg**.

For example, if the horse was cantering on the left lead the footfall would be right hind, followed by left hind and right fore together, finally the left foreleg reaching out farther indicating the left lead.

○ Just as the **left fore touches the ground** is a good time to ask for the flying change of lead to the right.

• If the timing is wrong, or your horse is not properly balanced and prepared, he might change leads in the front and not behind.
• This is called **cross cantering**, or **cross firing**. It is uncomfortable to ride because the horse's rhythm and balance have been changed.

This is usually only a problem, when the horse is asked to do something he is not ready for.
This may be due to:
  • Going too fast
  • Poor preparation
  • A sudden change of direction
  • Other rider error

Good flying lead changes are a natural progression for the horse.

They are important for jumping a course, whether in the ring or cross country. A good rider can change leads while the horse is in the air.

They are also important as a part of basic dressage. Eventually a really good horse and rider can do a flying change every three strides, then two, then change at every canter stride. This takes years to master, but you have already started to learn the basic skills.

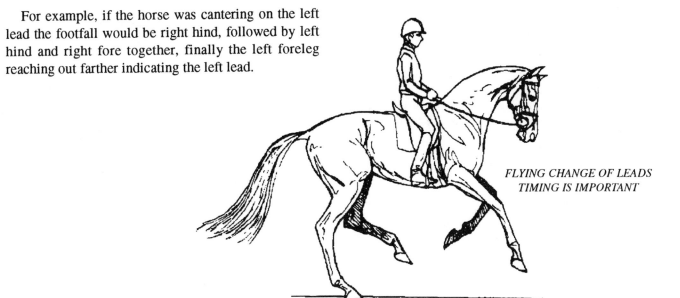

FLYING CHANGE OF LEADS
TIMING IS IMPORTANT

TURN ON THE FOREHAND

A turn on the forehand gives you control over your horse's hind legs. It teaches the horse to **move his hind legs sideways away from the pressure of your leg** when you give a leg aid. You can use a turn on the forehand to turn around at a standstill, to move a horse sideways, or to open and close a gate while you are mounted. In this turn, your horse's front legs will pivot in place while his hind legs step around in a bigger circle.

❍ Start at a **halt** with the horse relaxed and with good **simple contact** on the bit.

❍ To move his hind legs to the right, stretch your **left leg back** three or four inches behind its normal position with your heel down. This **leg presses against the horse** and tells him to take a step sideways with his hind legs each time your leg squeezes.

• **Sit up tall** and **deep** in the saddle and keep your **right leg relaxed**. You use your right leg only if your horse tries to back up instead of moving over.

• Your hands *don't pull the horse around*. You **lighten up on the right rein** enough for the horse to look a little bit to the left. **Be sure not to pull on the reins**, but ready to say NO with your hands if the horse tries to walk forward instead of moving over.

❍ **Squeeze or tap gently** on your horse's side with your stretched back **left leg**. Your leg tells him to take one step sideways for each squeeze.

• Each time he takes a step, relax your leg aid and give him a pat before asking for another step.

• If he doesn't understand your leg aids, your instructor can help from the ground by pushing on the side or by tapping his side gently with a dressage whip.

• When he has taken a few good steps, relax your reins and let him walk forward as a reward.

Practice moving his hind legs both ways. Most horses will move more easily to one side than to the other.

TURN ON THE
FOREHAND

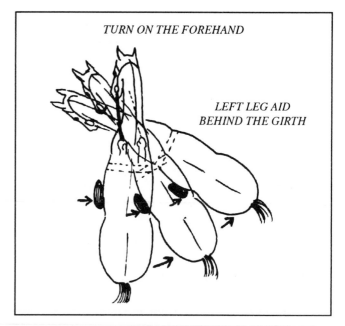

TURN ON THE FOREHAND

LEFT LEG AID
BEHIND THE GIRTH

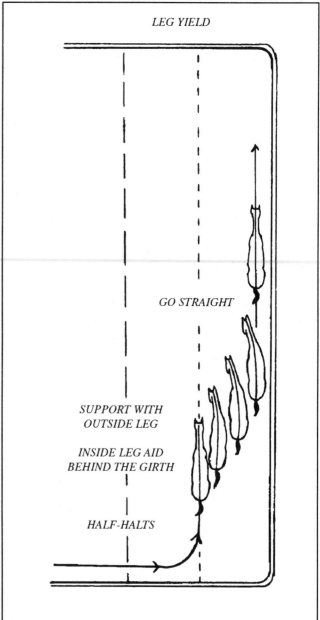

LEG YIELD

GO STRAIGHT

SUPPORT WITH
OUTSIDE LEG

INSIDE LEG AID
BEHIND THE GIRTH

HALF-HALTS

LEG YIELDING

To yield means to give in. Leg yielding means giving to the rider's leg.

• It can be practiced in all three gaits; at the walk to teach the leg yield; the trot for suppling and to help get the horse on the aids; less frequently, in the canter, as this can sometimes produce a crooked canter.

• It can not only be ridden on straight lines but on circles and curves too, the aids being virtually the same. It can also be used to pass a rider in front of you (leg yield away from wall / pass / leg yield back to wall), on trails, or anywhere you may need to move the horse over.

When a horse leg yields, he is moving approximately **2/3 forward** and **1/3 sideways** with the body fairly straight with a **slight bend in the ribs**, and the **poll slightly flexed in the opposite direction** of the way you are traveling. The shoulders of the horse may lead very slightly, but the haunches should never lead.

• Before teaching leg yields, your horse must be supple to the point that you can move his haunches in a larger circle than the forehand and you can block the forehand to keep it from moving to the same size circle as the haunches. It's along the lines of a turn on the forehand but you don't have to have the forehand remain completely immobile. The horse must also understand half halts.

❍ To begin leg yields, start by tracking left. Then **turn down the quarter line** of the arena.

• As you turn, you want to keep your body in *position left*; that is, your outside (right) seatbone sitting in the center of the saddle, lengthening your inside leg and keeping stretched up in your rib cage, turning your shoulders in the direction of the turn.

• You don't want to collapse your hip.

❍ Apply **half halts** for several successive strides to alert and balance your horse.

❍ Then another **half halt** to put the horse into the correct position for the leg yield.

• His body should be fairly straight with a slight poll flexion to the left (inside).

• The horse should be firmly on the aids with positive contact on the right (outside) rein.

❍ Keeping in **position left**, slide your inside leg slightly behind the normal position on the girth. This will influence the whole horse, not just one end (front/back) of the horse.

• Squeeze in with your inner calf and thigh in rhythm

with the inside hind leg (as the hind leg is coming forward) to direct the horse laterally into your outside rein.

❍ The **outside leg** is in the normal driving position maintaining forward impulsion.

• If the haunches begin to lead the leg yield, move your leg back to stop the haunches from leading.

• If the forehand moves sideways too quickly, then move your leg forward so it's on the girth to slow the shoulders down.

❍ The **inside rein** maintains poll flexion by squeezing and releasing towards your inside hip to keep the poll and jaw soft. You don't want to use an Indirect Rein of Opposition as this will cause incorrect bend, popping the shoulder and rubber necking.

❍ The **outside rein** limits the bend in the neck, keeps the shoulders from moving sideways to quickly, and maintains the frame and balance of the horse. Use a direct rein of opposition with your outside rein.

❍ As all your aids come together and you feel your horse is on the aids, **apply your inside leg aid** and **turn your shoulders** toward the wall or the direction you are traveling. This will adjust your weight in a way that the horse will understand which direction he is to go.

• Make sure you don't turn so much that you weaken your seat and leg aids.

SOME COMMON PROBLEMS

• Not enough outside rein allows **too much bend**. It allows the shoulders to pop so the horse can't move sideways because he's unbalanced and/or he may just go onto a circle.

• If you have contact with your outside rein and the **horse still won't move sideways**, you can use your outside rein and open it for a stride (leading rein) to lead the shoulders over. Then close it for a stride (direct rein), then open it again. If you hold it open, it becomes a crutch for both horse and rider.

• If the **shoulders are leading too much**, and there isn't too much bend, squeeze your outside rein as the outside shoulder of the horse moves forward. This will slow the shoulders down so the haunches can catch up. You may need to move your inside leg back farther to affect the haunches more.

USING YOUR SKILLS

There are many ways to put your advanced riding skills to work.

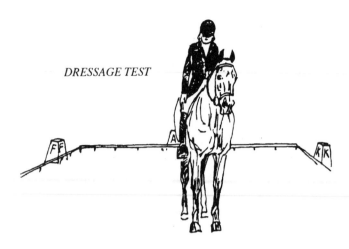

DRESSAGE TEST

DRESSAGE

One way is though Dressage, a French word that refers to the training that develops a horse's muscles and sensitivity until he can be ridden with almost invisible signals.

You may be surprised to learn that all your riding and training exercises are really elementary dressage.

You can put all the movements together in a dressage test. In the tests each movement is judged on its smoothness and perfection.

HORSE SHOWS

Competing in horse shows may be something that you are interested in.

EQUITATION CLASSES

You may ride in Equitation classes, in which **your riding form, smoothness, and control** are judged.

• In these classes on the flat, you compete in a group at a walk, trot, and canter around the ring, then reverse and repeat.
• In an class over fences you will jump individually.

The judge may break ties by requesting equitation tests such as a figure 8 at the trot or at the canter, a change of diagonals, or a simple change of leads. He may ask you to dismount and remount, ride without stirrups, back up, gallop and pull up, or perform a turn on the forehand. He can even ask riders to exchange horses and perform tests on a strange horse.

PERFORMANCE CLASSES

In Performance classes, your **horse** is judged on his **performance, smoothness**, and **way of going** at the walk, trot, and canter, and sometimes the hand gallop.

Performance classes include English Pleasure, Hunter Under Saddle, Bridle Path Hack and others.

The horse's manners and way of moving are also judged. He must take the correct leads. The rider's form doesn't count, but the better he rides, the better he will make his horse look.

Showing requires a knowledge of what a good performance is, what the judge is looking for, and how to properly present yourself and your horse to the judge and the public.

HORSE SHOWS

In Level 3 jumping, you learned to jump a variety of simple fences and to ride a course of fences. Now you can develop a stronger seat, better timing through gymnastics, learn to rate your horse for the proper takeoff and enjoy the challenge of more demanding courses and cross-country jumping.

Your **goal** should be for your horse to **jump better, not just higher**. As you progress, you will be able to handle whatever height is comfortable for your horse to jump.

POSITION CHECK AND REVIEW

Before you try more difficult courses be sure and review your jumping position and basics over several low fences or crossrails.
- *Do you stay up and balanced as your horse takes off and lands?*
- *Are your heels down and your legs firm on his sides?*
- *Do you always release properly, not catching the horse in the mouth?*
- *Are your eyes up and on target?*
- *Do you stay with the horse, not getting left behind or getting ahead?*

If you can do all of the above maneuvers well, you are ready to move on to advanced jumping.

GYMNASTICS

Gymnastics are **exercises over fences** and a **series of fences** that control your horse's pace, balance, and takeoff point. Gymnastics teach a horse to keep his balance and to develop his jumping style, which is why they are called gymnastics.

They also give a rider a **sense of rhythm and timing** and develop strong, supple legs and a secure seat.

If you are inclined to be stiff, gymnastics may help you relax.

The easier gymnastics are done in a lively but slow trot. Later, they can be done at a canter. Don't let your horse rush or he will not perform them well.

○ **The first gymnastic is over a *placing pole*.**
- This is a rail no more than six inches high placed twelve feet from the base of a fence for horses, ten feet for ponies or small horses.
- Canter over the pole and on over the fence. The horse will step over the placing pole and land in just the right spot to take off correctly.

○ **The next exercise is a bounce or a *no-stride*.**
- It consists of two fences about two feet high placed ten to twelve feet apart.
- The horse should jump the first one and just have room to touch down, then jump the second. It feels like he bounces in and then bounces out.
- Stay up in jumping position and leave your hands anchored on the mane through this gymnastic.

If your horse tries to take a stride between the fences, the bounce may be made a bit shorter or you may have to use a stronger leg aid.

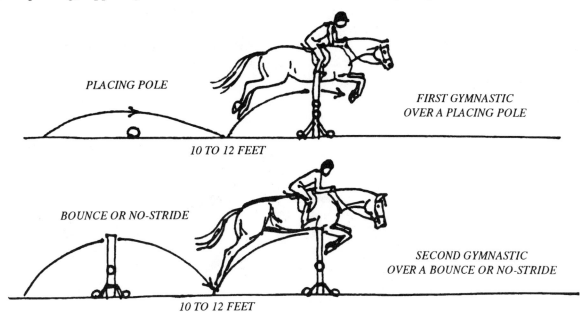

PLACING POLE

FIRST GYMNASTIC
OVER A PLACING POLE

10 TO 12 FEET

BOUNCE OR NO-STRIDE

SECOND GYMNASTIC
OVER A BOUNCE OR NO-STRIDE

10 TO 12 FEET

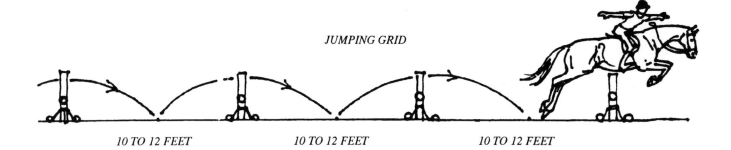

JUMPING GRID

10 TO 12 FEET   *10 TO 12 FEET*   *10 TO 12 FEET*

JUMPING GRID

After you and your horse are good at simple bounces, you can ride a jumping grid.

• This is a **series of three or four fences** in a **straight line** with the same distance between them as in a bounce.

These fences are set up along one rail of the ring and the other side opposite the rail is enclosed in a chute.

You need to ride into the grid with a lively trot or a controlled canter.

• At the first jump, release and hold the mane. You will feel the horse make your legs and body fold and unfold as he takes off and lands repeatedly.

• Keep your eyes up and your heels down.

Once your horse is taking the grid nicely in the chute, you can tie your reins and drop them as he enters the chute. This lets him jump freely while you practice balancing without holding onto the mane or the reins.

• The most advanced riders sometimes go through a jumping chute without reins or stirrups, but you must work up to this slowly.

• You will have to practice posting without stirrups and jogging over single crossrails without stirrups before your legs will be strong enough to jump a grid without stirrups.

Your instructor will tell you when you are ready to jump a grid.

COMBINATIONS

Gymnastics help prepare you and your horse for combinations. Combinations are **two or three fences** in a **straight line** placed closer than 39 feet apart.

The way you jump the first fence will determine how long a stride your horse must take in order to take off properly at the next fence.

◯ The most common combination is the **in-and-out** (*two fences set 22 to 24 feet apart*).

• The horse should take one stride between the fences.

An important consideration is that the distance between the fences is comfortable for the horse's stride, at least while you are learning.

• The distance may have to be shortened a bit, especially for ponies or small horses.

◯ Later on you may jump a **triple** combination (*three fences in a row*)

◯ Or you may jump a **two stride** combination (*fences set 30 to 36 feet apart to allow your horse to take two strides between them*).

Combinations require balance, rhythm and going straight forward.

ONE STRIDE COMBINATION OR IN-AND-OUT

22 TO 24 FEET

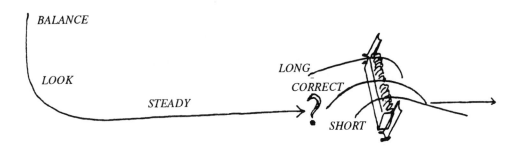

TAKEOFF POINT

Rating your horse for the correct takeoff point is very important. A horse should **jump in stride**, meaning that his jump is just as long as his canter stride and feels consistent.

- A horse's **canter stride** is usually about **12 feet**. This means that his jump should be 12 feet.
- **Small horses, lazy horses** and **ponies** may have a **10 foot** stride or so.
- **Half** of the **horse's arc** over the jump **is the takeoff**, so the right takeoff spot is five to six feet in front of the jump. This will make him land five or six feet away from the jump.

If you are jumping a **three foot fence**, the closest safe takeoff point is the same as the height of the fence, three feet away. If your horse jumps that close, he can get over safely, but his landing will be extra long.

- The closest he can land safely is the same, three feet away. He can take off as far back as nine feet and still make it, though he will be early and will land a little close. **Five or six feet away on either side is perfect**. Your finding the correct takeoff point every time won't happen all at once.

Your horse can see where he must take off, so don't worry if you aren't sure just where the perfect takeoff spot is. You can leave it all up to him.

- You must concentrate on bringing him into the fence straight, balanced and in an even canter. Your eyes must be up and your balance steady. When you have accomplished this, you have the best chance to get a perfect takeoff.

The distance exercise teaches you to see and feel a takeoff distance.

○ Set a simple jump, about 2' to 2'6", along the middle of the long side of the ring.

○ While you are cantering around the end of the ring, think **BALANCE**. Your horse must also be in good balance in a steady canter.

○ As you turn the corner, think **LOOK**. You look up and over the fence and let your eye take a flash picture of the distance between you and the fence.

○ Next, you think **STEADY**. Keep the canter straight and steady so that the horse won't speed up or slow down and fool you.

With practice, you will begin to see and think, *"We will be taking off long, short, or just right."* When you can *see your distance*, you can lengthen or shorten the stride to make it come out right. If you don't see your distance, be patient and remember, your horse will see it if you don't.

When you do adjust your horse's strides by making him lengthen or shorten, it's important to do it early, gently and in rhythm with his gait.

- If you kick, jerk, or disturb him, it will spoil his chances for a good jump and make him fight you.
- Don't make a last minute adjustment right before the fence. This can upset your horse enough to make him refuse or at least jump badly.

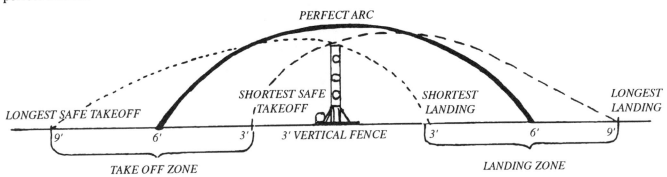

51

You can ride more interesting courses when you get good takeoff distances and ride your horse smoothly through combinations.

When you add more turns and changes of direction, you will have to be more precise about your lines and turns and be able to balance your horse for the turns. You may also include combinations or an in-and-out in your courses.

For variety when you ride a course, imagine you are competing in a horse show in Equitation Over Fences, Working Hunter, or Open Jumpers.

○ For an **Equitation course**, you are being **judged on your riding**. Your course should be as perfect, smooth and precise as you can make it, and your form over each fence should be correct.

○ **Working Hunters** are judged on the horses **smoothness**, **even pace**, **style of jumping**, and perfect **takeoff points** over the course. The rider's form isn't being judged, but the better he rides, the better he makes his horse look.

○ In **Open Jumpers**, the form of the horse and the rider doesn't count. The **horse is faulted** on **knocking down rails**, **touches**, or **disobediences**. Sometimes he is timed, so he must turn tight, save ground, and go as fast as he can without making faults.

• A good jumper rider is bold but smooth and precise. They allow the horse to jump its highest and fastest without being handicapped by rider errors. Don't let yourself ride wildly or sloppily just because rider form isn't judged.

• Bad form will eventually spoil your riding ability and the horse's jumping.

A HUNTER COURSE

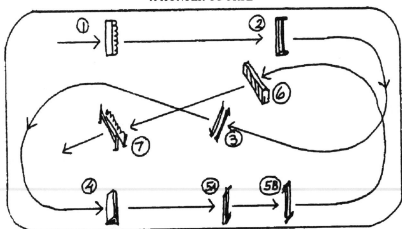

AN OPEN JUMPER COURSE

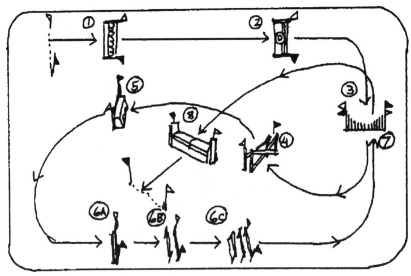

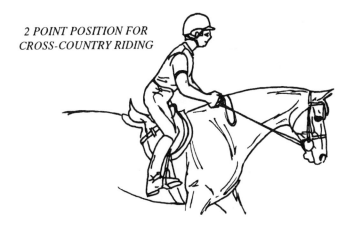

2 POINT POSITION FOR CROSS-COUNTRY RIDING

Cross country jumping can be fun for both horses and riders. Horses wake up and jump freely and happily outside the ring. A few jumps are a fun addition to a trail ride. Eventually you may want to compete over a cross country course in a combined training event.

Before jumping cross country, you must **build up** your **leg muscles** and **develop a strong galloping and jumping position**.

• The best way to do this is to ride cross country over gently rolling terrain at a trot while **balancing in a two point position**. The gentle uphill and downhill slopes will help you learn to shift your balance to stay with the horse. Staying up out of the saddle for long periods of time will strengthen your legs and back.

If your horse is easy to control outside the ring, you may practice galloping in a large field or other safe area.

• Start out cantering in two point position, then shorten your reins, squeeze your horse with your legs, and urge him to stretch out a bit. Close your body angle down and rest your hands on his neck as he strides out.

• Your galloping should be short, not too fast and under control, not an all out run!

• When you are ready to slow down, straighten up and open your body angle. Use a pulley rein if your horse is strong or hard to slow down.

NATURAL OBSTACLES AND JUMPS

When you have strong legs and good control, you can begin trotting over small natural obstacles like fallen logs. Keep your **eyes up** and **bring the horse in steadily**, as you would in the ring.

At first, the class may **line up** and **jump one at a time**. This keeps horses from getting excited.

• When you follow another horse at a trot or canter, your horse may want to go too fast to catch up, so be prepared to rate him.

• When you are waiting your turn, don't make him stand still facing other horses as they take off and leave him, this makes a horse frantic.

• Walk him in small circles instead, then ease him into a trot, and then a canter as you approach the fence.

Check both sides of anything you plan to jump. You might find wire, a hole, or a hazard on the landing side.

Because they are **solid**, cross country jumps frighten some riders. Actually, horses find these jumps easier and jump them better because of their solid, filled in look.

Cross country jumps are just as safe as ring jumps.

• As long as you don't ask your horse to jump:
 • In a slippery place
 • Under low tree branches
 • Where there are holes or wire to trip him

When you start jumping cross country, you should avoid jumping uphill or downhill at first. Jump only low fences that are well within your ability. As you progress, you can learn to jump uphill, downhill, and more difficult fences. Your instructor will safely guide your progress, step by step.

Safety rules for jumping cross-country:

1. Always wear a properly fitted jumping helmet, one with a harness-type chin strap. The chin strap must be fastened.

2. Check both sides of anything you jump before you try it.

3. Stay back a safe distance from the rider ahead of you, far enough back to stop if he had trouble at the fence.

4. Keep your speed under control. Don't let your horse race at fences.

5. Even if you have your own horse, NEVER go cross-country jumping alone!

53

CROSS COUNTRY JUMPS

STONE WALL

FALLEN LOG

CORD WOOD

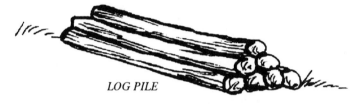

LOG PILE

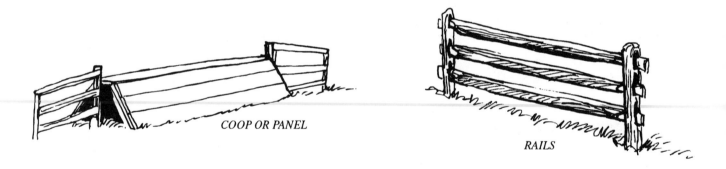

COOP OR PANEL

RAILS

TIRES

BRUSH PILE

Cross country jump materials are everywhere.
If you don't have many small cross country jumps, why not go out on foot and build a few?

HERE ARE SOME EASY TYPES OF JUMPS THAT CAN BE BUILT.

O **Fallen log or log pile**
  - Block the log or pile so it can't roll if it is hit
  - Saw off any protruding limbs

O **Stone wall**
  - Gather and pile large rocks into a moderately wide wall
  - Walls should be well filled in
  - They should be wide rather than high
  - Their should be no sharp rocks on top

O **Cord wood**
  - Cut short, even sections of wood and stack them like firewood, ends facing out
  - They will stack well between two trees

O **Coops and Panels**
  - In hunting country, a panel or coop is built into a wire fence to make the wire safe to jump
  - If you put a coop or a wooden panel in a wire fence,
    build a higher wing on each side so horses won't be tempted to run out and possibly run into the wire

O **Rails**
  - When you make fences of rails,
    cut them thick enough for horses to see easily, at least six to eight inches
  - Thin rails are hard to jump
  - Rails can be lashed in place with rope so that they can be removed if necessary

O **Brush pile**
  - Brush piles are easy to make but don't last long because horses learn to brush through them
  - You can use brush to fill in the front of a rail jump
  - Don't hide the solid rail. Be sure the horse can see it
  - Brush lasts longer if it is tied in bundles and lashed down instead of just being stuffed in place

O **Tires**
  - Tires can make a nice, round jump if they are held tightly together
    and placed in a shallow ditch to hold them

O **Oil drums**
  - Also make a good jump but they must be anchored so they won't roll under a horse if he hits them

O **Bales of hay or straw ARE NOT A GOOD JUMP**
  - A horse can get his foot stuck into a bale if he refuses and slides into it.
  - Bales also can roll under a horse
  - If the bales are very tight and anchored down, they may make a satisfactory jump

TRAIL RIDING

As you advance in horsemanship and trail experience, you should be able to handle yourself and your horse better on the trail. You will learn to condition horses for long distance riding, how to plan and carry out an overnight trail ride and how to care for your horse while out in the wilderness.

CONDITIONING HORSES

A horse must be **conditioned gradually** for any demanding activity. A fat, soft horse or a horse that is thin and run down can be injured by the stress of long or hard riding.

You may not be able to go through the process of conditioning a horse, but you should understand what it takes to get a horse into good working condition.

When a horse is out of condition, he first must be checked for health and soundness.

- He should:
  - Have his feet trimmed or shod.
  - Be dewormed.
  - Have his yearly inoculations.
(so that he will not be set back by health problems)

- If he is overweight, he will have to go on a diet.
- If he is thin he will need building up.

FEED AND GROOMING

His **feed** must **gradually be adjusted** to meet the needs of the exercise he is getting. This means that he will gradually get more grain as he is worked harder and becomes more fit.

Your horse's **skin** will also **need grooming**, care, and protection until he toughens up or he may develop sores where he is rubbed by the girth or bridle.

CONDITION GRADUALLY

CARE OF HORSES

When conditioning horses, it's especially important to be meticulous about horse care.

Long rides can produce bad saddle sores, so groom your horse thoroughly before riding and **be particular about the way the tack fits**.
- Your horse may need a special kind of saddle pad or protective padding on the girth or breast collar to prevent sores and rubs.
- Both the horse and the tack should be clean when you start out.

When you dismount after a long ride, the saddle pressure will have squeezed the blood out of the area right under the saddle.
- **Loosen your girth**, **lift the back of the saddle and pad** to let air get to the horse's back, but **leave the saddle in place for 15 minutes** to let the circulation return to normal slowly.

When you unsaddle, **wash your horse down** and **groom** him carefully. You should look for any rubs or swellings. Always cool him out carefully.

AZOTURIA

Horses that are **working hard** are subject to a condition called *azoturia* or *tying up*.

- It is usually caused by keeping a fit horse standing in a stall for several days while continuing to feed a high grain ration.
- When put back to work, the horse gets muscle cramps in his hindquarters, sweats, trembles and becomes unable to walk.

- He should be stopped and blanketed and kept quiet while a veterinarian is called.

Azoturia can be prevented by **cutting the grain ration by half or more** and by **turning the horse out** when he is not going to be ridden for a day or two.

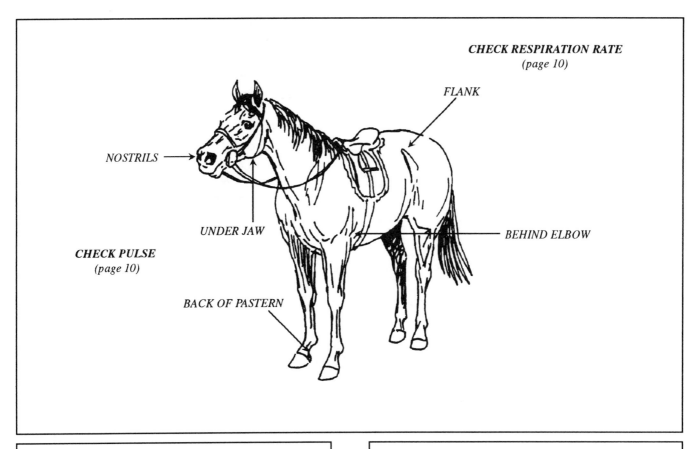

CHECK RESPIRATION RATE
(page 10)

FLANK

NOSTRILS

BEHIND ELBOW

UNDER JAW

CHECK PULSE
(page 10)

BACK OF PASTERN

EXERCISE

Exercise **starts** with **walking under saddle**, just long and hard enough to make the horse sweat a little.

• **Gradually** he is walked for **longer distances** and slow jogging is introduced.

• When he can jog for longer distances without sweating and puffing, he may be ridden at a long trot for short distances with intervals of walking for rest.

When conditioning a horse at the walk, he should be made to **move out with long strides** to develop his hindquarter muscles and trail gaits.

It is better for the horse to **work slowly for a long period than fast for a short time**, especially in the early part of conditioning. As he works, you should notice his muscles getting harder with less fat showing.

When a horse has developed good muscle tone and doesn't huff and puff and sweat up with ordinary work, he can:

• Begin doing more trotting.

• Do some cantering to develop his wind.

• Go on longer rides to develop his endurance.

• Work up and down hills to further develop his muscles and wind. Be sure to walk downhill as faster gaits are hard on the horse's legs.

TRAIL RIDE EXERCISE

You can **measure** out a **trail** about **five miles** long and **time your ride** over it at a walk and trot.

When you **stop to rest** at the five mile point, **take** your **horse's pulse** and **respiration rate**.

The exercise will **increase his heartbeat** and **breathing rates**, but in ten minutes of rest you should notice a drop in the pulse and the respiration rate. The recovery rate is the measure of your horse's condition.

• This is checked by veterinarians in judging competitive trail rides.

As you condition your horse, you should find that his recovery rate improves. Eventually you will be able to ride the five mile loop mostly at a long trot without overstressing him, and with a good recovery rate.

To condition him for a long trail ride of 20 to 35 miles, you will have to ride 5, 10, and 15 mile conditioning rides, with an occasional 20 mile ride near the end of the conditioning program.

OVERNIGHT TRAIL RIDES

An overnight ride or campout starts with good planning. You must decide **where you are going** and **how long you will be out** so you know what to take. If you plan to ride on private land or in a public park, get permission from the owner or check with the park ranger.

Check the weather forecast. If a storm is moving in or if fire danger is high, you might have to postpone your trip.

Be prepared in case of rain, extreme heat, humidity, and other conditions that can affect your ride.

WHAT TO TAKE

When planning what to take, you will have to think of the **needs of both people and horses**.

You will have to plan for food, cooking utensils, sleeping gear (*bedrolls and tents if you use them*), camping gear (*axe, shovel, latrine, etc.*), horse feed, rope to secure horses, grooming tools, etc.

The farther you go from civilization and the longer you will be out, the more critical it is to plan your needs well. Don't take more than necessary, but be sure you have the essentials.
• Remember to take a first aid kit.
• It is best to make two checklists.
One checklist for each person and his horse and a checklist for the entire group as a whole.

HOW TO CARRY IT

How you pack and carry your gear depends on whether you are using a truck, pack horses, or just yourself and your horse.

• Each person's **belongings** should be neatly **contained in a pack**. They can be rolled up in their bedroll or sleeping bag with the ground cloth outside to keep it from getting wet.
• **Saddle bags** can hold **trail food** and **personal items** you might want on the ride. If you don't have saddle bags, a feed sack can be a good substitute when rolled and tied across the front or rear of the saddle. Be sure to balance the load evenly.
• Everyone should have a **slicker** and **long sleeved shirt** rolled up on his saddle in case of rain.
• Carry a **canteen** or a clean bleach bottle for water.

Packing a pack animal is too complicated to describe here. You should have a demonstration from an expert. Someone experienced in packing, saddling, and handling pack animals should go along on the trip if you plan to use them. (*Packing is covered in the CHA Trail Manuals.*)

SELECTING A CAMPSITE

The place you ride to should have:
• Water
• A good place to camp, cook, and sleep
• A good place to secure the horses
• Good grass for the horses

Sometimes it is possible to send a truck to the campsite carrying camping gear, horse feed, personal items, and food. Other groups will *rough it* and carry everything they need on their saddles or on pack horses.

• The ride to the campsite should be pleasant and not too long nor too short.

• It is also nice to be able to take trail rides from the campsite once you have arrived and set up.

ARRIVAL IN CAMP

It is much easier to set up camp if everyone cooperates and it is set up in an organized fashion.

• The first to arrive should start to **set up a picket line or corral**. Others should **dig a latrine**.
• Riders arriving should put their **bedrolls** and **personal gear** in a neat pile in the sleeping area.
• Then they need to take their horse to the horse area and untack him. Horses should be cooled out, groomed, checked for problems and taken for water before being tied up or corralled.
• The **tack** should be hung with each horse's bridle and saddle together where it can be found again, even in the dark. Saddle pads should be turned upside down to air out. If possible, cover tack with a tarpaulin or plastic to protect leather from dampness. If you can't find a handy tree branch to make a saddle rack, try hanging saddles from a tree.
• Horse gear such as brushes, first aid items, and feed should all be kept in one spot so it won't be lost.

Your instructor or guide will check each horse to be sure it is properly tied or secured for the night.

CAMPSITE
SETTING UP CAMP

SUSAN E. HARRIS

BREAKING CAMP

Just like arriving in camp, you should be organized and each person should do his part.
- Cover the latrine.
- Drown and scatter the fire.
- Each person should check over his own area to be sure he has not left trash or personal items behind.

- Pack up any trash and take it home with you, never leave it to pollute the wilderness.
- Don't bury trash because wild animals will dig it up because they smell food.

- If your horses have been tied in a small area, try to rake and scatter or bury the manure.

- Never keep your horses near a campsite or picnic area, as the manure they leave will draw flies and spoil the area for others who may want to use it. Try to leave your campsite looking as natural as possible.

- When it is time to go home, **groom your horse** and **check his feet**.
- Be sure your **gear is balanced** equally on both sides, then make it secure so it won't come off as you ride.
- For safety, be sure to **check your tack as you saddle**.

Now you are ready to enjoy your ride home.

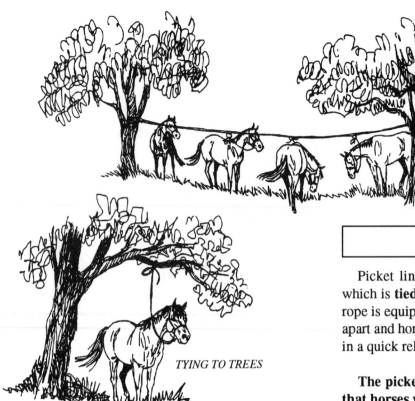

PICKET LINE

TYING TO TREES

SECURING HORSES AT CAMP

There are several ways to secure your horses at the campsite such as:
- Tethering
- Using a picket line
- Tying to trees
- Making a corral

Sometimes experienced packers hobble horses and turn them loose, but this is unsafe unless you know that your horses are used to it and won't get lost or even wander home.

TETHERING

Tethering is when a horse is **tied by a long rope** to a **stake or tree** to graze.

- This is dangerous unless your horse is broke to tether, as he can get tangled in the rope and get rope-burned or even break a leg.
- If the rope is run through a length of garden hose, it won't rope burn or tangle him but is heavy and awkward to carry.

Tethering is not a good way to secure most horses.

PICKET LINES

Picket lines require a strong, non-stretching **rope** which is **tied** tightly **between two or more trees**. The rope is equipped with **loops or rings** set about ten feet apart and horses are tied to rings with their halter ropes in a quick release knot.

The picket line should be above wither height so that horses won't get a leg over it.

TYING TO TREES

Tying to trees is **not as satisfactory as a picket line** because horses may wind themselves around the tree and will eat the bark, possibly killing the tree.

If necessary, **tie to an overhead branch** with just enough **slack** to let the **horse reach the ground** with his nose. USE A RELEASE KNOT.

CORRALS OR PERMANENT PASTURES

Corrals or permanent pastures are **excellent**. If not available, you may be able to make a temporary corral by **running a strong rope at chest height from tree to tree in a rough circle**. Horses that are broken to respect an electric fence will probably respect a rope corral.

- Any horses that fight, bite, or kick should be tied by themselves. It is a good idea to have a *horse guard* to keep an eye on the horses. This job can be alternated during the night.
- Be sure that any horses that are tied are safely **secured with a release knot** and cannot get a foot over the rope.
- If hay is available, it will help keep the horses quiet and contented.
- Horses should be taken for a drink before being tied up or corralled for the night.

LEVEL 4 REQUIREMENTS

To complete the Level 4 you must be able to pass each of the following requirements. This can be done by performing the Level 4 Ring Test, which includes all the movements in it (or an alternate test made up by your Instructor). or by having your CHA instructor may check off each **required item** as you pass it. This can be done in regular riding lessons, as a group test or in an individual test.

western instructors may prefer to make up a test incorporating western gaits and movements.

RIDING REQUIREMENTS

_____ 1. Demonstrate Level 4 riding in the following ways: (*without roughness*)
(*showing correct form, smooth and effective control, good balance and correct use of aids*)
___ a. Demonstrate the walk:
____1. on simple contact
____2. on a loose rein
____3. lengthen stride at the walk
___ b. Demonstrate the trot in the following ways:
____1. working trot
____2. medium trot
____3. lengthen stride to strong trot.
___ c. Demonstrating a simple change of leads at the canter on a figure 8
___   or while changing directions on the diagonal.
___ d. Demonstrate a turn on the forehand.
___ e. Execute a halt from any gait.
___ f. Demonstrate a transitions from one gait to another smoothly and promptly on command.
_____ 2. Ride through turns and circles with the horse bending correctly.
_____ 3. Explain and demonstrate:
___ a. Direct flexion (getting the horse to flex in the poll and jaw).
___ b. Correcting a faulty head set or head position.
___ c. Proper use of artificial aids (crop or bat, dressage whip, spurs).
_____ 4. Ride a ring test, dressage test, program ride, or one of the western performance patterns.

GENERAL REQUIREMENTS

_____ 1. Explain proper hoof care and demonstrate safely picking up and cleaning the feet.
_____ 2. Take a horse's pulse and respiration rate.
_____ 3. Know and explain the signs of health and illness in horses.
_____ 4. Evaluate a horse's conformation.
(pointing out desirable and undesirable points and any visible blemishes and unsoundness)
_____ 5. Make up a conditioning program for a horse.
If possible, carry out the conditioning of a horse according to your program.

TRAIL REQUIREMENTS

_____ 1. Explain (*demonstrate if possible*) how to:
___ a. Plan an overnight trail ride, including what to take.
___ b. Secure horses for an overnight campout
(using a picket line or other method approved by your instructor, showing tying safely).
_____ c. Demonstrate or explain the care of horses and equipment on arrival in camp for an overnight stay.

JUMPING REQUIREMENTS

NOTE: Jumping is not required to pass any CHA level.
Some Instructors programs may wish to include jumping in their testing or offer a special Jumping award.
(*CHA offers an unmarked badge picturing a jumping rider
which may be used as a Jumping award by programs that wish to do so.*)
This is an optional Jumping Checklist.

_____ 1. Demonstrate Level 4 jumping form and control: (*without interfering with horse*)
over single fences at least 2' 6" high (*not to exceed 3' high*).
(*correct form and jumping position, good timing, proper release and effective control*)

_____ 2. Jump low gymnastics at a trot:
 ___ a. Low single fence with placing pole.
 ___ b. Bounce or no-stride combination (*not to exceed 2' high*).
 ___ c. Jumping grid of three or more fences (*not to exceed 2' high*).

_____ 3. Jump low gymnastics at a canter:
 ___ a. Low single fence with placing pole.
 ___ b. Bounce or no-stride combination (*not to exceed 2' high*).
 ___ c. Jumping grid of three or more fences (*not to exceed 2' high*).

_____ 4. Jump combinations; in and out or triple combination (*not to exceed 2' 6" high*).

_____ 5. Jump simple fences cross-country with good control at trot and canter (*not to exceed 2' 6" high*).

_____ 6. Jump a course of fences (*minimum height 2' 6", maximum 3'; lower for ponies*) to be scored as:
 ___ a. Equitation Over Fences
 ___ b. Working Hunter Over Fences
 ___ c. Open Jumper or Stadium Jumping

WESTERN REQUIREMENTS

(*CHA offers an unmarked badge picturing a western performance horse.
Some programs may wish to use this badge as an additional award for achievement in western riding.*)
This is an optional western performance checklist.

_____ 1. Holding the reins in either split-rein style or California style,
ride with correct western form and good balance both ways of the ring,
 ___ a. At the walk.
 ___ b. At the jog.
 ___ c. At the lope.

_____ 2. Execute the following western movements, using correct aids:
 ___ a. Stop from the lope (*need not be a sliding stop*).
 ___ b. Pivot on the hindquarters
 ___ c. Roll-back
 ___ d. Figure 8 with simple change of leads at center.
 ___ e. Figure 8 with flying leads at center.
  (*Only if the horse is trained and capable of executing correct flying changes.*)
 ___ f. Back one horse length in a straight line.

_____ 3. Ride a western gymkhana pattern.
(*cloverleaf barrel race, pole bending, keyhole pattern or flag race or other gymkhana pattern*)

_____ 4. Ride a western performance pattern.
(*either reining pattern, western riding pattern or stock seat equitation test pattern*)

_____ 5. Demonstrate two training methods of holding the reins.

MULTIPLE CHOICE (select the best answer)

1. The most common fatal horse illness is:
   a) Thrush
   b) Colic
   c) Navicular disease
   d) Heaves

2. Cross cantering is:
   a) A ring pattern
   b) A balance and coordinated exercise
   c) Different leads in front and back
   e) A flying change of leads

3. If a horse is bleeding seriously from a cut on the heel of his foot, you should:
   a) Apply a tourniquet
   b) Soak the cut in warm water to clean it
   c) Apply pressure with a clean pad on the wound
   d) get him back to the stable before treating the wound

4. The underlying cause of many cases of colic is:
   a) Parasite damage
   b) Improper shoeing
   c) Dirty surroundings and neglect
   d) Infection passed from horse to horse

5. A horse should be checked for parasites and dewormed at least:
   a) Once a year
   b) Once a week
   c) Every six months
   d) Every two to three months

6. If a horse bucks when you are riding, you should:
   a) Stop him and stand still
   b) Stand up in your stirrups
   c) Sit up, lift his head up and drive him forward
   d) Hit him with a crop on the rump

7. The best way to handle a horse that shies is to:
   a) Punish him every time he shies
   b) Stop and pat him to quiet him down
   c) Never let him see the object that scares him
   d) Return to work as soon as possible without fuss

8. The most dangerous type of parasite is:
   a) Bots
   b) Strongyles or bloodworms
   c) Ascarids or roundworms
   d) Pinworms

9. When a horse is lame in the right front foot, he will:
   a) Refuse to move
   b) Throw his head down when the right fore leg hits the ground
   c) Throw his head up when the right fore leg hits the ground
   d) Take a longer step with the right foreleg

10. The best type of front leg conformation is:
    a) Long sloping shoulder, short canon
    b) Short straight shoulder, long cannon
    c) Long thin legs that toe out
    d) Short chunky legs that toe in

SHORT ANSWERS (fill in the missing word)

1. A(n) _____
   is a condition that makes a horse lame or damages his ability to do useful work.

2. A(n) _____
   is a condition that is unsightly but doesn't interfere with the horse's ability to work.

3. The horse's normal pulse rate is about _____ beats per minute.

4. The horse's normal breathing rate is about _____ breaths per minute.

5. The best indicator of a horse's fitness on a long ride is his _____.

6. A horse traveling with his weight mostly on the front legs is said to be _____.

7. When a horse moves with a very steady, noticeable beat, his gait is said to be _____.

8. A horse that is stiff on one side is not _____.

9. The horse's balance is effected by the riders:
   _____.
   _____.
   _____.

10. Conformation is: _____
    _____.

TRUE OR FALSE

___ 1.   A horse is supple if he will bend his neck when one rein is pulled.

___ 2.   In an extended gait, the horse takes shorter and quicker steps.

___ 3.   Stock type horses are built to be able to work cattle.

___ 4.   When a horse is collected, his balance is shifted to the rear.

___ 5.   Founder and Colic can both be caused by overeating grain.

___ 6.   The best way to secure a horse when camping overnight is to tie him with a slip knot around his neck.

___ 7.   Azoturia is a condition that can occur when horses are kept idle and fed too much grain.

___ 8.   Horses need shoeing only about once a year.

MATCHING
Match the following blemishes or unsoundness with the correct explanation:

_____ Navicular disease	A.	Serious sore caused by badly fitting saddle
_____ Splint	B.	Arthritis in the hock joint that causes unsoundness
_____ Quarter crack	C.	Arthritis in the bones of the pastern causing lameness
_____ Windpuff s	D.	Degeneration of the small bone within the hoof
_____ Bowed tendon	E.	Blemish often acquired by kicking
_____ Fistula	F.	Calcified lump on inside of cannon bone
_____ Ringbone	H.	Defect in the outside wall of the foot, may cause lameness if deep
_____ Capped hock	1.	Sprain or strain of flexor tendons which thickens the leg with scar tissue
_____ Bone spavin	G.	Hind leg locked in position because of loose ligament, often due to poor conformation
_____ Stifled	J.	Swelling on or near the ankles; a blemish that indicates hard work

LEVEL 4 WESTERN RING TEST

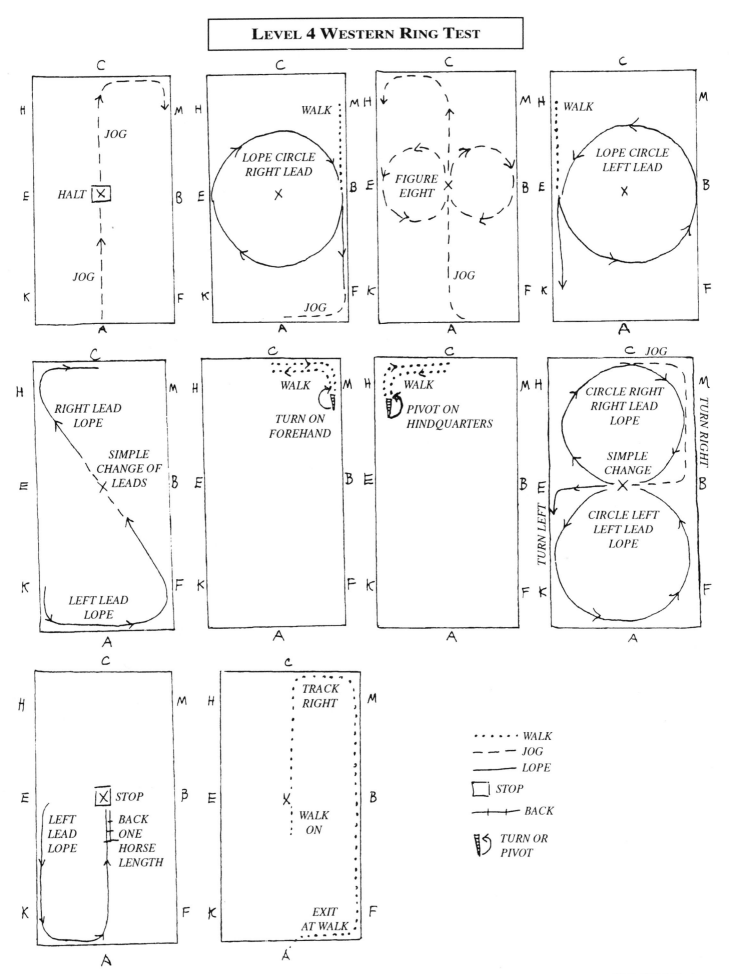

Panel 1: C, H, M, E, B, K, F, A — JOG, HALT ☒, JOG

Panel 2: C, H, M, E, B, K, F, A — WALK, LOPE CIRCLE RIGHT LEAD ✗, JOG

Panel 3: C, M, H, E, B, K, F, A — FIGURE EIGHT, JOG

Panel 4: C, M, H, E, B, K, F, A — WALK, LOPE CIRCLE LEFT LEAD ✗

Panel 5: C, H, M, E, B, K, F, A — RIGHT LEAD LOPE, SIMPLE CHANGE OF LEADS ✗, LEFT LEAD LOPE

Panel 6: C, H, M, E, B, K, F, A — WALK, TURN ON FOREHAND

Panel 7: C, H, M, E, B, K, F, A — WALK, PIVOT ON HINDQUARTERS

Panel 8: C, JOG, M, H, E, B, K, F, A — CIRCLE RIGHT RIGHT LEAD LOPE, TURN RIGHT, SIMPLE CHANGE ✗, CIRCLE LEFT LEFT LEAD LOPE, TURN LEFT

Panel 9: C, H, M, E, B, K, F, A — STOP ☒, BACK ONE HORSE LENGTH, LEFT LEAD LOPE

Panel 10: C, H, M, E, B, K, F, A — TRACK RIGHT, WALK ON ✗, EXIT AT WALK

Legend:
· · · · · WALK
– – – – JOG
——— LOPE
▢| STOP
+—+—+ BACK
↻ TURN OR PIVOT

CHA LEVEL 4

(Based on 5 points each, a total of 100 points)

Name: _____ **Place** _____ **Date** _____

		POINTS	COMMENT
1. A - X Jog to Stop	(5 pts.)		
2. X - M Jog to Walk	(5 pts.)		
3. M - B Walk	(5 pts.)		
4. At B Circle	(5 pts.)		
5 B - F Canter, right lead	(5 pts.)		
6. F - H through X Jog (with figure 8 at X see 7)	(5 pts.)		
7. Figure 8 at X	(5 pts.)		
8. H - E Walk	(5 pts.)		
9. At E Circle	(5 pts.)		
10. E through K Canter, left lead	(5 pts.)		
11. K - C Simple lead change at X	(5 pts.)		
12. C - M Walk at M Turn on forehand	(5 pts.)		
13. C - H Walk at H Pivot	(5 pts.)		
14. C - X Jog	(5 pts.)		
15. X Large figure 8, start to the right	(5 pts.)		
16. Simple change of leads at X	(5 pts.)		
17. E - X Canter and stop	(5 pts.)		
18. X Back	(5 pts.)		
19. Overall control	(5 pts.)		
20. Overall equitation	(5 pts.)		
Possible 100 points Passing score 70%	TOTAL SCORE		

Scoring: 1 = Not performed 2 = Unsatisfactory 3 = Sufficient, fair 4 = Good 5 = Outstanding

PASSING: _____ Yes _____ No _____ Instructor's signature _____

(Based on 10 points each, a total of 100 points)

Name: _____ Place _____ Date _____

	Letter	Directions	You are scored on		Points	Comment
1.	A	Enter at jog	Position, seat, aids			
	X	Stop, pause 5 seconds	Straightness, square halt			
		Continue at jog	Transitions			
	C	Track to the right	Accurate turn	(10 pts.)		
2.	M	Walk	Aids and transitions			
	B	Right lead lope	Seat and position			
		Circle right, width of ring	Correct lead			
		Then continue along rail	Not breaking gait			
	F	Jog	Accurate circle	(10 pts.)		
3.	A	Turn down center line	Accurate turn, figure 8			
	X	Figure 8 (left 1/2 width of ring	Position and seat			
		followed by circle right same size)	Aids and reining			
	C	Track to the left	Steadiness, not breaking gait	(10 pts.)		
4.	H	Walk	Aids and transitions			
	E	Left lead lope and circle left	Seat and position			
		Width of ring	Correct lead, not breaking gait			
		Then continue along rail	Accurate circle	(10 pts.)		
5.	F-X-H	Change of directions on the diagonal	Aids and control			
		Simple change of leads at center	Straightness	(10 pts.)		
6.	C	Walk	Seat and aids for walk			
	M	Stop, Turn on forehand 180°	Stop and turn on forehand			
		Walk along rail	Smoothness	(10 pts.)		
7.	H	Stop, *Pivot 180° on hindquarters	Seat and aids for pivot and stop			
		Walk along rail	Smoothness			
		*Turn-back on the rail is allowed		(10 pts.)		
8.	C	Jog	Seat and aids			
	B	Turn right into center of ring'	Transitions, correct lead			
	X	Right lead lope and circle right	Not breaking			
		Width of ring	Accurate circle	(10 pts.)		
9.	X	Simple change of leads to left lead	Seat and aids			
		Circle left width of ring	Smoothness of change of leads			
	X	Lope straight ahead to rail	Correct lead			
	E	Turn left along rail (at lope)	Accurate circle and turn	(10 pts.)		
10.	A	Turn down center line	Seat, balance and position			
	X	Stop, settle horse for several seconds	Aids; stop without roughness			
		Back one horse length in straight line	Straightness of stop and back			
		Continue at walk				
	C	Track to the right	Ability to settle horse			
		Continue along rail to exit at A	Walk quietly on loose reins	(10 pts.)		

Total = 100 pts

A score of 70% is considered passing

TOTAL
SCORE

Scoring: 0 = Not performed   3 = Poor   6 = Satisfactory   9 = Very good
            1 = Very bad   4 = Insufficient, not good enough   7 = Fairly good   10 = Outstanding
            2 = Unsatisfactory   5 = Sufficient, fair   8 = Good

Passing scores are 5 and over. Note: **10 means outstanding, not perfect** (10 is a possible score, though rare).

PASSING: _____ Yes _____ No _____ Instructor's signature _____

(Based on 5 points each, a total of 100 points)

Name: _____ **Place** _____ **Date** _____

	POINTS	COMMENT
1. A - X Walk (5 pts.)		
2. X Halt (5 pts.)		
3. X - M Sitting (5 pts.)		
4. M - F Posting trot (correct diagonal)		
At B Circle (5 pts.)		
5 F - H through X Sitting trot (figure 8 at X see 6) (5 pts.)		
6. At X Figure 8 (5 pts.)		
7. H - K Posting trot, Circle at E		
K - F Sitting trot (5 pts.)		
8. F - H Posting trot, lengthen stride		
H - C Sitting trot (5 pts.)		
9. C - M Walk, at M Turn on the forehand (5 pts.)		
10. C - H Walk, at H Turn on the forehand (5 pts.)		
11. M - A Canter, right lead (circle at B see 12) (5 pts.)		
12. At B Circle (5 pts.)		
13. A - C Flying change or simple change of leads (5 pts.)		
14. C - K Canter, left lead (circle at E see 15) (5 pts.)		
15. At E Circle (5 pts.)		
16. K - X Sitting trot (5 pts.)		
17. X Halt (5 pts.)		
18. X - A Walk and exit (5 pts.)		
19. Overall control (5 pts.)		
20. Overall equitation (5 pts.)		
Possible 100 points Passing score 70%	TOTAL SCORE	

Scoring: 1 = Not performed   2 = Unsatisfactory   3 = Sufficient, fair   4 = Good   5 = Outstanding

PASSING: _____ Yes _____ No _____ Instructor's signature _____

(Based on 10 points each, a total of 110 points)

Name: _____ Place _____ Date _____

Letter		Directions	You are scored on	Points	Comment
1.	A	Enter at working trot, sitting	Position, seat, aids and control		
	X	Halt, pause 5 seconds	Straightness, square halt		
		Continue at working trot, sitting	Transitions		
	C	Track to the right	Bending in turn (10 pts.)		
2.	M	Medium trot, posting	Position, balance		
	B	Circle width of ring	Correct diagonal		
	F	Working trot, sitting	Accurate circle, bending (10 pts.)		
3.	A	Turn down center line	Accurate turn, figure 8		
	X	Figure 8 (left 1/2 width of ring	Seat, position in sitting trot		
		followed by circle to right same size)	Bending and change of bend		
	C	Track to the left	(10 pts.)		
4.	H	Medium trot, posting	Posting and correct diagonal		
	E	Circle left width of ring	Accurate circle, bending		
	K	Working trot, sitting	(10 pts.)		
5. K-F		Working trot, sitting	Seat and position		
F-X-H		Change of direction on diagonal	Rhythm and lengthening of stride		
		Lengthen stride to strong trot, posting	Transitions		
	H	H to C, Working trot, sitting	(10 pts.)		
6.	C	Walk	Seat and aids for walk		
	M	Turn on forehand 180°, walk on	Turn on forehand (10 pts.)		
7.	H	Turn on forehand 180°	Seat and aids for walk		
		Walk on to C	Turn on forehand (10 pts.)		
8.	C	Working trot, sitting	Seat and aids for canter		
	M	Canter, right lead	Transition to canter, correct lead		
	B	Circle right, width of ring to E	Not breaking		
		Continue along rail at canter	Accurate circle (10 pts.)		
9. K-X-M		Change directions on the diagonal	Accuracy of change of directions		
		Between K and M,	Seat and aids for change of leads		
		Simple change of leads	Smoothness of change of leads		
	M	Left lead canter along rail	Correct leads/simple change (10 pts.)		
10.	E	Circle left, width of ring,	Seat, and aids in canter		
		Canter, left lead	Correct lead		
		Continue along rail to K	Accurate circle (10 pts.)		
11.	K	Working trot, sitting	Transitions and aids		
	A	Turn down center line	Straightness and accuracy		
	X	Halt, pause 5 seconds	Position and seat		
		Continue at walk to end of ring	Quietness of seat and aids		
		Track right along rail and exit at A	(10 pts.)		

Total = 110 pts

A score of 70% is considered passing

TOTAL SCORE [ ]

Scoring: 0 = Not performed   3 = Poor   6 = Satisfactory   9 = Very good
1 = Very bad   4 = Insufficient, not good enough   7 = Fairly good   10 = Outstanding
2 = Unsatisfactory   5 = Sufficient, fair   8 = Good

Passing scores are 5 and over. Note: **10 means outstanding, not perfect** (10 is a possible score, though rare).

PASSING: _____ Yes _____ No _____ Instructor's signature _____

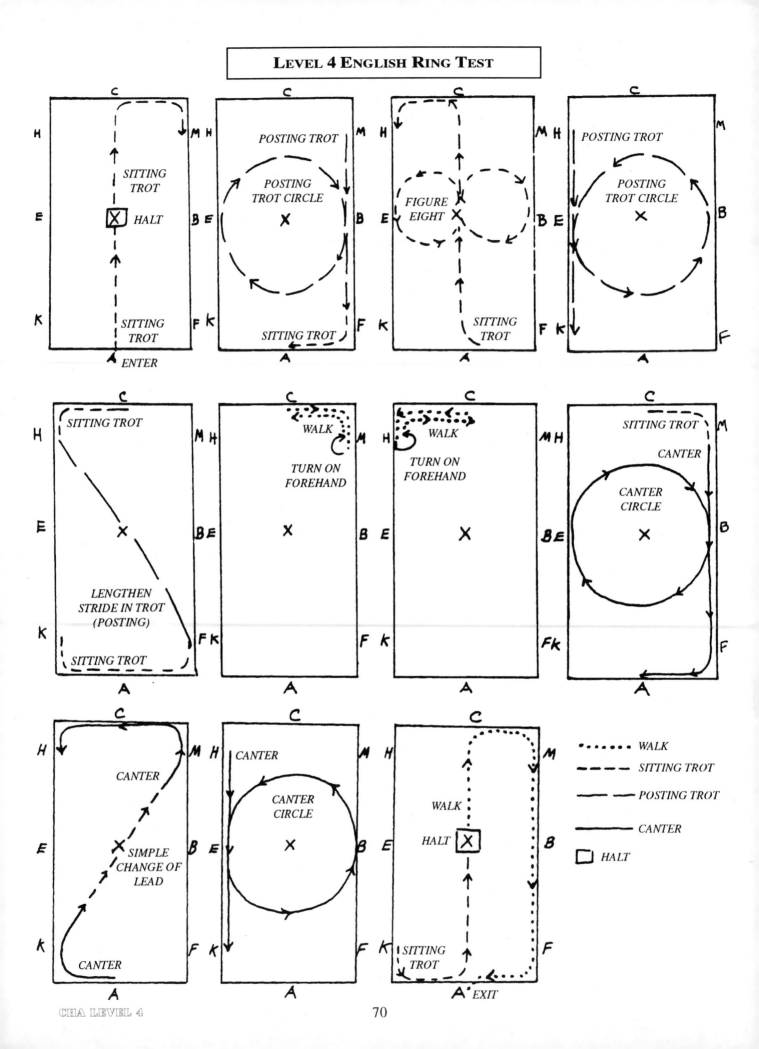

LEVEL 4 ENGLISH RING TEST

Panel 1:
C, H, M, E, B, K, F, A
SITTING TROT
HALT ☒
SITTING TROT
ENTER

Panel 2:
C, H, M, E, B, K, F, A
POSTING TROT
POSTING TROT CIRCLE
X
SITTING TROT

Panel 3:
C, H, M, E, B, K, F, A
FIGURE EIGHT
X
SITTING TROT

Panel 4:
C, H, M, E, B, K, F, A
POSTING TROT
POSTING TROT CIRCLE
X

Panel 5:
C, H, M, E, B, K, F, A
SITTING TROT
X
LENGTHEN STRIDE IN TROT (POSTING)
SITTING TROT

Panel 6:
C, H, M, E, B, K, F, A
WALK
TURN ON FOREHAND
X

Panel 7:
C, H, M, E, B, K, F, A
WALK
TURN ON FOREHAND
X

Panel 8:
C, H, M, E, B, K, F, A
SITTING TROT
CANTER
CANTER CIRCLE
X

Panel 9:
C, H, M, E, B, K, F, A
CANTER
X SIMPLE CHANGE OF LEAD
CANTER

Panel 10:
C, H, M, E, B, K, F, A
CANTER
CANTER CIRCLE
X

Panel 11:
C, H, M, E, B, K, F, A
WALK
HALT ☒
SITTING TROT
EXIT

Legend:
- · · · · · · WALK
- – – – – SITTING TROT
- — — — POSTING TROT
- ———— CANTER
- ☐ HALT

ACKNOWLEDGMENTS

CHA would like to extend its special thanks to
Dan Hemphill, founder of CHA.

Manual Revision Chairman 1983
Lewis Sterrett, Pennsylvania

Manual Revision 1995
Susanne Valla, North Carolina

Illustrations by
Susan Harris, New York

Layout and Typeset
Susanne Valla, North Carolina

Contributors

Judy Ale, California
Dan Arnold, Texas
Becky Blansett, Ohio
Cheryl Bradbee, Vermont
Rodney Brown, Washington
Fred Bruce, Texas
Chris Cochrane, Michigan
Carol Dobson, Canada
Cindy Drodge, Ohio
Amy Edwards, Michigan
Eddy Edwards, Michigan
Nan Edwards, Michigan
Sally Edwards, Michigan
Debra Glowik, Ohio
Audrey Grabfield, Massachusetts
Susan Harris, New York
Kristi Harris, Oklahoma
Sue Hughes, Michigan
Sharon Lindsay, Virginia
Denise Maxwell, Arizona
Gregg McEnroe, Michigan
Dale Miller, Texas
Bill Murrell, Texas

Audrey Nelson, Vermont
Lois Orr, California
Max Parrott, Indiana
Patti Pearson, California
Deborah Plimpton, Connecticut
Pam Prudler, California
Dallas Raab, Minnesota
Vivian Raab, Minnesota
Dodi Stacey, Colorado
Alice Steltenpohl, Indiana
Melodie Sterrett, Pennsylvania
Cindy Swanson, Minnesota
Margaret Taylor, Michigan
Daryl Thomas, Michigan
Eldon Toews, Washington
Bill Wiley, Ohio
Terry Williams, Ohio
Jane Wiley, Ohio
Mary Anna Wood, Missouri
Donna Woods, Missouri
Ruth Wright, Michigan
Timothy Wright, Michigan
Susanne Valla, North Carolina